COSTCO
WHOLESALE

Household
ALMANAC

Household ALMANAC

2007 Edition
Tips and advice from Costco

David W. Fuller and Anita Thompson

Editors

With a foreword by
MaryJane Butters

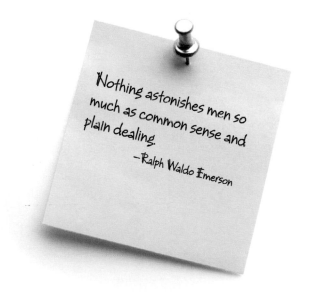

Nothing astonishes men so much as common sense and plain dealing.

—Ralph Waldo Emerson

Issaquah, Washington

**Senior Vice President
E-commerce and Publishing**
Ginnie Roeglin

Publisher
David W. Fuller

Editors
David W. Fuller, Anita Thompson

Art Director
Doris Winters

Graphic Designers
Ken Broman, Bill Carlson,
Susan Detlor, Robert Lehnhardt,
Chris Rusnak, David Schneider,
Dawna Tessier, Lory Williams

Staff Writers
Will Fifield, Steve Fisher,
T. Foster Jones, Stephanie E. Ponder,
Tim Talevich, Bill Urlevich

Business Manager
Jane Klein-Shucklin

Advertising Manager
Kathi Tipper-Holgersen

Advertising Assistant
Melanie Woods

Production Manager
Pam Sather

Assistant Production Manager
Antolin Matsuda

Color Specialist
MaryAnne Robbers

Print Management
Jim Letzel, Will Ting, GSSI

Proofreaders
Miriam Bulmer, Shana McNally

Indexer
Nan Badgett

Distribution
Rossie Cruz

FIRST EDITION

Printed by Toppan Printing Co. Ltd.,
Japan
ISBN-13: 978-0-9722164-7-0
Library of Congress Control Number:
2007924298

contents

Practical wisdom is only to be learned in the school of experience. Precepts and instruction are useful so far as they go, but, without the discipline of real life, they remain of the nature of theory only.

–Samuel Smiles
Scottish author and reformer
(1812–1904)

From the publishers

WE ARE PLEASED to present our first ever *Costco Household Almanac*! We have worked with our suppliers to compile a book of helpful tips to maximize the benefits and usefulness of our products. We also tried to answer many of the product-oriented questions that members ask us in our warehouses and call centers. For example, in the "Sight & Sound" chapter, you'll find everything you need to know about hooking up your new big-screen high-definition TV set to get a picture as good as the one you saw in our warehouse. And, in the "Hobbies & Leisure" chapter, you can finally learn how to get all of those pictures out of your digital camera and into frames and photo albums!

In the *Costco Household Almanac*, you'll find tips on everything from connecting complicated electronics to setting up your pantry, with some personal health advice in between. We thank our suppliers for their participation and invite you to keep it handy and refer to it often when you need a little advice from Costco!

Ginnie Roeglin
Senior Vice President
E-commerce and Publishing

IN PERHAPS THE MOST insightful biography ever written about Benjamin Franklin, Bernard Fay had this to say about almanacs: "These little books were faithful mirrors of the preoccupations of the times." As is, I hope, *The Costco Household Almanac*, a compendium of advice and pointers geared to life at the dawn of the 21st century.

Where Franklin in his *Poor Richard's Almanack* informed his readers of "Lunations, Eclipses, Judgment of the Weather, Spring Tides, Planets Motions and Mutual Aspects," our book takes you step by step through the process of shooting, editing, printing, archiving and e-mailing your digital photos. Where *Poor Richard's* noted, "Three things are men most likely to be cheated in, a horse, a wig and a wife," our almanac explains how to avoid identity theft. Although we have omitted noting the "Length of Days, Times of High Water, Fairs, Courts and observable Days," we do walk you through the "Seasons of Costco."

Which brings us to what this almanac really is about: helping Costco members navigate the complexities of today's world. Financed by Costco's suppliers, infused with the wisdom of Costco's members, organized, scrutinized and written by the editors of Costco's popular magazine, *The Costco Connection*, the *Household Almanac* has a simple two-part mission:

• To assist members in judging the quality of a product or service
• To help members get the most out of their purchases

We hope you enjoy this unique addition to the great tradition of almanac publishing, bearing in mind, as Franklin admonished, "We can give advice but we cannot give conduct."

David W. Fuller
Publisher

Foreword

THE WORD "ALMANAC" has been linked with farmers for hundreds of years. When Robert B. Thomas began issuing his *The Farmer's Almanac* in 1792 (the word "old" was permanently added in 1848), the idea of getting a grip on the vagaries of weather was its most compelling selling point. Like other almanac publishers, he added tips, shortcuts, quotes and witticisms, mostly to fill columns of weather charts that weren't quite fitting properly. Over time, as Americans began moving off their farms, the "useful tips, shortcuts and secrets" sections of some almanacs began to overtake the weather-prediction sections.

Almanacs continued to evolve. In 1888, we needed household help with things such as how to make fruitcake last a year or how to keep crepe de chine waists white. More than a century later, the lifestyle-savvy toolbox includes advice on home filing systems, storage of digital family photos, how to clean an AC system or how to reclaim a garage.

Nevertheless, we still need to know how to employ the same basic tenets that have always been an integral part of small farming communities, things such as frugality, efficient use of resources and neighborliness—the kinds of things that are part of the Costco community, what I call the "Costco way in the world." It's a vision of the future that includes recognizing the need to live in a more global economy while still maintaining a family atmosphere and investment in our communities—in short, to conduct commerce on a high moral plane.

The *Costco Household Almanac* sows the seeds of everything community—from how to start a book club to preparing for a weather-related disaster to improving your health to filtering your water to kicking a cigarette habit. It's the modern-day version of age-old helpful hints, homemade concoctions and darned good reading.

As a farmer for some 20 years, and most recently as an author, I know the importance of useful and entertaining information. As an Idaho farmer specifically, I also know the importance of potatoes! Here's my almanac tip from the past for today:

A good way to preserve flowers in bloom and keep them erect is to cut a flat surface on the long side of a raw potato and then stick the stems into holes bored into the top side using a pointed potato peeler. There is moisture enough in a large potato to support a bouquet of flowers!

May this 2007 version of a tradition that has played an important part in our nation's heritage help you put better food on your table and "sparklin' white linens" on your line! Let the old-time ways carry on.

MaryJane

Costco member MaryJane Butters has worn many hats (and aprons) in her day, but none more proudly than that of modern-day farm girl. She owns and operates MaryJanesFarm in northern Idaho and manages the "Farmgirl Connection," a Web site (*www.maryjanesfarm.org*) where both country and city women share their inner-farm-girl tips and inspiration. She is also the author of two books, *MaryJane's Ideabook, Cookbook, Lifebook* (Clarkson Potter, 2005) and *MaryJane's Stitching Room* (2007).

The reasons for the seasons

IN LATE **August**, when people are clinging to the last bits of summer, a most unusual sight appears in Costco: Christmas decorations, porcelain Santas and other holiday items—greens and reds in a season of yellow and brown. About as useful, it would seem, as gardening tools in December or a summer dress in January.

What gives? Christmas tree lights, gardening tools and hundreds of other items are seasonal products at Costco, available only during limited times of

The seasons of Costco*

January
Gardening tools and equipment, Easter gifts and décor, charcoal grills, beach towels, bathroom scales

Mid-February to March
Imported lawn furniture and umbrellas, Easter baskets, lawn and garden supplies, wheelbarrows, live plants, coolers, camping and water-sports equipment, swimsuits, car canopies, air conditioners, car-washing equipment

April
Bridal gifts

Late May to early June
Back-to-school supplies

*Exact arrival dates vary from region to region.

the year. These items appear early and are often gone before the end of the season. This "early in, early out" approach is one key element of Costco's formula to keep costs as low as possible—which translates into savings for members.

"One of the exciting things in the warehouses is the experience of change," says Dennis Knapp, who, as Costco's senior vice president of non-food merchandising, oversees many seasonal items. "There's a treasure-hunt feeling in the warehouses, with seasonal and opportunistic buys available for the members. We work hard to offer the right balance of exciting new products and our popular staples."

The seasons of Costco follow this general schedule: In **mid-July**, fall and winter sweaters, fleece and outerwear start arriving. They're followed in late **August** and early **September** by holiday items: imported home decorations, tree-trimming novelties, fancy food gift baskets, European housewares for gifts and much more.

Summer clothes appear in some regions as early as **mid-December**. Before New Year's, tax-related products are featured, such as organizers and software. Also in winter, the first home and garden goods for spring arrive, increasing in number by early **March**: lawn mowers, garden tools and supplies, roses and other plants, and much more. Coinciding with the arrival of these spring goods are the first summer recreational products, such as tents and camping accessories.

In late **May and June**, back-to-school products appear, increasing in number by July 4. And in summer, the whole cycle begins again.

Two smaller seasons are squeezed in during the year to fill in between the more popular periods. From **mid-December** through **mid-February** (between the holiday rush and the arrival of spring products), you'll find exclusive furniture sets and a collection of home and office containers for organizing. Those products are also brought in between **mid-July** and **mid-September**, between the summer and holiday seasons.

The exact arrival dates for these seasonal products vary from region to region to reflect different climates and shipping arrangements. For example,

What you'll find online

If shopping at a Costco warehouse is a veritable treasure hunt (you never know what you may find down the next aisle), Costco's Web site, *www.costco.com*, is a virtual one. That's because only 10 percent of the merchandise mirrors that of the warehouses.

Many seasonal items are available year-round on costco.com. For example, patio furniture, generators, grills and spas are all available online, whether the weather is right for them or not.

Here's some of what else you'll find.

Furniture. From individual pieces to complete rooms, hundreds of furniture items for every room of the house and office are available year-round.

Office products. Thousands of items, from corporate gifts and office furniture to a vast selection of ink and toner cartridges to paper clips, in most cases with next-day delivery.

Tires. An expanded selection of tires for almost any vehicle. A user-friendly search tool helps members find the wheels they seek and have them ▶

Early to mid-July
Furniture, fall and winter clothes (sweaters, fleece, outerwear), flannel sheets, down comforters, electric blankets

Mid-July to mid-September
Plastic storage organizers, calculators, educational software, scissors, globes, crayons and markers, binders

Late August to early September
Holiday décor, food and beauty gift baskets, toys, Kirkland Signature™ assorted cookies and candies, imported gifts, wrapping paper, tree stands, collectibles, snow tires and other winter automotive supplies

Mid-December
Spring clothes (sandals, shorts, short-sleeve knits and sleeveless dresses), furniture, organizers, tax-preparation software

shipped to their local warehouse for installation.

Sporting goods. A wide selection of outdoor, exercise and sporting goods equipment.

Special buys. Sometimes Costco's buyers find fantastic deals on spectacular items available in limited quantities. Members might find a one-of-a-kind diamond ring or a Cadillac Escalade electric golf cart.

Auto Buying Program. Research new cars and find a local dealer who offers special deals to Costco members.

Build a unique diamond solitaire. Learn everything you need to know about shopping for diamonds, then select shape, price, carat size, color and clarity to order a special ring.

Costco Cash card. Check your card's balance.

Costco cookbooks. Browse 1,000-plus recipes from Costco's five cookbooks to help make your next meal memorable.

Custom wine cellars. An easy-to-use online design template offers a simple way to create the perfect wine cellar for any home, restaurant or store.

Membership. Sign up for a new membership or American Express Card, or renew an existing membership.

Photo Center. Order prints for pickup at your local Costco warehouse or special photo gifts to be delivered.

Rebates. Submit a rebate request, check the status of an existing request and find out what rebates are being offered at any given warehouse.

Shopping list. Create a list of items to purchase online, now or later.

Travel. Choose vacation packages, rent a car or book a condo for a holiday getaway.

The Costco Connection. The *Online Edition* combines highlights of the print version with the added value of extended and supplemental content, including a searchable archive of recent issues.—*Steve Fisher*

spring clothing will appear in **mid-December** in warm regions and a month later in colder areas.

So why "early in, early out"? The approach is based partly on Costco's unique membership and partly on traditional retail principles. For starters, one key reason that seasonal items are brought in before the rest of the retail world is because many Costco members are business members who resell the products in their own stores.

Christmas decorations in **September** are a good example. "We develop many one-of-a-kind items from around the world and bring them in early for our gift-shop owners and our wholesale customers, so they can plan ahead for their own purchasing needs," explains Mitzi Hu, vice president and general merchandising manager of imports for Costco.

Another reason is to save costs at the factory. In many cases, particularly with clothes, Costco works directly with manufacturers to make unique products. With an early deadline, many of these products can be manufactured in factory downtimes, a move that helps keep costs low.

Having products in early also provides a helpful litmus test for Costco buyers. They can get a good idea of demand from early sales, then place their final orders accordingly. Ordering accurate amounts is a cost-efficient retail practice.

And as to "early out," the rationale is simple: It minimizes having extra stock on hand that must be marked down at the end of the season. Leftovers either have to be moved and stored or substantially reduced in price. For any retailer, these are huge expenses that can cut into or even consume profits made during the rest of the season.

"Because of the low margins we work on, we don't have the luxury of clearance sales," points out Knapp.

While it may be inconvenient to not find that bathing suit late in the season at Costco, the company's approach to handling seasonal items has many benefits for members. One is that in traditional retail stores prices are highest during peak demand.

"Buying early can save the consumer money," points out Tim Farmer, a Costco vice president who oversees the purchases of major appliances. "Retailers will charge full price for products—or even raise the price—during peak demand. So the price of an air conditioner in July could be at its highest. Also, you risk having it sold out because of the heavy and sudden demand."

He adds, "We hope our members come to trust that whenever Costco brings in a product it represents an excellent value. By buying early, we've been able to achieve savings that are passed on to our members. But for these seasonal goods, it's best to buy early—and not to wait."

The bottom line is that this approach helps Costco in its mission to offer top-quality products at the lowest possible prices for members. Buying products in large volumes, operating no-frills warehouses, fighting to prevent "shrinkage" (goods that are damaged or shoplifted) and bringing in seasonal products in the most efficient way all contribute to savings for members.—*Tim Talevich*

A plea
from the editors

We can't do this all by ourselves! And since there are some 50 million of you—the members of Costco—out there, we were thinking that, just maybe, you could:

Submit tips and household advice for our next *Costco Household Almanac*!

Here are some categories:

Cleaning tips: Ways to use products sold at Costco in safe, effective ways even the manufacturers may not have thought about

Storage tips: How do you handle all of our jumbo sizes and multi-packs?

Organizing tips: For the home, the office, your daily life in general

Safety tips: What to watch out for and what to do in today's surprisingly perilous home environment—electrical hazards, gas leaks, slippery floors

Technology tips: Ways to get the most out of your digital camera, home computer, HDTV, small appliances

For each idea we use in the next almanac, you'll receive a $50 Costco Cash card!

Tip tips:

1. The best tip is pithy, probably no more than 25 words.
2. Some tips will have to be lengthier.
3. Try your tip out yourself. If you survive, go ahead and send it.
4. Originality counts. If this is something you thought of yourself, let us know.
5. Venerability counts. If this was your grandmother's way of doing it, your mom's and yours, you're probably on the right track.
6. Fun. Always fun.

There are two ways to send us your tips:

By mail: Almanac Tips, P.O. Box 34088, Seattle, WA 98124-1088

By e-mail: *almanac@costco.com.* Please put "Tips" in the subject line.

Include your name, address, phone number, e-mail address and Costco membership number. In order to be considered, tips should be sent no later than **October 1, 2007**.

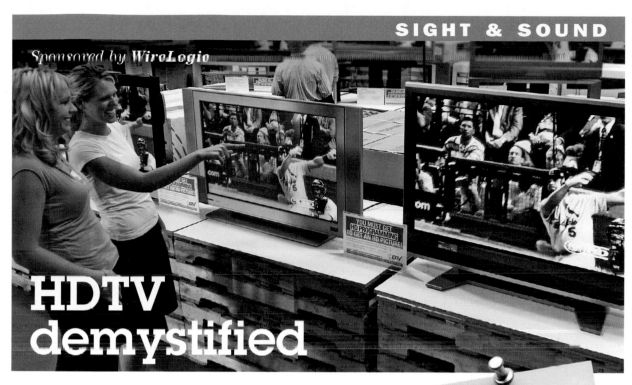

Sponsored by *WireLogic*

HDTV demystified

HIGH-DEFINITION TELEVISION (HDTV) is the hottest item in consumer electronics today, and, with an estimated 88 million sets expected to be sold over the next three years, there is no sign of slowing. Thanks to the picture quality and sleek look (especially flat-panel models), it is no surprise. Yet, despite HDTV's popularity, much of the terminology and technology behind that beautiful picture and amazing sound can still be confusing.

'To err is human—and to blame it on a computer is even more so.

—Robert Orben

What do all those numbers (and acronyms) mean?

Digital television (DTV) broadcasting is the new standard for delivering spectacular picture and sound. In 2009 it will completely replace television broadcasting as we know it. Most televisions capable of showing digital broadcasts offer high definition, while some offer a lower-resolution picture and are known as enhanced definition (EDTV). The displays are labeled based on their capability to show lines of resolution, such as 480i, 480p, 720p, 1080i and 1080p.

The number identifies how many lines run horizontally across the screen in order to make one complete picture; the higher the number, the more detail you will see. The "i" stands for interlaced, meaning the lines of resolution are drawn odd first (lines 1, 3, 5, 7, etc.), then even (lines 2, 4, 6, 8, etc.). The "p" stands for progressive, meaning the lines are drawn in order, yielding a smoother, more detailed picture compared to an interlaced version with the same number of lines. So, a set that's labeled 1080p can show up to 1080 lines horizontally across the screen, drawn progressively in numerical order from top to bottom, thus yielding a better picture than a set labeled 1080i, with interlaced lines.

HDTV starts at 720p, while EDTV sets usually display no greater than 480p resolution. Anything broadcast to EDTV sets at a higher level is down-converted (digitally downgraded) to 480p. ▶

Selecting your TV

You have practical decisions to make. Among them:
- Physical location
- Screen size
- Resolution
- Display and décor options

Start with deciding where you'd like to place your new HDTV. Flat-panel sets give you the flexibility to put the picture where it works best for your lifestyle. Plan on positioning the TV so the display faces the main seating area as straight on as possible.

When choosing screen size, think about how far most viewers will be from the screen. It's rare for people to wish they'd bought a smaller TV, but sometimes it makes the most sense. Being very close to a very big screen will reveal even the best TV's shortcomings.

Proximity is also a factor when it comes to deciding which screen resolution will work best for you; while HDTV is incredibly clear, lower-resolution broadcasts will not look as good up close.

Next, decide if you'd like to display the TV on a stand or hang it on the wall. You have many options with each. Many people are attracted to flat-panel TVs that hang on the wall like magic. If that is the best choice for your room, there are a few things to take into consideration. Make sure the wall you choose is up to the task. An alternating current (AC) outlet should be nearby, and you may want to hide the required cables. Consider engaging a professional installer.

Also ask about available brackets for your TV; typically they must be purchased separately. Several kinds are available. Choices include:
- Flat (allows for a basic, clean installation parallel with the surface)
- Tilt (if your room throws you a curve ball with its angles, this may the best bet)
- Articulating (swings out, rotates side to side and tilts up and down)

Feed your TV

With HDTV, like many things in life, you get back what you put into it. You must have quality sources supplying a video signal to your new set to fully enjoy its ability. To get high-definition television broadcasts from major networks, you can use an off-air antenna if you are in range for reception from the nearest tower. You will also need a set with a built-in HD tuner if you choose this as your source.

But most people want more than just local networks. The options are to subscribe to your local cable-TV provider or sign up with a provider that lets you receive signals from a satellite. Be sure to ask for HD programming and hardware! While not every HD station offers high-definition broadcasts 24 hours a day, the majority of the networks' prime-time offerings, most movie

Antenna options

The Web site *www.antenna.org* provides links to several sites selling antennas suitable for HDTVs.

channels and a number of specialty channels are available in HD, and the number of hours per day that HD is available is increasing all the time. If you're not watching programming broadcast in high definition, your HD set cannot provide true HD quality!

DVDs are another great source for HDTV. Standard DVD players display 480i, while "progressive scan" players show 480p. Two new formats deliver 1080p: HD DVD and Blu-ray.

Getting the picture you saw at the store

To get the picture quality you paid for, be sure to use high-performance video cables. Not all cables are created equal. Only two types of cable deliver HD signals: component and HDMI (high-definition multimedia interface). Component is a three-wire video cable capable of up to 1080i. The video signal is in three separate components, which are translated in the TV. HDMI is a high-bandwidth (10 Gbps, or 10,000 times faster than broadband Internet) digital format for delivering video up to 1080p, along with audio. While it may look simple, and is very simple to connect, it represents cutting-edge technology. Even though there is much going on within better-quality cables that you can't see, the construction and materials make a large difference. Look for silver-plated copper conductors for the best result.

Optimize your HDTV and turn your room into a home theater

The biggest impact you can make after getting an incredible picture is adding big sound to that big picture! Speakers come in many shapes and sizes. Listen to them with a multi-channel receiver capable of digital surround sound, such as Dolby Digital 5.1 or DTS. Look for helpful features such as component video switching or, even better, HDMI switching. Beauty can also be in the ear of the beholder. You are the one investing in and living with your system—select the one within your budget that sounds most pleasing to you.

Getting the sound you heard at the store

Invest in quality cables for your receiver, components and speakers. Digital coax and Toslink (fiber optic) are the only types of audio cables that can deliver digital, multi-channel surround sound. Don't forget to choose a high-quality speaker cable to maintain the performance throughout. Look for audio cables featuring solid-core center conductors.

Getting it home and making it work

For those ready to dive into the do-it-yourself pool, enjoy the satisfaction you can receive from putting your own sweat into your system. However, in order to get every bit of performance available, even if you are handy around the house, you will benefit from having your system professionally installed. Remember, the pros do this every day, and with that comes many an advantage.

Keeping your HDTV clean

YOU'VE MADE THE BIG MOVE to a new flat-panel TV. You've subscribed to a high-definition service to get the right signals. You've set up a surround-sound system for the complete theater-like experience. Given all the expense and steps it takes to enjoy the true HD experience, doesn't it make sense to keep that new big screen clean?

Of course! Big screens attract dust, which can dull the picture. However, keeping them clean requires very careful handling. The problem stems from the fact that many plasma and LCD TVs have a special antiglare coating that can be damaged by the wrong cleaning materials and techniques.

For information on your specific model, the first step is to check the user's guide or the manufacturer's Web site.

Here are some guidelines for keeping your TV clean.

1. Unplug the power cord from the wall or surge protector before cleaning the TV.
2. Use a soft, dry cloth to remove dust from the TV screen. Do not use an abrasive material such as a paper towel to do this.
3. Don't use liquid or aerosol cleaners unless they're especially intended for this purpose.
4. For tougher dirt or fingerprints, proceed with caution. Some manufacturers say you can use a slightly damp cloth with mild soap to lightly clean the screen's surface. Others say you should never use anything but a dry cloth. Check your user's manual.
5. Do not press hard on the screen while cleaning it.

To keep your entire entertainment center looking sharp, it's safe to dust the TV cabinet with a damp cloth or mild cleaner. Just make sure that no liquids drip down into the electronic equipment. You can use a compressed-gas duster (see page 171) to blow dust from hard-to-reach spots. Clean speaker grills by dusting them with a dry cloth: Wet cleaners can stain or damage them.—*Tim Talevich*

Safe power for home electronics

YOU WOULDN'T DREAM of filling a sports car with dirty gasoline, but many people plug their high-performance computers and audio/video components into unprotected outlets without considering the consequences. The electricity in your home was designed to run light bulbs, not sophisticated modern electronics. At best, unfiltered power is dirty, reducing performance and increasing wear and tear. At worst, it can damage electronics beyond repair.

The Electric Power Research Institute estimates that power problems cost American consumers up to $188 billion per year, but you can defeat that statistic with one simple, affordable solution. An uninterruptible power supply (UPS) system with automatic voltage regulation (AVR) protects your electronics with clean, safe, reliable power. Here are a few cases in point.

Problem: Surge/spike (short-term voltage increase from lightning, etc.) causes catastrophic equipment failure, data corruption and incremental damage.
Solution: UPS that provides built-in surge suppression for all outlets

Problem: Sag or brownout (low voltage caused by local or grid overload) causes malfunctions and incremental damage.
Solution: UPS with AVR that adjusts voltage to safe levels

Problem: EMI/RFI (electromagnetic and radio frequency interference) noise from local appliances and other sources causes data corruption and degrades performance, including sound, picture and stability.
Solution: UPS that filters EMI/RFI noise

Problem: Blackout (complete loss of power) causes reduced productivity, system corruption and lost data, settings and recordings. Can destroy projection bulbs due to sudden loss of cooling fans.
Solution: UPS that provides battery backup to support equipment and cooling fans until power is restored or systems are safely shut down

Clean, safe, reliable power from a UPS system with AVR offers you peace of mind and peak performance at a reasonable price, allowing your home computer and electronics investment to pay off for years to come. ▞

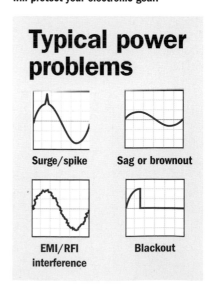

An uninterruptible power supply (UPS)/ battery backup, such as the one above, will protect your electronic gear.

Typical power problems

Surge/spike	Sag or brownout

EMI/RFI interference	Blackout

Why now is the best time to replace your old PC

HAVE YOU HAD a heart-to-heart with your home PC lately? If it's more than a couple of years old, it may be struggling to support your new digital lifestyle.

Don't believe it? Then ask yourself a few questions. Where do you store your photos today: in a shoe box, or on your hard drive? Are you still buying music on CDs, or picking just the tracks you want at iTunes? Have you made an Internet phone call on your PC? Used your Webcam to chat with the grandkids in Seattle? Instant-messaged your significant other while browsing airfares for a weekend getaway? Produced a home video and uploaded it to YouTube? Downloaded last week's episode of *Lost*? If you can't already answer yes to most of these questions, it probably won't be long before you can.

We're constantly inventing new things to do with our PCs, expecting them to act as our post office, newspaper, telephone, television, library, darkroom, video editing suite, jukebox, home theater and global flea market. And we're impatient—we want all of these jobs performed quickly, securely and simultaneously. Multi-tasking isn't just for working moms anymore.

Your PC processor needs a posse

The simple fact is that we're creating more new jobs for our PCs than most were built to handle. Machines that were state-of-the-art just a few years ago may be barely adequate today, and each new digital device that enters our lives adds a new straw to the camel's sagging back. Without downloads to the PC that nifty new iPod is just expensive costume jewelry. That 7-megapixel camera will churn out thousands of huge files to store, sort and process. Many new software programs are multi-threaded—games in particular—with several separate tasks attempting to run at once. In most PCs all of these workloads compete for execution space on a single microprocessor—the PC's silicon brain—and eventually even the fastest may struggle to keep up.

Enter the dual-core processor

Fortunately the PC industry has a high-throughput solution, a new generation of microprocessors built with two independent processing cores in a single physical package. Just like the proverbial two heads, dual-core processors are intrinsically better suited to complex computational challenges. They're ideal for multi-tasking. Compose a slide show while a virus scan runs in the background, download audio files while catching up on your e-mail—a dual-core system has the power to do more at the same time. And because a dual-core processor can distribute its work more efficiently, it may run cooler and consume less energy. They're available today in both desktop and notebook systems, so there's no need to choose between performance and mobility.

This is the PC you'll need tomorrow

Do you really need a dual-core processor for your near-term applications? Well, that's precisely the point. The role that PCs play in our lives and homes is continuing to change rapidly. It's becoming our primary gateway for rich, high-definition media, information and entertainment experiences. There's no end in sight for new PC applications or the workloads that go with them. Dual-core technology is actually arriving just in the nick of time.

It's very much like a new TV purchase decision. If you need a new TV today, do you buy standard or high definition (HD)? Even if HD content isn't immediately available you certainly still buy an HD set. That way, when HD content is ready to connect, your new TV isn't instantly obsolete. It's the same with dual-core PCs. Your digital world is evolving too fast for short-term purchase strategies.

Factor in the newly available Microsoft Windows Vista operating system, the growing list of software that runs better on dual-core processors and the wide range of speeds, cache sizes and price points to fit nearly every budget, and it becomes clear: Everything is coming together to make now a great time to replace your old PC.

What to look for in a new notebook PC

HOW ANCIENT IS your laptop? Is it the size of a dinner platter? Is the LCD on the verge of a twitchy collapse? Faced with the prospect of buying a new notebook PC, your biggest question should be, How will you use the notebook? Will you be traveling? Is it for work, for play or both?

Mobility. Between work and home, you need a notebook PC that works wherever you do. Long battery life is a must-have; sometimes it's not easy to find a power outlet when you're out and about. Internet connectivity is fundamental, as is having flexible options to make the connection. Wireless connectivity is especially important if you frequently inhabit coffee shops and airports, but the option of having a wired connection is handy too. Ultimate flexibility comes with the capability to use cellular phone networks that connect to the Internet when there isn't a hot spot around.

Readability. Working with documents and graphics frequently demands a top-drawer screen that has clarity, brightness and color reproduction that is easy on the eyes.

Today's advanced technology can provide brilliant colors, sharp contrast and crisp pictures. The high brightness level of a display means that black tones appear richer and deeper while white tones remain brighter. Graphics and text are displayed clearly, and colors appear more lifelike, providing a better representation of true colors than a standard LCD display or a standard tube display.

Entertainment. Life isn't all about work. When the day is done, whether you are traveling or relaxing at home, entertainment is a great way to unwind. A built-in DVD player is yet another reason to look for a superior LCD screen for viewing DVDs and home movies. You can enjoy your favorite TV shows on the road by selecting a notebook that has the capability of recording TV programs the way a digital video recorder does. Record shows and watch them later when it's convenient.

Capture, edit and share life. Downloading digital photos and video to a computer is as easy as popping a memory card into a slot or connecting a cable. Again, flexibility is important; you want a notebook that has plenty of hard disk space and port options for connecting your camcorders, such as USB and i.LINK/FireWire ports for digital video transfer. Photo and imaging software bundled with the notebook PC makes it easy to find, edit, share and print photos. Create virtual photo albums for viewing on your notebook PC or burn DVDs to share with family and friends.

On the video side, look for bundled video editing tools that help you capture and edit your home movies to make a Hollywood-style DVD. If you are into chatting and sharing video mail with family and friends, look for a notebook PC with a built-in camera and microphone that integrate with the free AOL AIM service. And finally, verify that the notebook PC is compatible with the Windows Vista operating system.

Style. Style is subjective, which is why you need to pick a notebook that reflects you and not you and a million other folks. Many notebooks on the market are bulky, heavy and on the clunky side. Remember, mobility is the primary reason people buy notebooks. They're looking for portability and functionality, but definitely not a trip to the chiropractor. Look for a notebook that is thin, light and performs. If you can personalize your notebook to reflect your sense of style, then you're adding beauty to substance. ▟

Transfer video and digital pictures to DVD—without a PC

Home movies and digital pictures have a tendency to end up languishing on tapes or memory cards, but now you can unlock new levels of home video enjoyment with a growing category of DVD burners that can be used in place of a computer to transfer video or digital photos to DVD directly.

These new devices have video and audio ports on the side for directly connecting to camcorders, VCRs, even digital video recorders (DVRs), and a little built-in screen to preview the video being transferred.

The DVD recorder works rather like a tape recorder: You press "Play" on the camcorder/VCR/DVR and the video appears on the DVD recorder's screen. When you're

at the piece of video you want to record, you press the red "Record" button and, presto, you are burning a DVD. When you're done recording, press the "Stop" button; a chapter will be created on the DVD. Recording occurs in real time, so five minutes of video on tape takes five minutes to record to DVD. You can repeat the process as often as you want until the DVD is full or you have captured all the video you want. The finished DVD will play in regular home DVD players.

Look for a DVD recorder that accepts the five most common digital camera memory cards—Memory Stick Duo, Memory Stick, Secure Digital (SD), xD Picture Card and Compact Flash [see page 152]—and

you can transfer and record all the pictures from a memory card to a DVD just by pressing the "Record" button on the DVD recorder. At the end, you can choose to have the pictures on the DVD as files or you can create a DVD slide show that will play on a home DVD player.

A DVD recorder can even connect with the new hard-disk-based camcorders (see page 132), which store video on an internal hard drive instead of a tape. Connect the camcorder to the DVD recorder via USB cable and, with a single button push, all the video can be transferred to DVD at up to six times the real-time speed (say, an hour of video in about 10 minutes).

Widescreen LCDs: The future of monitors today

MORE AND MORE, desktop monitors are being used for both work and play. And with desktop entertainment becoming more prevalent, a wide screen is the ideal choice. A major driver of widescreen popularity is the availability of movies, games and videos in 16:9 (wide) format. Matching your monitor to this wide content allows for the best possible picture quality for each of these entertainment choices.

In addition to the entertainment benefits, widescreen displays enhance productivity. Whether you're a business professional, student or casual Web surfer, having enough physical and virtual workspace is important, yet often hard to come by. Fortunately today's widescreen LCDs (liquid crystal displays) allow users to increase valuable workspace without great difficulty for much less than you may expect. And these new monitors are easy to set up: You basically just plug them in.

How widescreen displays improve productivity

Widescreen displays expand desktop real estate, allowing users to open multiple applications or manipulate two full-size Word or Excel documents side by side without toggling. With a widescreen display, users can surf the Internet and review accounting spreadsheets on the same screen.

While it's possible to view two full documents or work in two applications simultaneously on a dual-monitor setup, a widescreen display is a more affordable alternative.

Features to look for in a widescreen display

For all purposes, you should look for high resolution, high brightness and maximum contrast ratios. A nice added feature in your display is VESA® wall-mount compliance so that you can maximize desk space by mounting the display.

For entertainment, look for fast video response times, as well as digital and analog inputs for flexible component connectivity options. The faster the video response, the crisper and clearer gaming and movie images will be. With digital inputs, you can connect high-definition game consoles and DVD players to the display and immerse yourself in your favorite game or movie.

Displays with digital inputs with high-definition content protection

(HDCP) ensure that a monitor will be compatible with future digital content and technologies.

Windows® Vista™ and widescreen displays

Windows Vista complements the advances in widescreen displays. Monitor vendors who work closely with Microsoft offer Vista-certified displays that take business applications, home use and entertainment to even higher levels. Vista offers greater widescreen compatibility than ever before, with a host of new features suited for the widescreen format, thus further improving desktop efficiency and enhancing productivity.

For example, the Windows Sidebar feature is a pane on the side of the desktop that organizes "gadgets," giving users easy access to the applications they use most, such as calculators, Web services and media players. In addition, Vista's Windows Flip feature allows users to quickly flip through open applications using the Alt+Tab control, which provides a live thumbnail of each window. ⚡

Microsoft, Windows and the Windows logo are trademarks or registered trademarks of Microsoft Corporation in the United States and/or other countries. Windows Vista and the Windows Vista logo are trademarks or registered trademarks of Microsoft Corporation in the United States and/or other countries.

With widescreen monitors, movies and pictures shot in the new 16:9 format are displayed in their entirety—no more lost areas of the image. And for other purposes, you can display several programs on the desktop, enhancing productivity.

How to set up your wide-screen monitor

Refer to your monitor's user guide for the optimum screen resolution. To set the resolution, follow these steps:

1. Go to the "Settings" function on your Windows "Start" menu and select "Control Panel."
2. Double-click on the "Display" icon.
3. Select the "Settings" tab.
4. Click and drag the Screen Resolution slider until it reads "1680 x 1050" or matches the optimum resolution recommended in the user guide.
5. Click "Apply" or "OK" to set the resolution. Your screen might flicker momentarily as the resolution resets.
6. Click "OK" again.
7. After the screen settings are changed, a message box appears, asking whether you want to keep the new setting. Click "Yes" to keep the settings.

If you have difficulty setting the resolution, contact your vendor's customer support department for further assistance.

Flash media and the age of the "personal almanac"

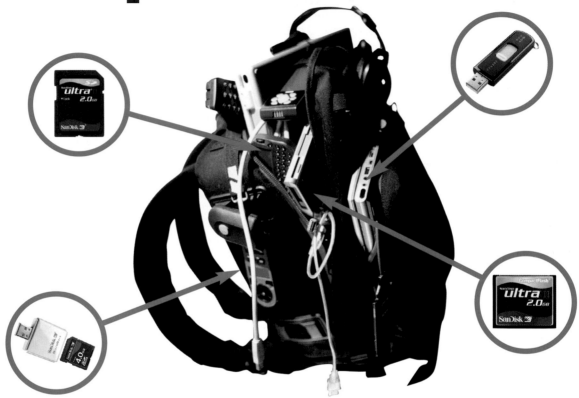

WOULDN'T IT BE USEFUL to have your own personal almanac—a collection of dependable and handy data and media files you could carry around with you and access at will?

Collecting—and transporting—large amounts of information is exactly what you can do with flash media (you know, those little cards you use in your digital camera or those data-storage doodads your friends carry around on their key chains). As opposed to the memory on your hard drive, flash media store information without a power source. Most commonly seen as "flash media cards" or "flash cards," flash memory cards are extremely stable and rugged, and have decades-long archival qualities. In addition to being handy, compact and durable, these cards allow you to erase old data and store new data.

Because of technological advances in flash memory, storage capacity for some formats now exceeds 12 gigabytes. SanDisk, the company that invented Compact Flash, will release a card later this year with an amazing 16 GB worth of memory capacity. You could literally record your entire world of data on just one card: photos, special events, music, video ... just about everything. *Voilà*, a personal almanac!

The evolution of flash media and rapid advances in flash technology have been impressive. In 1990, the first "flash chip" was shipped. Used in the manufacture of another product, this flash chip boasted a whopping 4 MB (yes, that's megabytes, not gigabytes) worth of memory. SanDisk shipped the world's first Compact Flash card in 1994, and the race was on. In 1998, the maximum flash-card storage capacity was 128 MB. Today, just nine years later, 16 GB is the maximum. Flash-memory storage capacity has doubled practically every year since 1998, outpacing even Moore's Law, which states that computing capacity doubles every 18 months.

Why is this increasing memory capacity for portable devices so important? Today our lifestyle can be described with one word: mobile. We are a world on the go. We want flexible hours, home offices, connected networks, constant communication. We want access to our data at any and all times, when and where we want it. We want to transfer and transport files, pictures, video, audio, text—our lives. We want to do this quickly, easily, securely and often. Flash media allows all of these things to happen. Right now!

Today, flash cards and USB 2.0 flash drives are used by millions of people around the world in digital cameras, MP3 players, PDAs, notebook computers and video game consoles. Possibly the largest market for flash cards is making its presence felt this year. The majority of cell phones produced from January 2007 forward will include flash-card slots for memory expansion.

As you might expect, consumer electronic devices that need flash media require varying flash-card designs and capacities. For precisely that reason, flash media come in a variety of forms, or form factors, as engineers call them. The most popular are:

Compact Flash. Popular with demanding photographers because of its large memory capacity. High-speed performance is important.

Secure Digital (SD). The most popular form factor. Used in almost every consumer electronic category. Most digital cameras use SD. A new format this year, SDHC (Secure Digital High Capacity), begins at 4 GB capacity but may not work in older devices. Look for devices with the SDHC logo.

Memory Stick Pro Duo (MSPD). Used mostly for Sony digital cameras, video recorders and PSP/PS-3 gaming consoles.

USB 2.0 Flash Drives. These have become very popular. The devices are about a half-inch wide and a quarter-inch thick, roughly the size of a large paper clip. These amazingly fast and convenient drives allow the user to store as much as 8 GB worth of data, transport it, then download it just about anywhere. New "U3" technology ensures the most secure use of these cool drives. Make sure your flash-drive purchase includes U3.

xD-Picture Card. This flash-card form factor is exclusively for use with Olympus or Fuji xD-compatible digital devices. Only the Olympus xD-Picture Card has the "panorama" feature.

Mobile products. The two key form factors are Mini SD and Micro SD. Currently, maximum capacity is 2 GB. Once you see the actual size of this fantastic product, you will not believe your eyes: It's about one-quarter the size of a postage stamp, and almost as thin! 🔊

Digitizing old videos

BACK IN THE "OLD" VHS video camera era, most of us thought the tapes bearing our cherished memories would last forever. Unfortunately, the truth is video lasts only 10 to 30 years. At some point in that life span, the quality will start to degrade and the memories may be gone forever. But technology has a way of providing solutions for its shortcomings. If you have a computer, you can protect your family history by converting those analog treasures to digital ones, and you don't have to be a technical wizard to do it. All you need is time and some techno-tools.

The right stuff

Digitizing video proves to be a memory hog. In order to minimize any potential frustration, your computer should have plenty of RAM (random access memory) and a decent processing speed. The general recommendation is no less than 512 MB of RAM and at least a 2.8 GHz CPU (central processing unit or processor). More of each is better. Many computers on the market today have at least 1 GB of RAM, but basic computers might have slower processors. It's not that you won't be able to achieve the task, but you may have to wait longer for it to be completed, and you can pretty much forget about multi-tasking.

When you transfer video from VHS to digital files, you'll want to store them on your computer for editing before burning to DVD. This takes an enormous amount of disk space, so be sure to have at least 40 to 120 GB of free space available. If your computer does not have a large disk drive, you can always purchase an external drive for a reasonable amount of money.

Video capture tools are a necessary part of the process. These enable the transfer of video from your camera or video player to the computer. There are three basic types.

Video capture cards. Capture cards record and convert the video to digital format and must be installed inside the computer. Capture cards can cost from less than $100 to thousands of dollars depending on the format and resolution required.

External capture device. This is a small "box" that connects the video source to the computer and enables the capture of VHS video without having to add anything inside the computer. External capture devices can run from $50 to $150 for home models.

Graphics cards with video capturing. These combine video capturing capabilities with graphics so nothing extra is needed. Many new computers come with built-in digital video connections. Internal and external TV tuners may also have ancillary capture capabilities.

Two other elements are important parts of the process.

Video editing software. Once your videos are digitized on your computer, you'll want to edit them to select the best parts, get rid of those shots of the ceiling and floor, and add video effects, titles and, perhaps, even music. With the editing suites available today, anyone can be a junior Spielberg, and many cost less than $100.

DVD burners. Once your "epic" is finished, you'll want to burn it onto a DVD for easy sharing. Many of the computers manufactured in the past couple of years have DVD burners as standard features, but if yours does not have one, you can get an internal or external drive for less than $100.—*Steve Fisher*

Making the most of your iPod

By Marc Saltzman

MARC SALTZMAN is one of the leading technology experts in the United States and Canada. Along with his regular tech column for The Costco Connection, *Saltzman writes weekly syndicated columns for Gannett News Service, CNN.com, USAToday.com and CanWest Media, and contributes to dozens of other leading publications. He also hosts two radio shows focusing on technology and has written 13 books, including* White Collar Slacker's Handbook: Tech Tricks to Fool Your Boss *(Que Publishing, 2005).*

APPLE'S MEGAPOPULAR IPOD PLAYERS are a wonderful product for music lovers on the go. Apple, along with other companies, has created incredibly cool accessories to complement the iPod. In fact, more than 2,000 add-ons have been designed for the popular player. A good many of them are sold at Costco.

One of my favorites is an FM transmitter/charger kit that enables you to listen to your iPod's songs, podcasts or audio books in your car—without risking your safety by a wearing headset. A dock for the iPod attaches to your car's cigarette lighter, which provides power and recharges the iPod. A clever FM transmitter in the dock wirelessly beams the audio to your car's FM radio.

Another area where iPod accessories shine is speaker systems. You can plug your iPod into a variety of systems, such as a bedside clock radio, a boombox for music on the go or a high-end home system, complete with subwoofer and 200 watts of power. The docks in these systems usually double as iPod chargers.

But the hottest iPod developments deal with video. The latest generation of iPods can display video clips—movies, TV shows, video podcasts and even your own home video, if converted into the right format. These video clips can be obtained through iTunes, Apple's media Web site. And with a simple cable, you can display these video clips on a TV or monitor.

In terms of taking care of your iPod, some simple steps can help out. You can save battery power by using the back-light and shuffle functions sparingly. And for protection, cases are on the market that can shield your iPod in case it's dropped. (It'll happen, trust me.)

Also, I recommend that you shouldn't be too extremely active with the hard-drive-based iPods. But the flash-memory-based players (iPod nano or iPod shuffle) have no moving parts, which makes them ideal for a workout.

Last, iPods are prone to scratching, so you might consider cleaning kits that can help restore them.

◆TDK

Capture and Share Your Memories

We look forward to celebrating holidays, birthdays, weddings and other important events, yet these exciting and memorable occasions pass all too quickly. Imagine being able to relive these special times again and again by making your own DVD movies. With TDK camcorder tapes and DVD media, you can create professional quality home DVD movies!

The process is simple and fun. Load a TDK DVC camcorder tape into your Mini-DV camcorder and capture your footage. Next, connect the camcorder to your computer and transfer the footage to its hard drive. Professional quality edits, titles, fades, special effects and much more can be done with a click of a mouse. Now, record your creation on a DVD. Voila! You've created a disc that's sure to impress friends and family.

Protect What Matters Most

TDK media products are formulated with premium materials, tested by broadcast and production professionals and trusted by countless everyday users like you. Protect what matters most with TDK.

DVC
8 Pack

VHS
10 Pack

DVD-R
100 Pack Spindle

DVD+R
100 Pack Spindle

Data CD-R80
100 Pack Spindle

Music CD-R80
75 Pack Spindle

A

B

C

D

E

A. TEAC Ultra-Thin Hi-Fi System
This elegant system features an integrated iPod® dock, CD player, AM/FM tuner, powered subwoofer and flat-panel speakers. Includes a full function remote control. iPod not included. Item #173631

B. iPod Car Kit
Charge, power and play your iPod on the road with stereo-quality sound. Includes all-in-one TuneBase FM transmitter/charger, AC travel adapter and a USB 30-pin sync charge cable. iPod not included. Item #195179

C. Logitech Harmony 720 Advanced Remote
One-touch activity control turns on your devices, sets inputs—even presses Play! Features color LCD display and rechargeable design. Item #104355

D. Franklin Covey Computer Tote
Featuring a full-grain cowhide leather exterior, this computer tote includes a secure flap-over closure, large padded computer pocket, full-length zipper pocket, removable accessory pouch and three padded pockets for computer accessories. Item #151676

E. KLH RSP-800 Outdoor Speakers
Disguised as landscape rocks, these high-fidelity, all-weather speakers feature two-way sound distribution utilizing an 8" with a coaxial 1" tweeter. Includes 125' of burial cable. Item #103329

Mount your flat-panel TV with Simplicity.

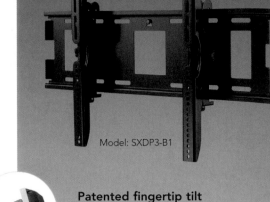

Model: SXDP3-B1

New flat-panel TVs offer a larger, crisper picture in a much thinner design… usually less than 4 inches thick. And thin is in! This opens new possibilities in home decorating. Possibilities such as hanging a TV on the wall, just like any piece of art. So, when buying your new flat-panel TV, don't forget the mount.

Safety and style

Simplicity mounts are strong and reliable. Their heavy-gauge steel construction supports even the largest flat-panel TVs. And the sleek, powder-coated finish offers a contemporary look. Add a padlock (sold separately) for extra safety and security.

Ease of installation

Simplicity mounts are designed for do-it-yourself installation. All mounting hardware is included. Simply mount two brackets to the TV and the wall plate to the wall, then lift the TV and set it onto the wall plate. In most cases, installation requires just one person, and even the heaviest TVs can be installed quickly and easily with the help of a friend.

Versatility

Simplicity mounts are dual purpose, with both low-profile and tilting brackets to provide multiple mounting options. Low-profile brackets position the TV just about 1 inch from the wall to maximize the sleek, thin lines of modern flat-panel TVs. This is a great choice when a clean, flush appearance is the main goal.

Tilting brackets can be angled up and down for better viewing from the couch, bed or even the floor. Innovative patented fingertip tilt technology allows effortless angle adjustment with just the touch of a finger; no tools needed! And the tilt motion is smooth, even under the full load of the heaviest TVs. Tilting brackets are also a great solution when reflections from windows or lighting interfere with TV viewing.

So, when you're ready to buy your new TV, make a simple choice… choose Simplicity!

Patented fingertip tilt offers effortless tilt motion without the use of tools.

Low profile positions TV ultra-close to the wall for a flush appearance.

Universal mounting brackets fit nearly all flat-panel TVs.

Lateral shift allows TV to slide left or right for perfect TV placement, even with off-center studs.

Wire management wall plate features cutouts, allowing cables to be routed into wall or J-box for concealed wire management.

simplicity ™

available in warehouses and online at costco.com

SONY

Sony brings high performance and sleek styling to your living room

46" Bravia KDL46V25L1 LCD Television
Spectacular picture, spectacular style

- BRAVIA Engine™ Technology: Full digital video processing system reduces unwanted digital artifacts for clear, crisp and clean images.

- Full HD 1080p LCD TV with native 1920 x 1080 panel resolution: Experience a clean, crisp picture with more than 6.2 million pixels.

- Live Color Creation Featuring WCG-CCFL: Combines a customized wide color gamut (WCG) backlight with special processing to create color filters to create deep, rich colors.

- 178° Wide Viewing Angle: Not a bad seat in the house! Now everyone gets a chance to see great color and contrast.

- Multiple Digital HDMI (High-Definition-Multimedia Interface) Inputs: Two digital inputs provide a pure digital/audio video connection.

- PC Input: Enjoy the convenience of being able to use your notebook or desktop PC with your home television[1].

1. Limited to resolutions supported by both the PC and the Sony TV. See Sony TV users manual.

DAV-HDX501W/C 5.1 Ch.
Home Theater System
HD Audio: Hear the big picture

- Five-disc DVD/CD player with HDMI output

- 1000 watts of power (RMS 10% THD)

- XM™ Connect and Play ready[1]

- iPod™ cradle included[2]

- DIGITAL MEDIA PORT interface

- Includes subwoofer plus two tall-boy front, slim center, and surround speakers

- Wireless speaker kit included

- Auto Calibration for simple set up

- Available late May 2007

1. XM Connect and Play requires subscription and antenna, which are sold separately. Antenna placement restrictions apply.

2. TDM-iP1 is compatible with iPod nano (2G/1G), iPod (5G/4G) and iPod mini. Please check for compatibility first. Design and specifications are subject to change without notice.

iPod is a trademark of Apple Computer, Inc., registered in the U.S. and other countries.

You will clearly see the difference.

67" Wide-Screen DLP® HDTV with 1080p Resolution: Featuring a thin bezel design that "fits where others won't," Samsung's 67" wide-screen DLP TV delivers an astounding HDTV experience. Samsung created the Cinema Smooth™ light engine that produces razor-sharp pictures in 1080p. The natural vivid colors of Samsung's HL-S6767W are achieved through our advanced Brilliant Color™ technology with a faster color wheel. Item #116767

HL-S6767W

DLP
TEXAS INSTRUMENTS

SAMSUNG

23" Wide-Screen LCD HDTV: Samsung's LNT2332 is the perfect answer for the savvy consumer who demands the highest quality and value in a wide-screen LCD HDTV. The slim, matte-black frame around the 23" screen incorporates side-firing speakers, two component video inputs, PC input and an HDMI input. Item #333323

LNT2332

Ideas You Can't Live Without

Crisp, colorful images that are amazingly lifelike. Powerful sounds that put you right in the middle of the action. Efficient connections that let you stay in touch like never before. These are just a few of the great ideas in store for you from Panasonic. Ideas for Life.

America's Best Selling Plasma Brand*

DMR-EZ475VK
DVD Recorder with VCR and AccuTune™ Digital Tuner

KX-TG6074B
5.8 GHz Digital Cordless Answering System

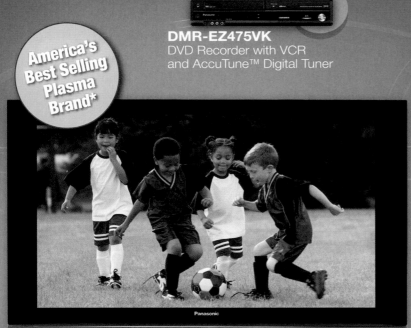

TH-50PE77U 50" Diagonal Plasma HDTV

SC-PT753
5-DVD Home Theater System with Rear Wireless Speakers

DMC-TZ3K
7.2 Megapixel Lumix® Digital Camera with 10x Optical Zoom and Stabilization

VDR-D220
DVD Camcorder with Optical Image Stabilization

Panasonic ideas for life

Turn up your viewing experience

PHILIPS

Philips 63" Plasma High-Definition Flat TV: Only 3.8" thick, this 63" plasma TV features easy connectivity with two HDMI inputs, two component inputs and a side A/V input with USB. Pixel Plus 3HD processes more than 4 trillion colors to give the most natural skin tones and brightest colors on both HD and non-HD programming. Native Panel resolution 1366 x 768p. Includes table stand and wall mounting bracket.

Philips 42" 1080p LCD High-Definition Flat TV: This 42" full HD LCD features three HDMI inputs, two component inputs, and a side A/V input with USB. Pixel Perfect HD engine, Philips' advanced picture processing, improves sharpness and colors on all video signals including current versions of 1080p (24, 25, 30, 50, 60 Hz). Native Panel resolution 1920 x 1080p. Includes table stand.

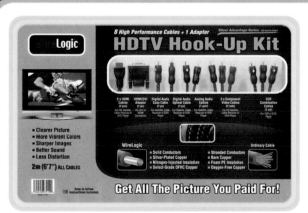
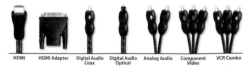

LC-60C52U
LC-60C46U

Experience Full HD 1080p

- **Full HD 1080p Resolution**
  provides OUTSTANDING detail.

- **10,000:1 Dynamic Contrast Ratio**
  optimizes the picture based on content black levels.

- **4ms Response Time**
  provides true film-like smoothness.

- **4-Wavelength Backlight System**
  adds deep crimson to the conventional colors of red, green and blue.

AQUOS®
THERE'S MORE TO SEE

The body as a topic of conversation

Health is worth more than learning.

–Thomas Jefferson

By Dr. Mehmet C. Oz and Dr. Michael E. Roizen

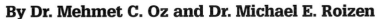

SURE, BECOMING AN EXPERT on your own body can save your life. As if that's not enough, your superior knowledge about health can change the lives of folks around you—not to mention give you gloating rights for having done so. The problem is, talking about how our bodies really work—what goes on in the digestive tract; the importance of paying attention to secretions of all sorts; the sizes, shapes and colors of diseased organs—can be uncomfortable in many situations and downright taboo in others. So the question is: How do you break the ice so you can talk with strangers about the act of breaking wind?

DR. MEHMET C. OZ (left) AND DR. MICHAEL E. ROIZEN

are the authors of the two spectacularly successful books: YOU: The Owner's Manual *and* YOU on a Diet. *Dr. Oz serves as vice chair of surgery and professor of cardiac surgery at Columbia University. He is known to millions of televsion viewers for his zestful appearances (in scrubs) on the* Oprah *show. Dr. Roizen is chair of the Division of Anesthesiology, Critical Care Medicine and Pain Management at the Cleveland Clinic, where he practices internal medicine and anesthesiology.*

It's tough to bring these subjects out in the open as we try to coax people along the path to health, but we're here to share our secrets for offering gee-whiz information that has wow-bang results.

First, the ground rules for talking medicine in social circles:

1. **No insults.** People won't remember anything useful if they're still stinging from a barb that insinuates that their waistline looks like a big bag full of gelatin.
2. **No scolding.** Nagging is about as effective as a two-legged table.
3. **Have fun.** People love imps, so use humor—perhaps directed at yourself—to initiate a touchy topic.

What now? Pick your spots for adding insight, information, inspiration—and a little body awareness—into the lives of others.

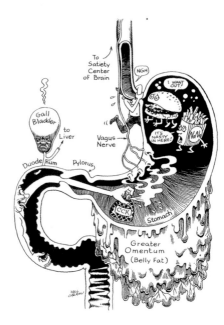

At the bar

Your insight: Women lack the enzyme that enables men to metabolize half of their ingested alcohol in their stomachs before it can enter the bloodstream. As a result, most women cannot withstand alcohol as effectively as men and become intoxicated more quickly or suffer such effects as constipation. **The fix:** A glass of water between drinks will help avoid intoxication and the constipation associated with dehydration.

At the water cooler

Your information: The canker sore he's trying to hide? It has nothing to do with being filthier than a corn-scarfing hog. His immune cells are overreacting to a virus (or even to his own cells), and the resulting collateral injury manifests as a canker sore oozing with the dead cells. **The treatment:** Zinc, vitamin C and stress reduction.

In the fast-food line

Your inspiration: A bulging waistline is made up of fat in the omentum (a fatty layer deep in the abdomen) that compresses the kidneys (causing hypertension) and paralyzes insulin production (causing diabetes). Mention that the omentum is like a fish net hanging off the stomach that catches digesting French fries, especially if they careen down on a stream of high-fructose corn syrup. **The awareness:** Hopefully, this appetizing metaphor will sour your friend on junk food forever.

In the end, inspiring health lessons resonate with everyone. When you find a defensible reason to educate a friend about health, you enter a no-embarrassment zone that could be life altering. Go ahead, try a little body talk and make a difference. /!\

How to feel good all over

WE THANK OUR good friends at that *great* great-granddaddy of all almanacs, *The Old Farmer's Almanac,* for this jaunty romp through a few classic home remedies.

From the top of your head ...

Feel a headache coming on? Pinch yourself. Specifically, put the squeeze on the webbed area between the thumb and first finger of either hand. Hold it for 30 seconds. Pressure applied here will stimulate nerve impulses to the brain and relax blood vessel dilation. Your headache won't have a chance to settle in.

up your nose ...

When your head feels under pressure and your nose is all stuffed up, and even your teeth hurt, you don't have a common cold. You have a sinus infection. To get relief, mix 1/2 teaspoon of salt into 1 cup of water. (Use cool water if you're stuffed up but have no discharge. If the mucus is thick, use warm water to help liquefy it.) Bring the mixture into the shower and set it to the side. Turn on the water and let it hit your face for three to five minutes. Hot water helps liquefy and drain the mucus. Now pour some salt water into a cupped hand and inhale, so the water goes up your nose. This alleviates irritation, washes out the mucus and kills bacteria. Spit out what goes down into your throat, and gargle with the rest of the salt water to clear your throat. You can do this snorting/gargling routine up to four times a day.

down your throat ...

A quick, easy way to quiet a dry, hacking cough is to chew gingerroot. Cut off a quarter-inch piece, trim off the peel and put it into your mouth. Chew it slowly: The juice will feel hot in the mouth and throat, and the cough will be gone in a minute. The ginger brings blood to the throat and helps soothe it. When you're finished chewing, spit out the pulp.

to the tips of your fingers and toes ...

When a painful blood blister forms under a fingernail or toenail, get a small metal paper clip (not a plastic-coated one) and straighten out one end of it. Light a match and, while holding the clip with a pair of tweezers or pliers, heat the straightened end. Touch the hot metal tip to the surface of the nail just above the half-moon, so that it goes through. The blood will drain and relief will be yours. ⧫

Source: The Old Farmers Almanac 2004, *"Home Remedies" by Steve Calechman*

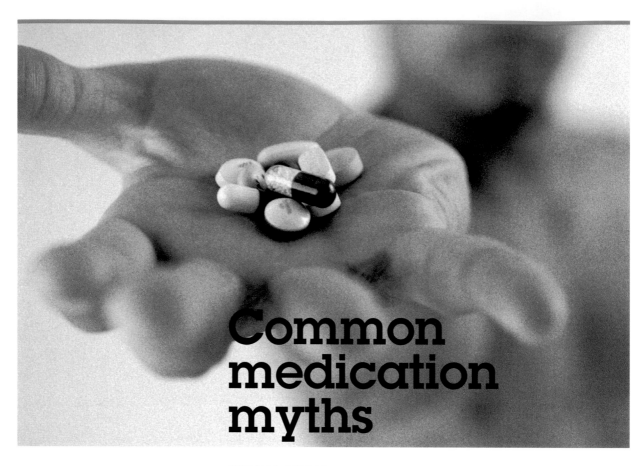

Common medication myths

SEVERAL COMMON MEDICAL myths can prove to be very dangerous to consumers. The American Society of Health-System Pharmacists aims at dispelling these myths and educating the public on the correct usage of medications. Here are a few of their top targets.

Myth: Nonprescription medications are safer than prescription medications.
Truth: All medications, even those sold without a prescription, have the potential to cause harm. Taking more than the recommended dose can cause serious adverse effects, such as stomach bleeding, as well as liver or kidney problems. Adverse reactions to nonprescription medicines can sometimes occur even when patients follow instructions exactly. In addition, the effects of certain prescription medications can be significantly bolstered or weakened if they are taken with some nonprescription medicines. Patients should tell their physician and pharmacist about all the medications they are taking, including vitamins and herbal supplements, to help avoid potentially dangerous drug interactions.

Myth: Splitting pills is a safe way to save money.
Truth: Consumers, especially seniors, often split pills to save money, but doing so can disrupt essential properties of the medications. For example, some medications contain a time-release property that is destroyed when a pill is cut, reducing the medication's safety. Also, because some pills are made with a protective coating to prevent nausea, an upset stomach may result if the coating is broken. Always ask your pharmacist if a pill is safe to split.

Myth: Children can take adult medications in smaller doses.
Truth: When it comes to medications, children are not small adults. Children may react differently than adults to the same medication. For example, antihistamines cause drowsiness in adults but may cause hyperactivity in children. The proper dosage for children may be lower than for adults; however, in some cases, children require larger doses than adults (such as with medications used to treat seizures). Always ask your child's doctor or pharmacist if you have questions about the correct dose of a medication.

Myth: The bathroom medicine cabinet is a good place to store medications.
Truth: Medications should never be stored in the bathroom because of the negative effects of excessive heat and humidity. Additionally, the bathroom is an easy place for children to explore, and medications should always be kept out of children's reach. Medicines should ideally be stored in a secure, dark location at 65 to 80 degrees, with little humidity.

Myth: Medication can be taken safely with any liquid.
Truth: Instructions on medications should be read carefully. Some liquids may enhance or diminish the effect of a medication. For example, grapefruit juice helps in the absorption of certain AIDS medications; however, it completely neutralizes some medications for high blood pressure. Always check with your pharmacist to determine which liquids are safe to take with your medicines.

Myth: Receiving a flu shot can give you the flu.
Truth: Although some people may feel ill after receiving a flu shot, it is impossible for a flu vaccination to cause the flu. Also, it's important to remember that the vaccination you receive only protects you from particular virus strains. You may still get sick if you are exposed to a different strain. Flu vaccinations are an invaluable tool to protect you from a dangerous illness.

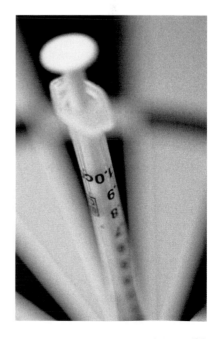

Myth: My spouse's prescription can help me if I have the same ailment.
Truth: Taking a medication that is not prescribed for you is never recommended. This is because physicians prescribe medications based on an individual's needs and circumstances, taking into consideration factors such as age, weight, existing medical conditions and other prescriptions.

Myth: My doctor knows which medications I'm taking.
Truth: In some cases, a doctor may not have your complete medical history. Take an active role in your own care by telling your physician about your medical history. When seeing your physician, bring along all of the medications you are currently taking, especially if more than one doctor has prescribed medications for you. Include nonprescription drugs. You should also feel free to ask your doctor or pharmacist any questions you have related to prescription and nonprescription medications. ♦

Source: American Society of Health-System Pharmacists (www.ashp.org)

Running hot or cold on pain?

YOU'VE GOT AN "owie." What's the best approach to treating that ache, pain or injury?

Heat and cold therapies both play a role in the treatment of muscle and tissue conditions, and both are used to help alleviate pain.

However, because body tissue responds differently to heat and cold, and because the cause of an injury—and therefore the source of pain—can vary, you should know when each treatment is appropriate.

How does heat therapy work?

By activating receptors found in tendons, muscles, ligaments and joints, heat inhibits pain receptors, reduces muscle tension and enhances blood flow to tissues. The increased blood flow improves healing by allowing an influx of cells involved in tissue repair. The effects of heat also decrease joint stiffness.

When should heat therapy be used?

Heat therapy is commonly used for everyday muscle aches, soreness, stiffness and spasms, backache and various forms of arthritis.

Heat is also often recommended to treat chronic ailments, including muscle tightness and tension, and may be effective therapy after four or five days following an injury.

How does cold therapy work?

The swelling and inflammation that result from an injury are primarily caused by fluid leaking from damaged blood vessels. Application of cold to the injury helps constrict the blood vessels, reducing their tendency to leak and restricting the amount of fluid buildup, thereby reducing the degree of swelling and inflammation. Lowering the temperature of the skin over the injury can also help reduce pain and muscle spasms.

When should cold therapy be used?

Cold therapy is recommended for treatment of acute or sudden injury, and is recommended as the immediate treatment for almost all sports injuries, including stress fractures, sprains, pulled muscles, tendonitis, hamstring injuries, runner's knee and tennis elbow.

Treatment with cold may be effective for acute flare-ups of chronic conditions, and cold therapy has also been used for many years for the relief of pain associated with migraine headaches.—*T. Foster Jones*

Sources: www.medicinenet.com; www.merckfrosst.ca; www.canadianpain society.ca; www.postgradmed.com

*Sponsored by **Johnson & Johnson Consumer Companies, Inc.***

For healthy healing, keep wounds covered

THERE IS A COMMON misperception that keeping minor cuts and scrapes uncovered to let them air out helps them heal faster, but extensive research has proven this to be untrue. In fact, if a wound is not covered, it may grow larger and deeper before it heals.

Keeping wounds covered protects them from infection and can make the wound less painful. Additionally, cuts and scrapes can heal faster in a moist environment than in a dry one. When left uncovered and exposed to air, wounds dry out and form a scab, which can lead to scarring. Scabs actually slow the healing process by creating a barrier between healthy skin cells. Bandages that absorb fluids and maintain natural moisture let skin cells travel seamlessly and form new, smooth tissue.

When a wound is covered, the body sends a signal to the skin that it can heal at a regular, more organized pace, so the skin is less likely to scar. In essence, keeping a wound covered with a bandage can enhance nature's healing process.

Meanwhile, keeping wounds covered helps prevent exposure to water, dirt and germs while providing extra cushioning for added comfort and protection from reinjury.

No matter the type of cut, scrape or laceration, experts suggest this easy-to-follow, three-step process to promote better healing:

- **Clean.** Thoroughly flush and clean the affected area with mild soap and water or an antiseptic wash and allow to dry.
- **Treat.** Apply a small amount of antibiotic ointment to the affected area to help prevent infection.
- **Protect.** Put on the bandage and keep the wound covered until it is completely healed.

The first three to five days of healing are key, so keep it covered! 🅰

You can learn more online at www.band-aid.com.

Uncovered wound

Moisture escapes

- Scab forms.
- Wound dries out.
- Epidermis slides underneath scab.

Covered wound

Bandage

- No scab forms.
- Moisture is retained.
- Epidermis grows across a flatter wound.

Protecting your eyes the natural way

By Joyce Tellier Johnson, N.D.

ACCORDING TO A STUDY conducted by the National Eye Institute (*www.nei.nih.gov*), Americans fear blindness more than any other disability, including cancer and heart disease.

More than 3.5 million Americans over the age of 40 suffer from some sort of vision loss. The chances of developing eyesight problems increase dramatically with age, due partly to environmental conditions such as cigarette smoke and ultraviolet radiation damage from the sun and partly to the body's inability to synthesize nutrients that protect and enhance eye health and vision. Cataracts and age-related macular degeneration (AMD) are the top two age-related causes of blindness or reduced vision.

Age-related macular degeneration

Macular degeneration is a descriptive term for any condition that leads to loss of function of the light-sensitive cells at the center of the retina. Peripheral vision is preserved, but reading becomes impossible. Blurred or distorted vision and trouble discerning colors can be symptoms of AMD. The Amsler grid test is one of the simplest and most effective methods of monitoring macular health. The Amsler grid is a pattern of intersecting lines (identical to graph paper) with a black dot in the middle. One stares at the central dot. With normal vision, all lines surrounding the black dot will look straight and evenly spaced, with no missing or odd-looking areas. When the macula is not healthy, as in macular degeneration, the lines can look bent, distorted and/or missing.

You can order a free Amsler test grid online at *www.ixm.us* or take the test at *www.eyesight.org/Eye_Test/eye_test.html*.

Cataracts

A cataract is a clouding of the lens in one or both eyes that affects vision. Most cataracts are related to aging. In a normal eye, light passes through the transparent lens to the retina, where it is changed into nerve signals that are sent to the brain. The lens must be clear for the retina to receive a sharp image. If the lens is cloudy from a cataract, the image will be blurred.

Cataracts can be caused by clumps of protein that reduce the sharpness of the image reaching the retina or by a general changing of the color of the lens from clear to yellowish/brownish. Most age-related cataracts develop from protein clumps. Cataracts tend to "grow" slowly, so vision gets worse gradually. Seeing may become more difficult. Vision may get duller or blurrier. If lens discoloration is the cause, you may not be able to identify blues and purples, but vision will remain clear.

Many Americans aren't waiting for symptoms to escalate; they are using natural nutritional and herbal supplements to protect their eyes from the effects of aging.

Antioxidants

Studies using antioxidant vitamins and other nutrients that fight free-radical damage have shown excellent results. A 2001 U.S. National Eye Institute study of 5,000 people between the ages of 55 and 80 showed a 25 percent reduction in the risk of developing advanced AMD through the use of an antioxidant-and-zinc combination with vitamins C and E as major components.

Lutein and zeaxanthin

Lutein and zeaxanthin—carotenoids, or plant components, known for their color and antioxidant capacity—are found in the macular region of the eye. The body can't make lutein or zeaxanthin, so supplementation is recommended to protect the eyes from ultraviolet light—a leading cause of cataracts—and free-radical damage.

A Tufts University study in 2004 showed that generous intakes of lutein and zeaxanthin reduced the risk of macular degeneration by as much as 40 percent and the risk of cataracts by up to 20 percent. While no recommended daily allowance currently exists for lutein, positive effects have been seen at levels of 6 mg per day.

Blueberries, bilberries and eyebright

Blueberries and bilberries (huckleberries) are extremely high in anthocyanidin bioflavonoids—the blue pigments in fruit, which have natural health benefits, especially the ability to strengthen capillaries.

Bioflavonoids, such as those in blueberries, are essential for the proper absorption and use of vitamin C and other antioxidants, and should be part of a lifetime regimen to help prevent loss of sight.

Bioflavonoids also help maintain collagen, the intercellular "glue" that strengthens connective tissues throughout the body. Bilberry jam was fed to fighter pilots in the Second World War to enhance their night vision.

Eyebright is a European wild plant used since the Middle Ages to treat eye irritation. It has antibiotic and astringent properties that tighten membranes and mucus surrounding the eyes, which can strengthen and improve circulation. Rich in vitamins A and C, eyebright also contains tannins that help reduce inflammation. ✯

Does your child need an eye exam?

In a word, yes. School vision screenings, or even the quick checks at the pediatrician's office, are not intended to be a substitute for a full vision exam. Generally, such screenings catch only the squinters—the children who can't see the blackboard from the back of the room. While that's great, it's not enough.

About one-third of the population has myopia, or distance-vision problems. If your child complains about not being able to see the board or can't identify objects in the distance well, schedule an eye exam.

But another one-fourth of the population has near-vision problems— and many cases go undetected. In fact, near-vision problems are sometimes diagnosed as behavior problems. Symptoms might include difficulty concentrating on seat work at school, difficulty or impatience with reading and headaches after reading.

Some children also have accommodative problems, meaning their eyes don't adjust as quickly when switching focus back and forth between near work and distance work. Many of these problems become more noticeable as children move to higher grades, away from picture books with big print.—*MB*

What's new with contact lenses

By Marjolijn Bijlefeld

REMEMBER WHAT your first computer was capable of doing? Probably not much, at least compared to what most office and home computers today can do.

Similar kinds of changes have taken place in contact-lens technology in the past decade—even if they're not obvious to the casual observer. Yet the advances in materials make the contact lenses of even a few years ago as obsolete as that old clunker computer still sitting on a shelf in the garage.

The point is, if you haven't talked with your eye doctor in the past two years about what's new in contact lenses, you're in for some surprises. Your independent doctor of optometry, located in or near your Costco Optical Department, can not only examine, diagnose and treat vision conditions, but also recommend the best contact-lens option for you. In many cases, you can leave the office with a trial pair of lenses.

Here's a look at the new contact-lens technologies that are giving people more choices than ever.

Single-wear lenses

For those people who like to wear contact lenses only on special occasions or for sports, there are single-day lenses designed to be worn for a day and then thrown away.

These lenses are also an excellent option for teens and children, providing parents a worry-free way of making sure their children are wearing clean lenses each day. Because they come in a 90-day supply, there's no need to fret over an occasional lost lens. It's an economical option for part-time or full-time contact-lens wearers.

Continuous-wear lenses

For those who like to wear contact lenses but don't want to be bothered with the daily rituals of inserting, removing and cleaning them, there are lenses the U.S. Food and Drug Administration has approved for up to 30 days of continuous wear.

These lenses offer a great deal of flexibility. You can wear them continuously for 30 days and nights, or take them out once a week. You can even take them out every night, if you like. Talk to your eye doctor about the schedule that works best for you.

Two-week replacement lenses

Continuous wear is possible now because new materials allow a far greater supply of oxygen to pass to the eye. Contact lenses made of a special silicone hydrogel allow eyes to "breathe" normally—almost like not wearing contact lenses at all. The result is that contact-lens wear is more comfortable for a longer period. An added benefit is that many people find the whites of their eyes stay white, instead of reddening. Silicone hydrogel lenses are available for patients who want to replace their lenses every month or every two weeks.

Colored lenses

If you're interested in wearing colored lenses for cosmetic reasons, today's colored lenses look more natural than ever. Some are available as single-wear lenses, too, for those who want an occasional enhancement. Select one color or choose several. There's no easier way to experience life as a blue-, brown- or green-eyed beauty. Some people like these lenses just because the color pattern makes it easier to see and handle them.

Mix and match

Don't feel you're limited to just one kind of contact lens. You and your optometrist can select a lens type for your primary wear and also choose colored or daily disposable lenses for specific needs.

There are so many possibilities that you have every reason to ask your optometrist about contact lenses—whether it's your first time ever or the first time in 10 years. In fact, even if you're wearing contact lenses now, ask your optometrist this simple question: What's new?

Is your child ready for contacts?

Even young children can be successful contact-lens wearers. Here are some ways to gauge a child's readiness.

- Is your child generally responsible for personal belongings?
- Does your child demonstrate good hygiene habits, such as washing hands?
- Is your child motivated? Being able to wear contact lenses instead of eyeglasses can help boost a child's self-esteem and may be motivation for other good behaviors.
- Would contact lenses be better in some circumstances? If your child is a part-time athlete or performer, contact lenses could be preferred over eyeglasses on the field or on the stage.—MB

Battling the sounds of silence

Symptoms of hearing loss

People with hearing loss may experience some or all of the following problems.

- Difficulty hearing conversations, especially when there is background noise
- Hissing, roaring or ringing in the ears (tinnitus)
- Difficulty hearing the television or radio at a normal volume
- Fatigue and irritation caused by the effort to hear
- Dizziness or problems with balance

If any of these symptoms apply to you, visit your physician, who may refer you to an otolaryngologist (ear, nose and throat doctor) or audiologist. Visit your local Costco Hearing Center for a free hearing test to determine if you could be helped by hearing aids.

IN THE NOT-TOO-DISTANT PAST, when someone talked about a hearing aid, the image conjured was of Grandpa holding a large funnel-like device called an ear trumpet to participate in conversation. Even after electric hearing aids were invented around the turn of the last century, they were often obtrusive and a source of embarrassment. People would even shun diagnosis of a hearing problem for fear of being branded as "handicapped" and, especially for children, being teased or misunderstood.

Today, hearing loss is out of the closet. According to the National Institute on Deafness and Other Common Disorders, "approximately 28 million Americans have a hearing impairment." It is "one of the most prevalent chronic health conditions in the United States, affecting people of all ages, in all segments of the population, and across all socioeconomic levels."

Thankfully, due to technology, hearing loss no longer has to attach a stigma or a feeling of being a social pariah to the person afflicted. Today, hearing aids come in different forms, many of which are almost unnoticeable. Since "one size fits all" does not apply, there are things you should know if you think your hearing needs an assist.

Different kinds of hearing aids

Today's hearing aids use digital programmable technology. A technician programs the hearing aid with a computer and can adjust the sound quality and response time on an individual basis. Digital hearing aids use a microphone, receiver, battery and computer chip. Digital circuitry provides the most flexibility for the hearing professional to make adjustments for the hearing aid and can be used in all types of hearing aids.

There are three basic types of hearing aids currently being used and they come in various sizes.

In-the-ear (ITE) aids. ITE instruments are crafted from a custom mold of the ear. They are available in a wide variety of shell sizes, ranging from a full shell down to the smallest of sizes, called completely-in-the-canal (CIC) instruments. Custom hearing instruments are built based on the size and shape of the ear canal and the degree of hearing loss. Some features of ITE aids are:

- They offer a more secure fit, with easier insertion and removal than with behind-the-ear (BTE) aids.
- There are improved cosmetic benefits with smaller styles.
- Less wind noise is heard than with BTEs.
- Directional microphone technology, enabling the listener to focus on a more specific source, is available for most styles, except CIC aids.
- Components are integrated into a one-piece shell, which some find easier to handle and operate than BTE aids.

Behind-the-ear aids. As the name suggests, BTE aids are worn behind the ear and are connected to an earpiece that is molded to the shape of the outer ear, although some models do not use a custom earpiece and, instead, use rubber tubing inserted directly into the ear. BTE aids are usually flesh colored and can be used by people of all ages for mild to profound hearing loss. Other features are:

- BTEs may be better for young children, as only the earpiece has to be replaced as the child grows.
- BTEs are generally the most powerful hearing aids available.
- FM and direct auditory input is available with BTEs.
- Telecoil circuitry, to enable using the aid with telephones, tends to be more powerful with BTEs than with ITEs.
- BTEs use larger batteries, which may be easier to handle for people with manual dexterity or vision challenges.

Open-fit aids. Open-fit hearing aids are the latest technology and have proven very successful for high-frequency hearing loss, the most common type of loss. They are incredibly small and offer several features that may be more appealing than the other styles.

- They are more discreet and cosmetically appealing.
- They do not block the ear canal, allowing voices to sound more natural.
- The small size and light weight provide greater comfort.
- Since no custom molding is necessary, they can be fitted and worn on the same day you get your hearing evaluation. No waiting to enjoy the benefits of better hearing.

Your licensed hearing professional can help you select the hearing aid that is best for you. Don't miss out on the sounds that can add so much to your life. Get your hearing checked as soon as you think something's missing from your life.

—*Steve Fisher*

(Note: Costco carries only digital aids at about 50 percent of the cost elsewhere. Prices range from $899 to $1,899.)

Sources: The National Institute on Deafness and Other Common Disorders (www.nidcd.nih.gov); *Better Hearing Institute* (www.betterhearing.org)

Passing the test

Costco's Hearing Centers provide free testing for members. Appointments are recommended. Here's what to expect.

First, the licensed professional asks questions to determine your symptoms and the circumstances surrounding them (injury, illness, etc.).

Then you're given a set of headphones and a small unit with a push button on the end. The technician will advise you to push the button only when you actually hear a tone. Don't guess! Each ear is tested individually. Tones come in three short blasts, starting relatively loud, then diminishing in volume.

The next test is for speech recognition. A computerized voice says a series of words, one at a time, with the patient repeating after each one. First the right ear; then the left; finally, both together.

A third test establishes the highest volume you can tolerate.

When the testing is over, the licensed professional will consult with you to give the results. The entire process takes about 60 minutes.

Costco believes it is in the best interest of the purchaser to consult a physician prior to being fitted with hearing aids. The use of hearing aids cannot restore natural hearing or prevent further loss.

To find the location and phone number for your local Costo Hearing Center, go to costco.com, click on "Costco Connection Magazine," then look under "Resource Guides." Or call toll-free 1-800-774-2678.—*SF*

Psyched about scent

By Angela Pirisi

SCIENCE HAS BEEN finding out how certain scents can affect memory, learning, emotions, physical performance, pain, appetite and sexual attraction. That may explain why aromatherapy—the use of aromatic extracts (essential oils) from herbs, flowers and spices by inhalation or topical application—is growing more popular. It's a no-brainer, suggest smell researchers, who explain that scent has the power to positively alter mood and behavior, and heal the body.

An answer to drugs

The growing fascination with aromatherapy has created a huge interest in fragrance-based products, such as room fragrances, scented candles, essential oils, and bath and spa treatments; even scented leg wax and feminine hygiene products have recently appeared on the market.

"There's a strong movement away from expensive drugs that have many side effects to herbs and essential oils that have little to any side effects and that have promise," says Glen Nagel, N.D., an assistant professor of botanical medicine at Bastyr University in Seattle.

For example, some scents, such as ylang-ylang and rose, may help to reduce pain, theoretically by eliciting relaxation. (Painkillers work similarly through a sedative effect.)

Research from the University of Kiel, Germany, showed that dabbing peppermint oil on the forehead and temples for three minutes reduced tension headache pain. Similarly, sniffing the fresh scent of green apple reduces the severity and duration of migraine, suggested findings from the Smell & Taste Treatment and Research Foundation in Chicago.

Meanwhile, research sponsored by the Sense of Smell Institute in New York City found that sniffing lavender increased the amount of time subjects spend in deep (or slow-wave) sleep, the restful, restorative phase of sleep. Other studies have found that the smell of spiced apple, nutmeg or sandalwood can lower blood pressure.

Emotional rescue

Aromatherapy also seems to be a good antidote to stress, depression, anxiety and other emotional upheaval.

"Smell affects mood or emotional state more than any of the other senses," says Dr. Alan Hirsch, director of the Smell & Taste Treatment and Research Foundation. "That's because the olfactory bulb [smell center located in the brain] is part of the limbic system, which is the emotional brain."

For example, says Hirsch, lavender increases alpha brain waves, which induce calm. Jasmine increases beta waves, which are associated with a more awake, alert state and better mood. Scent can even make people friendlier, suggest findings from Rensselaer Polytechnic Institute in Troy, New York. Results showed that people smelling something pleasant, such as freshly baked cookies or roasting coffee, were twice as likely to help a stranger at the mall by doling out a dollar when asked or picking up a ballpoint pen someone had dropped.

Smell can even trigger memory. Hirsch did a study looking at 989 people in 39 countries, and found that the No. 1 "nostalgic" odor people recalled was baked goods. The reason for scent's powerful ability to reach back into the recesses of the memory may have to do with the fact that the hippocampus (the part of the brain where memory resides) is also part of the limbic system.

Smelling smarts

Certain odors can also sharpen mental acuity, which may translate into better marks or increased productivity. One study, at the University of Cincinnati, which asked people to perform stressful computer tasks for 40 minutes, found that breathing peppermint or lily-of-the-valley scent through an oxygen mask resulted in people making fewer errors than those breathing unscented air.

As for the mating game, research suggests that the way to a man's heart is not just through his stomach, but also his nose. According to Hirsch's research, for men the No. 1 smell that attracted them to women was the combination of lavender and pumpkin pie, followed by doughnuts and licorice; strawberries apparently increased sexual satisfaction. So maybe men can hold off filling their Viagra prescription and opt for a tastier tactic.

For women, the No. 1 smell that attracted them to men was Good & Plenty licorice candy and cucumber, followed by Good & Plenty and banana nut bread. These smells work individually too, but even better together, says Hirsch.

But what if an individual doesn't like cinnamon or apple or lavender? Like art, smell works very much on a gut level—you either like it or you don't. In most cases, it works only if you like it, says Hirsch. However, in a mating context, he adds, certain smells work at an unconscious level, regardless of what a guy thinks of pumpkin pie or a woman thinks of banana nut bread.

If you're starting to explore essential oils, try a few drops in a bath or diffuser, or mix in with a massage oil (e.g., sweet almond, jojoba or mineral oil). Just don't use essential oils alone (undiluted), since they're pretty potent concentrations of herbs and can cause skin reactions, suggests Nagel. "Keep in mind, it may take 100 pounds of fresh herb to get 2 ounces of essential oils," he says. Also, don't take them internally or during pregnancy without consulting a qualified health-care provider. ⚕

The aroma of relief

As any aromatherapist can tell you, there's a scent for whatever ails you, physically or mentally. Here are just a few scents to brew, sniff or soak in if you are under the weather.

Depression. Ylang-ylang, geranium, jasmine, sandalwood
Anxiety. Clary sage, bergamot, nutmeg, pine
Respiratory ailments (cough, colds, asthma). Eucalyptus, peppermint
Muscular pain. Clary sage, eucalyptus, rosemary, chamomile
Mental fatigue. Lemon, rosemary, orange
Indigestion. Anise, basil, fennel, ginger, peppermint

What is good oral hygiene?

GOOD ORAL HYGIENE results in a mouth that looks and smells healthy. This means:
- Teeth are clean and free of debris.
- Gums are pink and do not hurt or bleed when brushed or flossed.
- Bad breath is not a constant problem.

How is good oral hygiene practiced?

In between regular visits to the dentist, there are simple steps that you can take to greatly decrease the risk of developing tooth decay, gum disease and other dental problems. These include:
- Brushing thoroughly twice a day and flossing daily
- Eating a balanced diet and limiting snacks between meals
- Using dental products that contain fluoride, including toothpaste
- Rinsing with a fluoride mouth rinse if your dentist recommends it
- Making sure that your children less than 12 years old drink fluoridated water or take a fluoride supplement if you live in a non-fluoridated area

It takes more than just brushing

OK, so you know about brushing and flossing. But there are other steps you should take if you want to keep your teeth for a lifetime. Some people assume they will lose their teeth as they age, but that doesn't have to happen. Joan Gluch, Ph.D., director of community health at the University of Pennsylvania School of Dental Medicine, suggests these steps to keep your teeth and your mouth healthy.

Understand your own oral-health needs

"Everyone's mouth is different," Gluch says. "Talk to your dentist or dental hygienist about special conditions in your mouth and the ways your general health affects your mouth." Changes in your health status should lead you to a dental office. "For example, pregnant women will have special oral-health needs," Gluch explains. "Or, if you start taking a new medication that can dry your mouth [as more than 300 common drugs do], you should ask your dentist or dental hygienist about how that will affect your mouth."

Commit to a daily oral-health routine

Based on discussions with your dentist or dental hygienist, come up with an effective oral-health routine that's easy to follow and takes your situation into account. For example, if you are taking medication that dries your mouth, you may want to use fluoride every day. Pregnant women, people with underlying health conditions, such as diabetes, and people in orthodontic treatment also may want or need special daily care.

Use fluoride

Everyone can benefit from fluoride, not just children. Fluoride strengthens developing teeth in children and helps prevent decay in adults and children. Toothpastes are good sources of fluoride. Your dentist can prescribe stronger concentrations of fluoride through gels or rinses if you need it.

Brush and floss to remove plaque

Everyone should brush and floss at least once a day, preferably twice or after every meal. These activities remove plaque, which is a complex mass of bacteria that constantly forms on your teeth. If plaque isn't removed every day, it can combine with sugars to form acids that lead to decay. Bacterial plaque also causes gingivitis and other periodontal diseases. It's important to brush and floss correctly and thoroughly. Otherwise, some plaque may remain.

Limit snacks

Every time you eat, particles of food become lodged in and around your teeth, providing fuel for bacteria. The more often you eat and the longer food stays in your mouth, the more time bacteria have to break down sugars and produce acids that begin the decaying process. Each time you eat food containing sugars or starches (complex sugars), your teeth are exposed to bacterial acids for 20 minutes or more. If you must snack, brush your teeth or chew sugarless gum afterward. A balanced diet is also important. Deficiencies in minerals and vitamins can also affect your oral health, as well as your general health.

If you use tobacco in any form, quit

Smoking or using smokeless tobacco increases your risk for oral cancer, gingivitis, periodontitis and tooth decay. It also contributes to bad breath and stains on your teeth.

Examine your mouth regularly

Even if you visit your dentist regularly, you are in the best position to notice changes in your mouth. Your dentist sees you only a few times a year, but you can examine your mouth weekly to look for changes that might be of concern. These changes could include swollen gums, chipped teeth, discolored teeth or sores or lesions on your gums, cheeks or tongue. A regular examination is particularly important for tobacco users, who are at increased risk of developing oral cancer. If you smoke or use smokeless tobacco, your dentist or dental hygienist can show you where lesions are most likely to appear.

Visit the dental office regularly

You and your dentist should talk about the frequency of your visits. Some people need to visit a dentist more frequently than others.

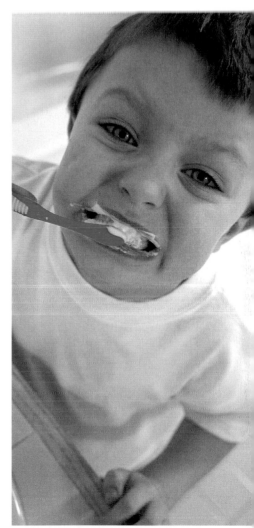

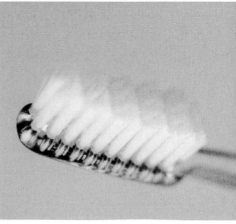

Making sense of sensitive teeth

SOMETIMES ONE'S FAVORITE foods and beverages, whether hot, cold, sweet or sour, are impossible to enjoy. The culprit? Sensitive teeth.

One in every five adults, 45 million in the United States alone, suffers from sensitive teeth, experiencing pain that ranges from mild discomfort to sudden, sharp and shooting pain deep in the nerve endings of the tooth.

Tooth sensitivity occurs when the underlying layer of the teeth—the dentin—becomes exposed, probably due to receding gum tissue or worn enamel caused by aggressive brushing, revealing the tooth roots. When the sensory nerves in the tooth roots are exposed to things such as ice cream, citrus, tea, soup or even just cold air, then … ouch!

Not treating sensitive teeth can bring on even more anguish. Tooth pain might diminish one's brushing and flossing, and that, in turn, can lead to plaque buildup, gingivitis, periodontal disease or eventual tooth loss.

On the other hand, treating sensitive teeth can be easy and quite painless. Sensitivity toothpastes containing potassium nitrate can help reduce discomfort by desensitizing the tooth nerve directly. Fluoride mouthwashes can also be beneficial. After using these for a few weeks, many people find that their tooth sensitivity goes away. However, even when the pain does stop, continuing to brush with sensitivity toothpaste will help prevent tooth pain from coming back.

There are other steps to take to help relieve tooth sensitivity.
• Moderate sweet or acidic food intake.
• Reduce tooth abrasion by brushing teeth gently in a circular motion with a soft-bristle toothbrush.
• Floss carefully below the gum line in an up-and-down motion.
• Limit cosmetic whitening and bleaching.

Above all, it's important to follow your dentist's or hygienist's advice about caring for sensitive teeth. And, of course, have regular checkups to keep your teeth from becoming a more serious problem. /A\

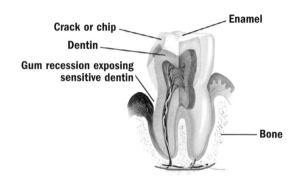

Crack or chip — Enamel
Dentin
Gum recession exposing sensitive dentin
Bone

Clear signs: cold or allergy?

IT CAN BE DIFFICULT to tell what's causing your runny, stuffy, itchy nose or your coughing, fatigue and headache—especially when cold viruses and allergens may be hitting hard. After all, allergy and cold symptoms are similar, but there are clear signs that can help you get to the bottom of your symptoms—and on the road to relief.

A good clue might be the timing of your symptoms. If those cold-like symptoms occur all at once, you're most likely experiencing allergies. But if the symptoms appear one at a time (first sneezing, then runny nose), it's probably a cold.

For more ways to distinguish between cold and allergy symptoms, check out the chart below.

Allergy or cold?

Symptoms	Allergy	Cold
Symptoms occur all at once or within a few hours	x	
Symptoms may occur one at a time (first sneezing, then runny nose)		x
Generally clear, thin, watery mucus discharge	x	
Runny, stuffy or itchy nose	x	x
Sneezing	x	x
More likely to have yellowish mucus discharge		x
Coughing	x	x
Fatigue	x	x
Headache	x	x
More common in the spring or fall	x	
More common in the winter, except in the southeast United States		x
Symptoms generally clear up within 7 to 10 days		x
Symptoms last more than 8 to 10 days	x	

Congestion relief at your pharmacy

Whether you're suffering from allergies or a cold, you want to breathe freely again. Try taking a product with pseudoephedrine (PSE) to help relieve nasal congestion. PSE is found in Claritin-D and some other cold and allergy products. It works by shrinking the blood vessels and allowing the sinuses to drain.

How can you ensure that you're taking a product with PSE? Check the ingredients list on the package before purchasing and look for pseudoephedrine.

Recent federal legislation requires products containing PSE to be sold to consumers from behind a pharmacy or service counter. In compliance with this law, Costco sells cold and allergy products containing PSE, such as Claritin-D, at the Costco Pharmacy counter (not available at all locations). No prescription is required to purchase these products except in Oregon.

Vive la vitamin!

VITAMINS PLAY AN important role in maintaining health, but, gee whiz, there are so many of them. I mean, there are 12 B vitamins alone, for goodness sake. How is a person to keep track of which vitamin does what, and how to get the best source? We hope this handy primer, based on resources from the U.S. Department of Health and Human Services and Health Canada, will help simplify selecting and stocking what you need to keep healthy.

Vitamin A is important for the growth and development of bones, teeth and gums. It is also essential for night vision, healthy skin, hair and mucous membranes. Good sources of vitamin A include liver, fish oil, eggs and vitamin A–fortified foods.

Vitamin B_1 (thiamine) contributes to the body's ability to use protein and carbohydrates to produce energy. It also aids metabolism, especially of carbohydrates. Good sources of thiamine include whole-grain and enriched grain products, such as beans, rice, pasta and fortified cereals.

Vitamin B_2 (riboflavin) is found in every cell of the body and is necessary for energy production. It is also needed to maintain metabolism and the functioning of skin and nerves. Good sources of riboflavin include milk and other dairy foods, enriched bread and other grain products, eggs, meat, green leafy vegetables and nuts.

Vitamin B_3 (niacin) is found in every cell of the body and is needed for DNA formation and to maintain normal functioning of skin, nerves and the digestive system. Good sources of niacin include poultry, fish, beef, peanut butter and legumes.

Vitamin B_6 influences many body functions, including regulating blood glucose levels, manufacturing hemoglobin and aiding the utilization of protein, carbohydrates and fats. It also aids in the functioning of the nervous system. Good sources of vitamin B_6 include chicken, fish, pork, liver and kidneys. It may also be found in whole grains, nuts and legumes.

Vitamin B_{12} is essential for normal growth, healthy nerve tissue and blood formation. It is also a crucial element in the reproduction of every cell of the body. Good sources of vitamin B_{12} include meat, fish, poultry, eggs, milk and other dairy foods.

Vitamin C plays a role in collagen formation, neurotransmission and tissue repair. Good sources of vitamin C include oranges, grapefruit, tangerines and many other fruits and vegetables, including berries, melons, peppers, dark green leafy vegetables, potatoes and tomatoes.

Vitamin D helps the body properly utilize calcium and phosphorus, necessary to build strong bones and teeth. Good sources of vitamin D include fortified milk, cheese, eggs and some fish (sardines and salmon).

Vitamin E is important for the proper functioning of nerves and muscles. Good sources of vitamin E include vegetable oils such as soybean, corn, cottonseed and safflower, as well as nuts, seeds and wheat germ.

Vitamin K helps the blood clot when the body is injured and is important in bone metabolism. Good sources of vitamin K include green leafy vegetables, such as spinach and broccoli.—*T. Foster Jones*

Comparing arthritis supplements

FIVE MILLION Americans already use them. In Europe they're dispensed as prescription drugs. Now the U.S. medical community is taking a serious look at glucosamine and chondroitin for arthritis pain relief.

If you, a family member or friend are among the 20 million sufferers of osteoarthritis, you'll want to stay current with alternatives for dealing with this painful and degenerative joint disease that destroys cartilage.

Supplement	Daily dosage in mg	What it's supposed to do	Where it comes from
Glucosamine Also: • Combined with MSM	1,500 1,500 + 1,500	• Rebuild cartilage • Improve joint mobility • Slow deterioration of cartilage	• A natural component of shellfish
Chondroitin sulfate and glucosamine	1,200 + 1,500	• Improve joint comfort and function • Slow disease process	• Chondroitin comes from beef cartilage
SAMe (S-adenosyl-L-methionine)	400 to 1,600	• Reduce osteoarthritis pain and inflammation • Repair cartilage • Treat depression	• A natural compound in all living cells • Supplement comes from fermented yeast
MSM (methylsulfony-methane) Also: • Combined with glucosamine	1,500 to 6,000 1,500 + 1,500	• Provide pain relief from osteoarthritis and rheumatoid arthritis	• Occurs naturally in fresh fruits and vegetables, milk, fish and grains • MSM supplement is derived from DMSO (dimethyl sulfoxide)

Super fruits to the rescue

By Kathryn M. D'Imperio

WHAT WOULD YOU DO if you suddenly had an extra hour in your day? Or maybe an additional five hours? To many people, this extension of free time in their jam-packed lives would be a godsend, a dream come true. And while you can't just multiply the amount of time in a given day, you can enhance the quality of your life without missing a beat.

Boosted energy levels, increased productivity and overall health are just the beginning with "super fruits," one of nature's best-kept secrets. Super fruits offer exceptional health benefits and natural, medicinal advantages for the human body. The antioxidant characteristics of super fruits make them highly effective in improving the immune system and preventing the activity of free radicals. (Free radicals can cause damage to the body by targeting and attacking certain cells.) For this reason, the succulent nectar of various super fruits can provide an excellent advantage in cancer prevention.

Exotic and rich in color, super fruits—the distinctive and tasty pomegranate, mangosteen and noni—deliver delicious nutrients and healthy results to youthful and mature bodies across the globe.

- Super fruits add variety to your diet.
- Super fruits supplement your vitamin intake without the addition of sugars and calories.
- Super fruits, by providing antioxidants, aid the body in many ways, from enhancing the immune system to aiding in proper digestion and circulation to helping to prevent cancer and beyond.

Pomegranates appear in mythology and ancient history. In Egypt, pomegranates symbolized safe passage from physical life to the next life. Pomegranate juice contains more polyphenol antioxidants than green tea, red wine, blueberry juice, cranberry juice or orange juice.

Healthy benefits of pomegranate
- Pomegranates are rich in antioxidants, which help to reduce the activity of free radicals.
- An increase in antioxidants also keeps the cardiovascular system running in tiptop shape.
- Pomegranate improves the circulatory system, again thanks to those antioxidants.

Noni, also known as *Morinda citrifolia*, hails from the Polynesian Islands and brings with it an abundance of healthful, healing properties. The region's volcanic soil creates a unique, fertile environment where noni can grow and flourish. In the tropics, noni is a household staple on the table, raw or cooked, as well as a natural remedy for many maladies. The bark, leaves, root and seeds all contain vital nutrients and important therapeutic elements. Noni trees grow to between 15 and 20 feet, boasting creamy white blossoms and ripened fruit kissed with yellow and white hues.

Medicinal uses of noni
- Has been shown to support digestive health and increase the body's ability to absorb nutrients from food
- Useful in promoting healthy skin, joints and a general feeling of well-being

Mangosteen may be one of the healthiest exotic fruits known to man, and is grown plentifully in Thailand. The combined juice, pulp, seeds and rind of the mangosteen not only taste great, but also contain more xanthone, an organic antioxidant compound, than any other fruit, according to research. In other words, the fruit offers extremely high antioxidant qualities through biologically active plant parts. Not to be confused with mangos, mangosteen has a smooth, brownish outer skin and fleshy, pure white pulp inside.

Tasty advantages of mangosteen
- Mangosteen's high xanthone content enhances its antioxidant qualities and medicinal properties.
- For its delicious taste, mangosteen quickly became the favorite fruit of Queen Victoria.

Super fruits provide the body with enhanced energy levels and add balance to a normal diet. These vitamin- and nutrient-packed fruits also contribute to radiant skin, healthy joints and a generally positive mood. The nutrients that can be extracted from the juice, seeds and rinds of pomegranate, noni and mangosteen produce a healthful elixir to enhance the diversity of anyone's diet.

Hoodia gordonii— is it right for you?

OVER THE LAST year, *Hoodia gordonii* has become a very popular natural supplement for those trying to lose weight. For many people, managing their weight is an ongoing life challenge. We are all aware of the physical and emotional health risks associated with being overweight, such as diabetes, heart disease, lethargy, low self-esteem and depression.

Along with a balanced diet and a regular exercise program, many people experience dramatically improved results in their weight-loss efforts with the proper use of *Hoodia gordonii*. Benefits they experience include:
- A reduction in appetite
- Loss of pounds and excess body fat
- Heightened energy levels

What is *Hoodia gordonii*?

Hoodia gordonii comes from a leafy and spiny succulent plant native to the Kalahari Desert in southern Africa. It is often confused with a cactus plant because they look quite similar. According to folklore, the hoodia plant has been used for centuries by the San Bushmen to help them stave off hunger during hunting expeditions and nomadic cycles. The *Hoodia gordonii* plant is difficult to grow due to its four- to five-year maturation rate and southern Africa's extremely hot growing conditions.

The chemical component in hoodia is a substance known as P57. This substance interacts with the brain's hypothalamus to trigger a full and satiated feeling. Hoodia has also been found to reduce cravings and appetite. Research conducted in 1997 by scientists in South Africa's national laboratory found that individuals using hoodia had a significant daily caloric reduction—by as much as 1,000 calories per day. Further, participants who were given hoodia experienced body-fat reduction as compared to those in the study using the placebo.

Words of wisdom when using *Hoodia gordonii*

First and foremost, all situations that involve taking a pill, powder or liquid supplement to aid in weight loss require prior consultation with a medical professional. With reduced food consumption, there is a challenge of maintaining a well-balanced diet combining a full array of proteins, carbohydrates and antioxidants. In order to achieve any kind of successful and healthy weight loss, a well-balanced diet is crucial.

To enhance weight-loss efforts, *Hoodia gordonii* should be used in a liquid form because the absorption rates in liquid supplements versus pills have been shown to be 30 to 50 percent higher. The vast majority of naturopaths and herbalists prefer liquid extracts over pills and powders because they are absorbed into the bloodstream almost immediately and do not need to be digested.

Eat healthfully when using *Hoodia gordonii*

Believe it or not, eating healthfully is one of the simplest ways to make the best use of *Hoodia gordonii* and lose weight. An easy way to determine what and how to eat comes down to asking one important question: "Will my body burn and use the foods I eat as energy, or will they be stored as fat?"

Eating healthfully means choosing lean proteins, fresh fruits and vegetables and whole grains, while minimizing consumption of sugars, fats, starches and processed carbohydrates.

Eat lean proteins. Proteins are the best things you can eat to help manage your cravings and control your weight. Proteins such as chicken, turkey, seafood, eggs, low fat yogurt, cottage cheese and legumes are on the top of the list. Consuming an adequate amount of protein daily helps manage energy, glucose levels and cravings.

Exercise regularly. It is recommended that you exercise three to four times per week anywhere from 20 minutes to an hour. The type of exercise you want to do is your choice. Again, see your physician before starting any exercise program.

There are two basic types of exercise: aerobic (heart and lung conditioning) and resistance (weight bearing). It is most beneficial if you can combine the two. Great exercises that combine both aerobic and resistance training are swimming, yoga, in-line skating and cycling.

Drink plenty of water. The body is mostly made up of water, and it uses water in all of its functions. One of the most common causes of fatigue and lethargy is dehydration. Keeping your body hydrated is one of the most important health moves you can make. Depending on your activity level or environment, you should drink anywhere from 48 to 64 ounces of water per day.

Keep a food diary. When using *Hoodia gordonii* in your daily regimen, you will most likely experience a reduction in your appetite. The goal is not only to reduce calorie intake, but to make sure that the calories going into your body are balanced and beneficial. Restricting your caloric food intake to less than 1,000 calories a day to lose unwanted pounds is not a healthy solution. An ultra-low-calorie diet can lead to reductions in bone density, muscle mass, scalp hair, energy and mental acuity, because your body can quickly become malnourished.

Take before-and-after pictures. Seeing is believing. Believe it or not, you can quickly forget what you looked like when you started your program. A photo timeline will help you fully embrace the changes you have made. The pictures say it all!

Did you know?

Weight gain can sometimes be attributed to factors other than diet. For this reason, it is most important to see your family physician, as weight gain can be a sign of a medical condition in need of treatment. Consult your physician before starting any new exercise or diet regimen.

Medical matters while traveling

FOR MILLIONS OF PEOPLE suffering from chronic illnesses or allergies, the idea of travel can be a first-class nightmare. However, with proper reparation, there's no reason anyone can't enjoy a trip.

Medication

Be sure to take enough to last approximately double the time period you will be away. Place medication in containers in separate travel bags to prevent spoilage or loss. If you are taking liquid medication, be sure it is placed in a leakproof plastic bag.

Food

If there are certain foods that you know will precipitate problems, write up a list of them and refer to it throughout your trip. Many times, when people dine out, they have a tendency to overlook or not recognize ingredients. Notify the hotel, tour operator or airline in advance if you are on a special diet.

Contact information

Have your physician provide you with an extra prescription and also the generic and chemical name for the drug. Also have on hand your health insurance company's name, address and phone number; the name of a person to notify in case of an emergency; your blood type; and a list of your drug allergies. If you have a medical alert card, be sure to carry it at all times.

Health-care providers

Take along a short medical report from your health-care provider describing your illness and mode of treatment. This is essential so that, if you have a relapse and need medical attention, the attending health-care provider has a point of reference and can assist you promptly and effectively.

Adjust dosage schedule

If you are flying long distances, ask your health-care provider about your dosage schedule. Find out if it should be adjusted for high altitudes, lack of activity, different time zones and/or different climates.

Plan for medical help abroad

The International Association for Medical Assistance to Travellers (IAMAT) is an organization that can supply a list of English-speaking physicians overseas. Contact IAMAT at (716) 754-4883 or *www.iamat.org*.

Check to see if your health insurance policy covers overseas travel. Medical assistance overseas can be very expensive. If you are not covered, your travel agent should be able to help you purchase travel health insurance from any of a number of companies.—*T. Foster Jones*

Medical Information

Health insurance company
Name_____
Address_____
_____
Phone No._____

Emergency contact:
Name_____
Address_____
_____
Phone No._____
Primary-care contact_____
Blood type:

Drug allergies:

Other special conditions:

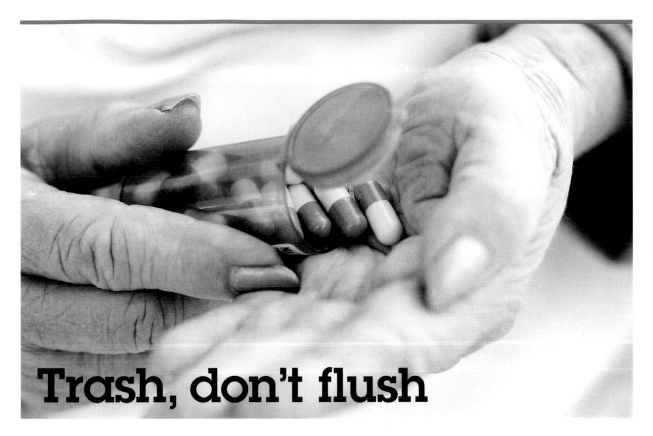

Trash, don't flush

SCIENTISTS ARE INCREASINGLY warning us not to flush expired medicines. At issue are the pharmaceutical and personal-care items that defy traditional wastewater treatment—such as antibiotics, painkillers, estrogen, anti-depressants and blood-pressure medicines—leaving traces in waterways and raising worrisome questions about potential health and environmental effects.

While the Environmental Protection Agency studies whether to develop formal recommendations, here are a few tips for disposing of old meds.

Crush it, bag it, trash it

Trash is better than sewer, with precautions in case children or animals get into it. Break up capsules and crush tablets, then put the remains back in the original container with its child-resistant cap. Tape it up and double-bag before tossing.

Ask when the trashman cometh

Check with your local hazardous waste collection agency—where you're supposed to take motor oil and batteries—to see if they accept expired medicines.

Check your drugs at the door

Ask your pharmacy if it will take back expired drugs, as is common in Canada and Australia. Some pharmacies have programs to incinerate or otherwise dispose of inventory they can't sell, as well as consumers' leftover medicines. (Costco Pharmacies will accept expired medications for disposal.)

—*T. Foster Jones*

Be sun smart every day

WE ALL KNOW that lying on the beach exposes you to the sun's harmful ultraviolet (UV) rays. But so can walking down the street on an overcast day, driving in your car or having fun in the snow. In fact, just by following your regular routine, it's not uncommon to be exposed to up to 20 hours of UV rays a week. Are you properly protecting yourself?

There are two types of UV rays that you need to be concerned with—UVA and UVB. Both can harm the skin.

- Can pass through window glass and can penetrate deep into the layers of the skin
- Contribute to premature signs of aging—including fine lines and wrinkles
- Can play a part in the formation of skin cancer

- Penetrate the outer layer of skin, causing damage to skin cells
- Are the primary cause of sunburn
- Can play a part in the formation of skin cancer

Protection is prevention

Wearing sunscreen every day is one of the most important steps you can take to protect your skin from the harmful effects of the sun. However, not all sunscreens protect equally.

You'll want to choose a sunscreen that offers a high sun protection factor (SPF). But SPF only measures protection against UVB rays. In addition to a high-SPF sunscreen, you'll need one that protects against UVA rays. Typically, sunscreens labeled "broad spectrum" do this.

Unfortunately, many sunscreens on the market today may not shield against a lot of UVA radiation. And, ironically, many sunscreens can start to lose their ability to deflect the sun's rays the moment they are exposed to the sun.

Patented Helioplex™ technology is a new approach to sunscreen. Helioplex not only shields skin from the UVA rays that penetrate deep into the skin, but also maintains this protection, even under high-intensity sun exposure. Helioplex stabilizing technology provides superior UVA protection that lasts. Sunscreens with Helioplex provide balanced broad-spectrum protection against both UVA and UVB rays.

Too much sun means aging skin

The immediate signs of sun damage are not always obvious; however, sun damage is cumulative and can worsen over time. This means the signs of sun damage will likely develop as you grow older.

Moderate sun damage
- Fine wrinkling: Shallow indentations or lines, typically on the forehead and around the eyes and mouth
- Roughness: A change in skin texture from soft and supple to rough
- Mottled hyperpigmentation: Light, patchy discoloration, including brown spots

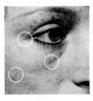

More severe sun damage
- Coarse wrinkling: Deep lines, furrows and creases on the forehead, chin and around the nose and eyes
- Yellowing: A change in skin tone from rosy to sallow or pale
- Laxity: Loose, thin skin that can result in a sunken appearance

Your sun-smart checklist
- Avoid the sun whenever possible. Wear protective clothing, including a wide-brimmed hat, sunglasses, a long-sleeved shirt and pants during prolonged periods of sun exposure.
- Use SPF 15 or higher sunscreen every day.
- Make sure your sunscreen offers both UVA and UVB protection.
- A full ounce (about the size of a golf ball) is required in order to adequately cover the entire body of an average person. Reapply every two hours, especially after swimming, towel-drying or perspiring.
- If your skin is sensitive, use sunblocks containing titanium dioxide or zinc oxide.
- Lips get sunburned too, so don't forget to apply a lip balm with an SPF of 15 or higher.

Sun-smart facts

- More than 90 percent of skin cancers are caused by sun exposure, yet adults, teens and children routinely expose unprotected skin to the sun during the middle of the day, when the sun's rays are most harmful.

- SPF (sun protection factor) is a measurement of how long you can stay in the sun without sunscreen before getting burned. With SPF 15, it takes 15 times longer for a burn to begin. Remember, sunscreens should not be used to increase the time you spend in intense sunlight.

- Even on a cloudy day, 80 percent of the sun's UV rays pass through the clouds. Don't reserve the use of sunscreen for sunny summer days only.

• Check your skin monthly and be on the lookout for new skin spots or changes in existing spots. Visit your dermatologist regularly for a full-body skin examination.

Early detection can save your life

Melanoma is the most serious form of skin cancer. However, melanoma is almost always curable in its early stages. Melanoma usually starts as a flat, dark-colored spot that looks like a freckle. The edges are irregular and the whole spot is most likely asymmetrical. There are often two or more colors to the spot (gray, red, black and brown mixtures).

To help distinguish between normal moles and malignant melanoma, apply the ABCD rule. Usually, melanomas share one or more of these criteria:

Normal mole

 • Symmetrical shape
 • Even coloration
 • Even border

Abnormal mole

 • **A**symmetry: One half does not match the other.
 • **B**order: irregular, ragged or blurred edge
 • **C**olor: multi-colored black, tan, gray, brown and possibly blue, red and white
 • **D**iameter: larger than 6 millimeters, or smaller but growing

The American Cancer Society recommends regular self-exams of moles and freckles so that individuals can track any changes in their skin. It is important to see a dermatologist if any growth, mole or discoloration appears suddenly or begins to change, or if a sore does not heal. Early detection and treatment are the best defense against skin cancer.

Perform a monthly self-exam

One of the best ways you can help take care of your skin is to perform a monthly visual exam of your body. Just follow these easy steps every month to identify any skin changes or new skin spots. And be sure to see your doctor if you notice anything different from the previous month.

What you'll need: a bright light, a full-length mirror, a hand mirror, two chairs or stools and a blow-dryer.
   1. Examine your head and face, using one or both mirrors. Use the blow-dryer to inspect your scalp.
   2. Check your hands, including nails. In a full-length mirror, examine elbows, arms, underarms, neck, chest and torso. Women: Check under breasts.
   3. With your back to the mirror, use the hand mirror to inspect the back of your neck, shoulders, upper arms, back, buttocks and legs.
   4. Sitting down, check your legs and feet, including soles, heels and nails.

Make sure to ask your dermatologist about skin-cancer prevention, including regular skin exams. To find out more about ways in which you can help in the fight against skin cancer, visit *www.cancer.org* or *www.neutrogena.com.* ⒶⅤ

Bloom into beauty

SPRING IS THE TIME to think about updating your health and beauty routine to fit the changing seasons. Step into spring with these helpful tips that will bring you out of hibernation and into bloom!

Hair

Spring is all about fun, flirty styles. Welcome warm weather with a new haircut. Try a bouncy bob or layering to change things up. Not gutsy enough to get a cut? Try a fun updo.

Bump up the volume for spring by turning limp hair into luscious pumped-up locks with a bodifying shampoo.

Skin

As the days get warmer, it's good to be out breathing fresh air and being active, but beware of the sun: Its ultraviolet rays are no friend to your skin.

Spring is the time to exfoliate the dry skin left over from winter's harsh temperatures. Use a gentle exfoliant to wipe away dead skin, which can prevent moisturizers from working and cause makeup to look caked on. Exfoliate twice weekly and you'll have the kind of soft, smooth skin you've always wanted.

Spring is all about what's in bloom. Invigorate your senses with the smell of freshly cut flowers or ripe fruits. Let the scents of spring transport you to a different place—right in your shower. Try a moisturizing body wash that leaves skin not only silky soft but fresh and fragrant too.

Indulge yourself in skin that shines. Try a moisturizing body wash that leaves skin radiant. Your gorgeous glow will give you the confidence to take on the new season.

Break out that razor. Warmer days mean you get to show some leg! After shaving, be sure to apply a moisturizer. You'll feel more comfortable and your skin will glow. Alcohol-free lotions will reduce dryness and irritation.

Hands and nails

Do your hands always seem dry, no matter what the season? Before you go to bed, try using a heavy lotion or petroleum jelly. Then, slip on a pair of cotton gloves or even socks. Your hands will be amazingly soft by morning.

Lifestyle

Spring is the perfect time to reassess your lifestyle. Drinking too much, smoking, stressing out and skimping on sleep and exercise will show on your skin. If you're healthy, your skin should be smooth and soft, with a rosy glow. Jump-start the season with new beauty and health routines!

The real skinnies

Remember, no matter what season it is (or age you are), it's important to keep your skin protected. Follow these basic guidelines every season and your skin will be healthy and smooth.

- Start moisturizing at an early age. The earlier you start, the better you'll be able to protect your skin from the signs of aging.
- Strengthen skin by choosing moisturizers that contain vitamins A and E.
- Lock in moisture after a bath or shower by applying lotion to your skin.

Putting your best face forward

By Georgette Mosbacher

STUDIES HAVE SHOWN that when a woman feels she looks good, she does better at work and in her personal life. I believe that's true. Additionally, you can't hide your face from the world. If you take care of your skin it shows, and if you don't take care of it, it shows.

Makeup and skin care have always been a passion of mine. I'd like to spread that passion by sharing some of my beauty secrets.

Skin-care regimen

Before applying makeup, make sure you cleanse and hydrate. This is essential for smooth, flawless skin. I suggest this simple daily facial regimen.

Morning
- Step 1. Cleanse with a moisturizing cleanser.
- Step 2. Apply age-defying wrinkle serum.
- Step 3. Apply moisture lotion with SPF protection (a minimum of 15 is recommended).
- Step 4. Apply protective eye cream.

Evening
- Step 1. Cleanse with a moisturizing cleanser.
- Step 2. Apply age-defying wrinkle serum.
- Step 3. Apply restorative night cream.
- Step 4. Apply protective eye cream.

It's important to follow a complete skin-care regimen—one that includes cleansing and moisturizing—because doing so effectively provides both reparative and preventative treatment for your skin. Most cleansers and moisturizers are designed to work individually, but they provide maximum benefits when used together. For additional benefits, complement your regimen with targeted, area-specific skin care—for your nose, forehead, cheeks, etc.

Steps to perfect makeup

Perfect makeup complements perfect skin. Follow these simple and easy makeup steps to achieve that perfect radiance every woman deserves.

Concealer. A concealer is the best-kept secret you will ever have. It is the perfect cover for dark circles. Start application under the eye, then move up to the lash line and into the inner corner of the eye. Gently blend with fingers or a concealer brush to meet your complexion needs. To freshen up your face late in the day, add more concealer. It works wonders.

Foundation. After the concealer, layer with foundation. Always use foundation, because it protects your face from harmful environmental elements. Select a foundation that includes a sun protection factor of at least 20 as well

GEORGETTE MOSBACHER

is president, CEO and chairwoman of the cosmetics company Borghese. She started honing her business skills on a budget in college—where she balanced three jobs to pay for classes. In the early 1990s, she purchased the failing cosmetics company La Prairie, turned it around and sold it three years later. In 2000, she began consulting with Borghese, a venerable cosmetics brand, and streamlined its business model. The Kirkland Signature™ by Borghese line, exclusive to Costco, was launched in 2006.

as multi-minerals and vitamins A, C and E. Apply around the nose and mouth first, and then blend outward.

Many women have a difficult time deciding which shades will work and look good. Start by selecting a hue that matches your complexion well; blending is essential, and you are on your way to achieving a beautiful look that is right for you.

Translucent pressed powder. Powder sets your foundation and takes away shine. Gently pat a puff or brush onto the powder. Shake off any excess. Apply gently over nose, chin, forehead and cheeks.

Natural bronzing powder. Lightly sweep a brush over the bronzer; tap off excess. Apply to cheeks, forehead, nose, chin and neck for a sun-kissed look. Reapply, if necessary, to achieve the desired shade.

Blush. Blush adds a sheer, shimmery glow to your face. To apply, smile and sweep your cheeks with the darker shade. Follow up with a lighter shade on the apple of your cheeks for an extra pop of color.

While bronzing powder and blush may seem similar, a blush enhances the contour of your cheekbones, adding a sheer, shimmering glow to your face. Bronzers give you a sun-kissed look and can be used on particular areas of the face. Blush can be used on top of the bronzer for a bit more color.

Eye shadow. An eye shadow base is an essential primer to ensure the perfect application of eye shadow. Place a small amount of the base on the fingertips and blend it over the eyelid area up to the brow.

When adding color, sweep on the lightest shade first, using the fuller side of a dual-ended brush, from lash line to brow. Follow with a semi-light shade from lash line to brow; then a medium shade from lash line to crease. Dampen the eyeliner brush (it's the thinner side of a dual-ended brush) with a darker shade and apply along the lash line.

If you're having trouble choosing eye shadow colors for day or evening wear, consider the following. For day, colors should look natural and beautiful to complement your features. For a dressier look for the evening, play up your eyes by creating a smoky, smoldering look. Shimmery tones reflect light, which makes facial lines and wrinkles less noticeable.

Mascara. To lengthen and define lashes, roll the mascara brush from the base to the tips.

Always cap mascara tightly and do not dilute. Look for mascara with proteins to strengthen and guard lashes against breakage.

Once a tube has been opened, replace mascara every three to four months to ensure hygiene.

Lipstick and liner. For a natural look, line lips with lip liner after applying lipstick. For a more dramatic look and to keep color from bleeding, line lips before applying lipstick.

Again, the ideal colors for daytime wear are more natural shades. In the evening, you can add drama on the lips with a deeper, brighter shade, shimmer and sparkling gloss. ⚡

Make a plan and live by it

Pick a quit day. Mark a day on your calendar when you will completely stop smoking.

Clean house. Prior to your quit day, throw out all cigarettes and smoking accessories, such as ashtrays or lighters.

Remind yourself why you want to quit. Discuss your reasons with a friend or write them down on a piece of paper you can carry with you.

Identify your barriers to quitting. Think about what has kept you from quitting before. Use past quit attempts as a reference.

Learn to beat your cravings. The easiest way to beat cravings is to prevent them. Familiarize yourself with the available tools—nicotine patches, lozenges or gum—and select the tool that is right for you.

Learn to beat trigger situations. Understand your habits and what situations may cause you to smoke. Next, plan how you will deal with these triggers.

Review the directions. When using nicotine replacement therapy, ensure that you read all the directions and understand how to properly use these products.

Get support. Find people who can help you successfully make it through your quit attempt.

Have a quitting ceremony. The night before your quit day, celebrate by throwing away your cigarettes and making a commitment to stick with your plan.

Stay positive! You can do it.

Want to quit smoking?

WHAT DOES IT TAKE to quit smoking for good? Most people think it takes willpower. Wrong. If you've tried to quit and failed, chances are what was working against you was not a lack of willpower, but a lack of knowledge. This guide is intended to give you the knowledge needed to quit for good.

There are two sides to a smoking addiction: the cravings for nicotine and the habit of smoking.

The cravings caused by cigarettes are similar to those associated with other drugs such as alcohol, cocaine or even heroin. Receptors in the brain respond to certain substances in cigarettes. The more the brain is exposed to these substances, the more the receptors get used to them. Over time, it takes more and more to satisfy those receptors. When you feel a craving, it's actually these receptors asking for more nicotine.

The other side of a smoking addiction is habit. People tend to smoke when they are in certain situations, such as when they're relaxing, when they're with friends or when they're stressed. The brain associates these situations with nicotine. To successfully stop smoking, one has to break both the addiction and the habit.

One popular and proven method to fight nicotine addiction is to use nicotine replacement therapy. This method has helped millions by reducing their cravings and allowing them to focus their efforts on breaking the habit.

With nicotine replacement therapy, another source of nicotine is substituted for cigarettes. The substitute nicotine might come in the form of a patch applied to the skin, gum to chew or lozenges to suck. When used correctly, these products provide nicotine to help relieve the cravings and the withdrawal symptoms that can derail even the most determined quitter.

Nicotine replacement therapy does not contain the harmful chemicals found in cigarettes. However, in order for nicotine replacement therapy to work properly, it is important to use the product as instructed on the label and to break the habits you have always associated with smoking. You also need to decide which form of nicotine replacement therapy will work best for you.

As with any medication, you should consult a health-care provider before starting a new program.

The last step is to develop your own "quit plan" based on your needs and characteristics. ⚄

Embrace Health. Embrace *Life.*

Naturally Noni is useful for promoting healthy skin, healthy joints and a general feeling of well-being. Noni also helps support proper digestion which is vitally important for your body to receive the nutrients from the food you eat.*

Naturally Pomegranate combines the best of science and nature into a supplement. Naturally Pomegranate helps keep your circulatory system healthy and provides antioxidants that play a key role in cardiovascular health.*

Naturally Thai Mangosteen—the Xanthone Fruit. Xanthones are found in abundance in this fruit from Thailand and research supports the role of xanthones in microbiological balance, supporting a healthy immune system, joint flexibility and positive mental support.*

AGRO LABS

HILLSIDE, NJ 07205 • www.agrolabs.com

* These statements have not been evaluated by the Food and Drug Administration. This product is not intended to diagnose, treat, cure or prevent any disease.

A. Cetaphil
Gentle Skin Cleanser

Cetaphil is great for daily makeup removal or as a part of a skin-care regimen to treat the dryness caused by topical medications used in the treatment of acne, fine lines and wrinkles. Originally formulated for dermatologists, it is gentle and will not strip the skin of natural protective oils or emollients, or disturb the skin's natural pH balance. Fragrance free and noncomedogenic, Cetaphil Gentle Skin Cleanser is an excellent choice for daily facial cleansing. Item #92182

B. Extra Strength
Tylenol® Caplets

When used as directed, no other pain reliever has been proven safer than Tylenol. Item #449832

C. Advil PM

Stop hurting and start sleeping with the multi-pain-relieving power of Advil plus a gentle sleeping aid. Item #164450

A

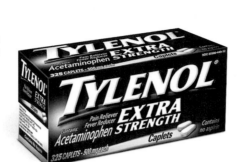

B

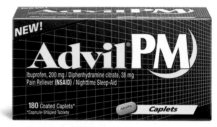

C

COMPLETE BEAUTY, COMPLETE HEALTH, COMPLETE VALUE.

Health & Beauty Care for the Entire Family.

Moisturize. Cleanse. Protect. Soothe. Your family has many different needs. At Costco, you'll find more than just the favorite brands they want — you'll find great savings. Come in to Costco to stock up on the very best brands at the very best prices.

©2006 Unilever UBNC06 9898

Spring Forward to Good Health.

STAY HEALTHY THE NATURAL WAY.
TruNature® premium-quality herbal and
dietary supplements are made to the highest
quality, purity and potency standards.

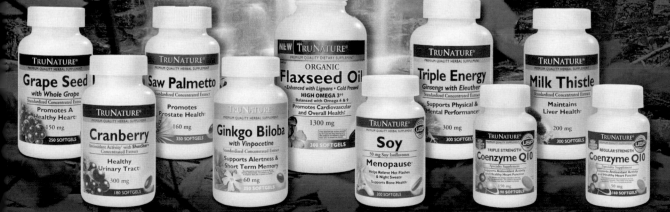

Exclusive to Costco Wholesale and costco.com

Body Choice

Weight Loss Solution

made with

100% Certified African Hoodia...

...a natural plant source which clinical research shows may help decrease appetite.

Weight Loss Never Tasted So Good!

Body Choice

Cortisol Hoodia Weight Loss

With 100% African Hoodia

· Curbs
· Boost

32 FL OZ (946 ML)

Enriched With Real Bluebe

HOODIA EXTRACT 100% CERTIFIED

Loaded with green tea and antioxidants, **Body Choice** liquid Weight Loss Formula is designed for maximum absorption. For an effective and healthy way to lose weight, make **Body Choice** part of your daily weight loss solution.

"Building Better Bodies For Life"

AVEENO® has been dermatologist recommended for 60 years.

THE LEADING LIQUID FOR JOINT SUPPORT*

Per Day

JOINT MOVEMENT
Glucosamine
With Chondroitin + MSM
2000mg OF GLUCOSAMINE HCl

For Healthier
Joint Function*

△SYMTEC®
Mixed Berry Flavor 33.8 FL OZ (1000 ml)
Liquid Dietary Supplement

- Easy to swallow
- Fast absorbing
- 2 tablespoons daily

For more
information, visit
www.symteclab.com.

△SYMTEC

*This statement has not been evaluated by the Food and Drug Administration.
This product is not intended to diagnose, treat, cure or prevent any disease.

Joint Juice.
Dietary Supplement

Hydrate &
Lubricate
Your Joints.

Glucosamine
1500 mg per can

7 Ways To Protect Your Joints

1. **Maintain your ideal body weight.**
   Extra weight puts more stress on your joints.
2. **Exercise.** Strong muscles help protect your joints.
3. **Pace yourself.** Start any new exercise
   program slowly and let your body adjust.
4. **Mix it up.** Try different exercises and
   activities to avoid overuse.
5. **Listen to your body.** Don't overdo
   it, and take a break if you need to.
6. **Use good posture.** Use proper
   technique when lifting, moving
   and sitting.
7. **Try dietary supplements.** Studies
   show glucosamine may help joints
   function better.† Ask your doctor if
   glucosamine is right for you.

Joint
Juice
Tropical
Fruit

Proud sponsor of the
🅰 ARTHRITIS
FOUNDATION®
www.arthritis.org

† These statements have not been evaluated by the FDA. This product
is not intended to diagnose, treat, cure or prevent any disease.

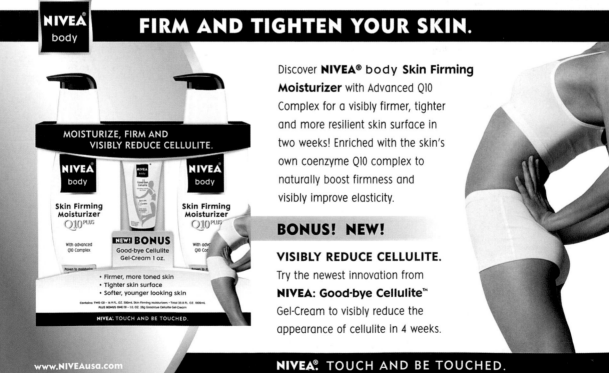

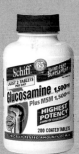

HOLD YOUR HEALTH TO THE HIGHEST STANDARD.

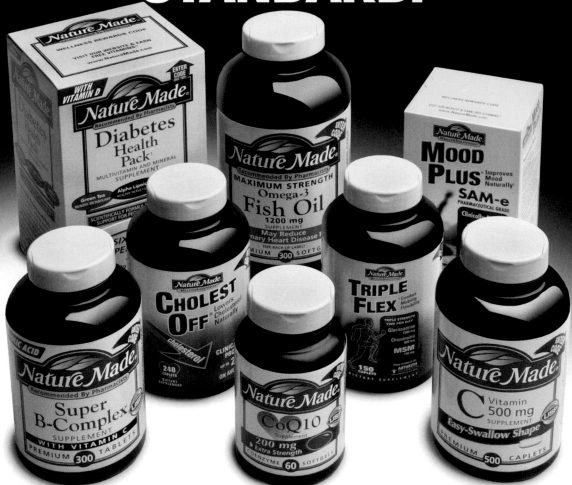

For more than 30 years Nature Made has offered high-quality vitamins, minerals, herbals and other nutritional supplements for nutritional needs.

That's why so many health-conscious people trust Nature Made. Each Nature Made item is specially formulated with the most beneficial ingredients to enhance health and well-being.

And we guarantee that Nature Made vitamins, minerals and supplements contain no artificial flavors or preservatives. So when you're looking for the best prices and best selection of Nature Made supplements, the best place to look is Costco.

hold your health to the highest standard
For more information,
visit www.naturemade.com.

Cleanliness and order are not matters of instinct; they are matters of education, and like most great things, you must cultivate a taste for them.

—Benjamin Disraeli

Laundry 101

By Linda Cobb

LAUNDRY SHOULD BE EASY, RIGHT? You've got a washer, a dryer and detergent; you throw the clothes in the washer; they come out clean and you toss them in the dryer, praying you won't have to iron them. Not so fast. Laundry is easy, but follow these guidelines and you'll be doing laundry like a pro every time.

The basics

• Sort. Don't just pick up an armful of clothes and dump them in the washer. Sort the clothes, not only by color, but also by fabric type and weight. Rough fabrics, such as heavy denim, can snag and damage delicate fabrics.

• Choose a detergent that best suits your needs. Laundry detergent is available in powder or liquid form, and many brands have additives to help brighten and protect the color of your clothes. Or you might prefer products that are free of extra additives.

Once you've picked a brand that works for you, the most important thing is to read the instructions on the package and make sure that you're using the right amount of detergent and the correct water temperature. With detergent, using more doesn't mean that it will clean better. Too much detergent can leave fabrics coated with a soapy residue. If you are using powder detergent, be sure that it dissolves well. If it does not completely dissolve or if you are using too much, you will find white powdery residue on your

LINDA COBB, the Queen of Clean®, is the bestselling author of seven books about the joys of cleaning. Cobb began earning her title when she owned and ran of one of Michigan's biggest cleaning companies. The company specialized in some of the most difficult cleaning challenges, including disaster restoration and fire and smoke damage. More information about her, along with additional cleaning tips, is available at www.queenofclean.com.

Too much detergent can leave fabrics coated with a soapy residue.

clothes. With liquid detergent you can pre-treat a heavily soiled area with part of the measured amount of detergent you will use in the wash.

• Pre-treating spills and heavy soil is vital, so keep a good laundry spotter on hand. You can also make your own laundry spotters. For a great all-purpose spotter, combine 1 part rubbing alcohol and 2 parts water in a labeled spray bottle. Spray on spots and spills, wait a few minutes and then launder as usual. For oily stains, such as salad dressing, combine 1 tablespoon of glycerin, 1 tablespoon of liquid dishwashing soap and 8 tablespoons of water in a squeeze bottle. Work the solution into grease and oil stains. Let it sit a few minutes, then flush with water and launder as usual.

• Fabric softener is available as a liquid or a sheet. Liquids help to ensure equal coating on all of your clothing. They also help reduce wrinkles and retain colors. Dryer sheets control static cling and can add a fresh scent. You may want to have both kinds on hand for different fabrics and for those that don't go in the dryer.

Now that you have the basics down, here are the tricks of the trade to help you do laundry faster, easier and more successfully. These tips will help you extend the life of your clothing and succeed at removing tough stains every time.

Tricks of the trade

• Catch the spills and spots before you launder the clothes. Treating a spot when it is fresh makes it easier to remove, and treating it properly before laundering is vital.

Try this trick: Keep colored plastic clothespins near the laundry hamper. When you take off something with a spot on it, clip the clothespin to the spot. It's so easy, even the kids will do it. When you are ready to do the laundry, you will easily spot the colored clothespin and know exactly where to pre-treat the spot. You'll never again miss one and find a stain when the clothes come out of the dryer.

• Speaking of the dryer, always remove the clothes from the dryer immediately. Prompt hanging and folding will eliminate the need for ironing in many cases.

• If you forget to take the clothes out immediately, eliminate wrinkles by tossing in a damp towel and letting the dryer spin for five or 10 minutes to steam out the wrinkles. Hang or fold the clothes promptly, and hopefully you won't have to iron.

• And, of course, read the label in each piece of laundry. The Federal Trade Commission requires that all garments have a label that identifies how to properly care for the item; look for it in the neck or side seam. For best results, follow the laundering directions on that label. If it says, "DRY CLEAN ONLY," you should do that.

Almost anyone can learn to do some part of the laundry. Even children can sort and fold their own clothes, as can Dad. The job will go faster, and it's great training for the kids later in life.

You spend a lot of money on your clothes, so next time you do laundry take a few extra minutes to do it right and your clothes will last longer and look better. ⚡

Cleaning special fabrics like a pro

Cashmere. This expensive fiber comes from the undercoat of cashmere goats. Treat it with respect. Dry-clean these prizes or hand-wash with care in cool water and well-dissolved gentle soap. Adding a little hair conditioner to the final rinse and rinsing well is important. Do not wring. Dry flat, reshaping the garment as it dries. Iron on the "wrong" side while still damp with a cool iron, if necessary.

Down. Down is the soft under-feathers of waterfowl that are often combined with adult feathers. It is machine washable and dry-cleanable. Be sure to follow the care label closely. Do not air-dry down: It dries too slowly, and mold or mildew may form in the process. Dry in your dryer, using a large-capacity dryer if needed. Set temperatures low (less than 140°F), fluffing and turning the item often. Make sure to dry the item thoroughly. This can take time. Want really fluffy down jackets and bedding? Put a clean tennis shoe or tennis ball in the dryer with the item to fluff it up!

Linen. A tough fabric that withstands high temperatures, linen is made of natural flax fiber, and ranges from light to heavyweight. Hand-wash or machine-wash linen in warm water (be sure to read the care label). If the fabric is color-fast you may remove stains and brighten the garment with oxygen bleach. Do not use chlorine bleach. Iron while still damp; to help prevent creasing you may want to treat linen with starch or sizing. Press heavy linen with a hot iron; for lighter-weight linen and blends, press with a warm iron. Linen may also be dry-cleaned.

Silk. This natural, delicate fabric requires special care to avoid damage. Check the labels, but you may be able to hand-wash crepe de Chine, thin, light-weight and medium-weight silk in lukewarm water with mild soap or detergent. You can also use cold water with cold-water detergent. Do not use chlorine bleach. Do not wring or rub silk. Rinsing well is vital. Rinse several times in cold water to remove suds. Blot with a towel and dry flat. Iron on the wrong side of the fabric with a warm iron. Silk may be dry-cleaned, and that works best for suits, pleated silks and silks that are not colorfast. Do not use strong spotters or enzyme spotters on silk.

Spandex. Spandex is an artificial fiber that is added to other fibers to give them stretch and elasticity. Machine-wash spandex in warm water on the delicate or gentle cycle. Do not use chlorine bleach. Do not put spandex garments in the dryer or iron; high heat will break down spandex fibers. Line dry or dry flat, per the care label. If you have exercise clothes containing spandex, be sure to launder each time you wear them. Body oil can break down spandex fibers.

Wool. This natural fiber comes from the fleece of sheep. Hand-wash wool sweaters and other knits in cold water with cold-water detergent. Rinse several times, and do not wring or twist. Blot with a towel and dry flat, reshaping as needed.

—Linda Cobb

Stain removal

THERE'S NOTHING LIKE a little coffee, wine or lipstick stain to ruin your mood and a favorite piece of clothing. The good news is that, by following a few basic guidelines, many, if not most, stains are treatable.

These are the basics most of us already know:

- Before you treat any stain it's a good idea to treat a small part of the fabric that's not readily visible to make sure the treatment won't damage the fabric.
- Be sure to read all fabric-care labels before treating a stain.
- As a general rule, fresh stains are easier to treat than old ones, and heat tends to set a stain. Be sure any stain is completely out before drying the garment.

Here are some down and dirty hints about stain removal that you might not be as familiar with.

Antiperspirant/deodorant. For light stains, pre-treat with a liquid laundry detergent. For heavier stains, pre-treat by allowing to sit in laundry detergent for up to 10 minutes, then launder.

Baby formula. Dab stain with cold water, followed by soaking the item in an enzyme wash before laundering as usual.

Blood. Soak the item in cold water. If the blood does not come out, treat with the appropriate bleach for that particular fabric.

Candle wax. Harden wax by freezing or using ice. Scrape off as much wax as possible. Place paper towels on both sides of the stain and, with the stain side down, press with a warm iron. Change paper towels frequently to soak up more wax. Do not put an item in the dryer until all of the wax is removed.

Chewing gum. Harden gum with an ice cube, then scrape off as much as possible. Soak in dry-cleaning solvent until the rest of the gum can be removed.

Chocolate. Pre-treat by soaking in warm water with a stain treatment. If laundering does not remove the stain, wash again with the appropriate bleach.

Coffee/tea. Soak the item in cold water, then pre-treat with stain remover or laundry detergent. If the stain does not come out after the first wash, rewash with the appropriate bleach.

Berries. Soak in cool water and wash in warm suds. If, after rinsing, the stain is still visible, use the appropriate bleach.

Grass. Pre-treat spot with an enzyme product. If the stain does not come out after the first wash, rewash with the appropriate bleach.

Grease. Pre-treat the fabric with a stain remover or laundry detergent, followed by laundering with the hottest water safe for the fabric.

Ink. Sponge with rubbing alcohol and launder as usual.

Ketchup and other tomato-based products. Soak in cold water before laundering. If a greasy stain remains, treat with dry-cleaning solvent.

Lipstick. Pre-treat with stain remover and launder as usual.

Makeup. Pre-treat with stain remover and launder as usual.

Mildew/mold. Wash in bleach safe for the fabric in the hottest water possible.

Paint. For water-based paint, soak the still-wet item in warm water and launder as usual. For oil-based paint, use turpentine or other suggested thinner, then rinse and treat with a stain remover or laundry detergent before laundering.

Rust. Treat with commercial rust remover before laundering

Scorch mark. If the fabric has not been damaged, wash item in warm water using the appropriate bleach.

Urine (human). Rinse the stain with cold water and wash in warm, sudsy water with the appropriate bleach.

Wine, red. Soak the item in cold water and treat with stain remover or laundry detergent. Wash in warm water with the appropriate bleach.

Wine, white. Sponge the stain with cool water, rub with liquid laundry detergent and launder as usual.

Sources: Cleaning Plain & Simple, *by Donna Smallin,* and *Good Housekeeping's* The Complete Household Handbook.

No stain, no pain

Stain removers are designed to help treat a spot before it sets and becomes a permanent feature on an item of clothing. Typical use means they can be left on for a few hours—or even a few days—before washing. They come in store-bought (such as Oxiclean, which is available at Costco) and homemade varieties, which can include as ingredients rubbing alcohol, white vinegar, dry-cleaning fluid, mild synthetic laundry detergent, household ammonia, bleach, hydrogen peroxide or enzyme detergent.

Linda Cobb, better known as the Queen of Clean, has several recipes for stain removers. See page 72 for instructions on making all-purpose and oil-stain removers.

Caring for clothing

CARE LABELS ARE sewn into clothing to provide three pieces of information: fiber content, country of origin and care instruction.

The labels offer insight into the ideal temperature for washing, drying, ironing and whether the item should be bleached.

Below is a list of the most common fabric-care symbols and what they mean.

WASHING Instructions	Machine Wash, COLD	Machine Wash, COLD Permanent Press	Machine Wash, COLD Gentle Cycle	Hand Wash
	Machine Wash, WARM	Machine Wash, WARM Permanent Press	Machine Wash, WARM Gentle Cycle	Do Not Wash
	Machine Wash, HOT	Machine Wash, HOT Permanent Press	Machine Wash, HOT Gentle Cycle	

| BLEACHING Instructions | Bleach as needed — Any bleach may be safely used. | | Do Not Bleach — No bleach product should be used, Including detergents with bleach—or follow bleach-package test procedures to test for bleach safety. |
| | Non-chlorine bleach as needed — Use only a color-safe bleach. | | |

DRYING Instructions	Tumble Dry NO HEAT	Tumble Dry Permanent Press NO HEAT	Tumble Dry Gentle Cycle NO HEAT	Do Not Tumble Dry
	Tumble Dry LOW HEAT	Tumble Dry Permanent Press LOW HEAT	Tumble Dry Gentle Cycle LOW HEAT	Line Dry
	Tumble Dry MEDIUM HEAT	Tumble Dry Permanent Press MEDIUM HEAT	Tumble Dry Gentle Cycle MEDIUM HEAT	Drip Dry
	Tumble Dry HIGH HEAT			Dry Flat

IRONING Instructions	Iron, Steam or Dry, with LOW HEAT	Do Not Iron with Steam
	Iron, Steam or Dry, with MEDIUM HEAT	Do Not Iron
	Iron, Steam or Dry, with HIGH HEAT	

| DRY-CLEANING Instructions | Dry-clean — May appear with additional letters and/or lines. Take this item to a professional dry cleaner. | Do Not Dry-clean |

Source: Reprinted with permission of Textile Industry Affairs.

All is vanity

YOU'VE DECIDED TO update your bathroom with a beautiful new free-standing vanity/sink combination unit you recently purchased. The only things standing between you and your family enjoying the improved aesthetics and function is your old vanity—and the unfortunate reality that you're not an especially adept handyman or handywoman.

Not to worry. If you make adequate preparations, which includes reading this article, you can handle the installation.

Out with the old

Before you begin removing the vanity, turn off the water to the sink. In most cases you can do this by closing the shut-off valves on the water feed lines to the vanity located under the sink. If you don't have shut-off valves in your current vanity, you will have to shut off the water to the whole house and hire a plumber to install the necessary fittings.

After you shut off the water, place a bucket under the sink to catch any water still left in the supply lines or drain. Then, with an adjustable wrench, disconnect the water supply tubes from the base of the faucet and, with a large wrench, remove the drain.

Before you can remove your old vanity, you have to determine how it was fastened to the wall. Vanities are often attached with screws or nails through a rail or wood panel that runs along the wall. Other common spots bathroom vanities are attached are in the corners nearest the wall.

While you're looking inside your old vanity, note how its countertop and sink are held together. They may be held down with screws, or held in place with glue.

Next, run the blade of a utility knife along the seam where the vanity joins your bathroom wall, cutting through any caulking that might be holding the vanity edges or counter backsplash to the wall.

Next, take out the aforementioned screws or nails holding the vanity to the wall. If it was fastened with nails, you'll have to pull them with a nail puller such as a cat's-paw. Use a thin scrap of wood against the wall if your nail puller will come in contact with the wall, to prevent damaging it.

At this point you should be able to pull the vanity away from the wall. If doesn't pull away freely, use a pry bar. Again, use a thin scrap of wood to protect the wall from the pry bar.

Once your old vanity is removed, inspect the open area for damage and place a level on the floor to make sure it's level. If you suspect water damage in the walls or floor, now is the time to make the repairs.

If your old vanity was larger than your new vanity, you'll want to make sure that the newly exposed bathroom wall matches the rest of the room. If the texture or paint color doesn't match, consider hiring a professional to resolve these problems.

In with the new

If the new vanity/sink unit you purchased doesn't have the faucet installed, you'll need to purchase a faucet that matches your bathroom's décor and carefully follow the instructions included. If the faucet on your new vanity is already installed, hooking up the new vanity is not especially difficult. Place it where the old vanity was, with the faucet spout lined up above the drain.

If the back of the new vanity is open, as many free-standing units are, connecting the water supply lines and drain is especially easy. If the back is not open, carefully measure the locations of the water pipes and drain line coming out of the wall and transfer those measurements onto the back of the vanity. Measure up from the floor for horizontal reference point, and use a mark from the center of the drain for vertical reference. Use a hole saw with fittings at least a half inch larger in diameter than the pipes, and drill the holes for your water lines. Cut the hole for the drain with a larger hole saw or a jigsaw.

Flatten the cardboard packaging in which the vanity came or use some other layer of protection for your bathroom floor, and slide your new vanity into place. Before you reconnect the water lines and drain, it's a good idea to use new, flexible water feed lines to the water supply valves. Make sure you purchase lines that are the proper length. Apply a layer of Teflon tape over the water supply outlets before tightening the fittings. When tightening the fittings, use pliers until the connection is snug, but don't over-tighten the fittings. Then connect the sink tailpiece to the trap drain.

Finally, turn the water on and check the water supply lines for leaks. Hold a small wad of toilet paper near the connection. The paper will detect leaks efficiently.—*Will Fifield*

Tools of the trade

Before you try to tackle this project, make sure you have the following tools:
- Adjustable wrenches
- Tape measure
- Teflon tape
- Carpenter's level
- Utility knife
- Appropriately sized hole saws
- Power drill
- Water bucket
- Pry bar

A

B

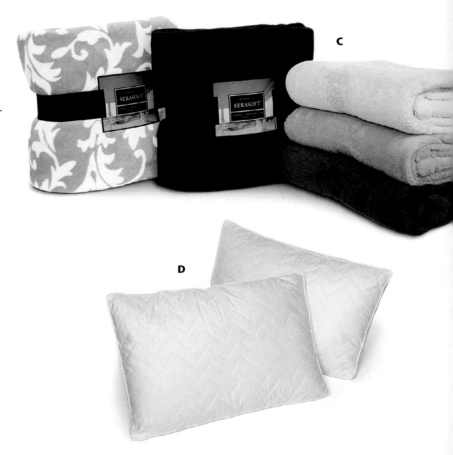

C

D

A. Royal Sateen Cotton Sheet Sets

These 450-thread-count sheets are made with 100% Egyptian cotton, woven with a delicate sateen dobby pinstripe and finished with solid hems and piping. Item #105415 Queen, #105441 King, #105442 California King

B. Space Bag Storage Packs

Triple your storage space with this 15 vacuum-seal bag combo set. Includes four medium bags, four large bags, three extra-large bags, one jumbo bag, two suitcase-size bags and one carry-on-size bag for travel. Easily seals with your own vacuum. Airtight and waterproof, these bags protect against bugs, dirt, mildew and odors. Item #896466

C. Berkshire Serasoft Throw

You can lose yourself in this decadently soft and plush throw. Durable and non-pilling, it can be thrown in the wash—presuming you can get yourself to let go of it. Item #660766

D. Comforel Pillow 2-Pack

Filled with soft fiber clusters that move freely to cradle your head, neck and shoulders. Accommodates all sleeping positions. Hypoallergenic, washable and dryable. Item #662756 Standard/Queen, Item #662757 King

PURE COMFORT...GUARANTEED

At Pacific Coast® we have more than a century of experience crafting irresistibly fluffy bedding.

Our Hyperclean® down is carefully selected to provide cozy warmth and adjustable support. And our Barrier Weave™ down-proof fabrics assure easy care.

A dream come true? Yes, and only Pacific Coast® guarantees it.

🌙 30-Night Comfort Guarantee

www.pacificcoast.com

Comfort with a touch of class

This ultimate eight-piece comforter collection made by Divatex includes two regular shams, two Euro shams, two Euro pillows, bedskirt and comforter. Presented in 420-thread-count, this elegant arrangement is single-ply, 100% Pima cotton and is shown here along with our 540-thread-count, single-ply, 100% Pima cotton Kirkland Signature™ sheet set. The comforter set is offered in white with chocolate trim and sage, canvas or icy blue border. A classic touch to complete the look of any bedroom with sophistication. Comforter set: Item #178403 Queen, #178404 King, #178405 California King
*Comforter sets arrive mid summer

HoMedics® SBM-360 Therapist Select™ Shiatsu Plus Massaging Back Cushion
This memory-foam seat houses a state-of-the-art mechanism that travels fully up and down the back with deep-kneading shiatsu and soothing rolling massage. The easy-to-use control provides targeted relief, width control and six programs. Item #777990

Conair Tourmaline Ceramic Styling System
This unit generates infrared heat that works on molecules inside the hair, drying it from the inside and out while minimizing heat damage and promoting more manageable hair. Item #109314

'Tis the Season for Sneezin'!

Get ready for Allergy Season with KLEENEX® Facial Tissue at Costco!

Thank goodness for **Kleenex** *tissue*

Support you trust.
Comfort you'll love.™

WHY PURCHASE A SEALY MATTRESS AT COSTCO

SELECTION: A complete range of comfort choices to meet your individual requirements.

QUALITY: Comfort, Support, and Durability. Only Sealy Posturepedic can provide the comfort and support for a truly restful and healthy nights sleep. Sealy uses only the finest materials and the best workmanship so that the Sealy Posturepedic mattress will provide years of comfort.

CONVENIENCE: You'll never have to "flip" your mattress again. In addition to comfort and durability, Sealy's "Unicased Edge Design" technology also offers the convenience of a one sided non-flip mattress. Now you can have both durability and convenience of a non-flip Sealy Posturepedic.

SEALY COMFORT STORY

All Sealy mattresses are designed and built to provide unsurpassed comfort. Sealy starts with the patented Posture*pedic* inner spring, which delivers both conformance and support. The finishing touch is the high quality foams and fibers that Sealy uses in every Sealy Posture*pedic*.

SUPPORT VS. FIRMNESS

Support and firmness do not mean the same thing. Support is determined by the overall sleep system, primarily the innerspring unit and the box springs. Regardless of which firmness you select, you will get the maximum support you require from Sealy's new "Comfort Support System" (CSS). Firmness describes the comfort or feel of the top "quilt system" of the mattress. One of the Sealy choices available at Costco will be the right one for you and will give you the "**Support you trust. Comfort you'll love**".

Sealy. **Posture***pedic®*

Featuring:

C S S
comfort | support | system

exclusively by **Posture***pedic*

- *Proper back support*
- *Relieves pressure points*
- *Retains its comfort*

Three ways to purchase Sealy Mattresses from Costco

1| Warehouse
Pick up your Sealy mattress directly from our warehouse.

2| In-store Kiosk
Order your Sealy mattress at the Special Order Kiosk and have it delivered to your home.

3| Online
Order online at costco.com and have your Sealy mattress delivered directly to your home.

Relax in luxurious comfort

Comforel® Ultima Down-Alternative Pillow Twin-Pack

Filled with Comforel down-alternative fiber, this pillow molds to your every sleep position, providing you with a comfortable night rest. With its 340-thread-count, 100% cotton quilted sateen cover and generous 2" side gussetts for extra support, this pillow keeps both luxury and comfort in mind. Item #662756, 662757

MARTEX®

Martex Commercial Towel Packs

Easy-pick packs of bigger, thicker, thirstier, pure white bath towels, hand towels and washcloths. The cotton-rich blend has just enough polyester for added durability.

Martex Bare Necessities Egyptian Bath Sheets

It's the supreme bath sheet — extra-large, sensuously soft, instantly absorbent — with luxurious Egyptian cotton loops for outstanding performance.

Healthy living

Did you know that good oral health contributes to good overall health? From expecting mothers to people managing diabetes, recent studies suggest that proper oral health can play an important role in your overall health.

Including the **Philips Sonicare Elite** power toothbrush in your oral routine, with its dynamic fluid cleaning action and patented sonic technology, can contribute to a healthier lifestyle. Plus, Philips Sonicare guarantees noticeable results and better check ups or your money back – guaranteed.

The **Philips Sonicare Elite** power toothbrush is available at costco.com and a Costco warehouse near you.

For more information, go to www.sonicare.com

PHILIPS
sonicare
the **sonic** toothbrush

PHILIPS
sense and simplicity

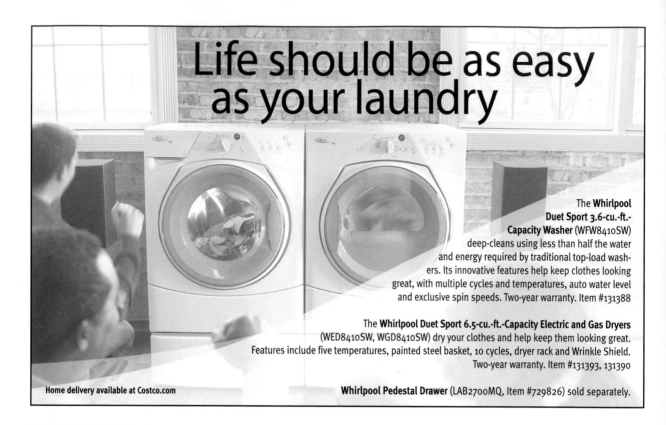

Life should be as easy as your laundry

The **Whirlpool Duet Sport 3.6-cu.-ft.- Capacity Washer** (WFW8410SW) deep-cleans using less than half the water and energy required by traditional top-load washers. Its innovative features help keep clothes looking great, with multiple cycles and temperatures, auto water level and exclusive spin speeds. Two-year warranty. Item #131388

The **Whirlpool Duet Sport 6.5-cu.-ft.-Capacity Electric and Gas Dryers** (WED8410SW, WGD8410SW) dry your clothes and help keep them looking great. Features include five temperatures, painted steel basket, 10 cycles, dryer rack and Wrinkle Shield. Two-year warranty. Item #131393, 131390

Home delivery available at Costco.com

Whirlpool Pedestal Drawer (LAB2700MQ, Item #729826) sold separately.

Costco and TIDE® bring innovation to you.

TWO BREAKTHROUGH TECHNOLOGIES FOR COSTCO MEMBERS
Tide® Advanced Power and 2X concentrated Tide® HE (High Efficiency)

TIDE ADVANCED POWER HAS ADDED COLOR SAFE BLEACH FOR EXTRA STAIN-REMOVAL POWER.

2X CONCENTRATED TIDE® HE

Tide HE is a high efficiency detergent designed specifically for use in high efficiency washers. HE washing machines are different because they use less water and tumble, rather than agitate, the clothes. Tide HE is formulated with special dirt-capturing ingredients and is low-sudsing to maximize the cleaning performance in an HE washer.

 Was 78 loads   Now 96 loads

TIDE® ADVANCED POWER – A FORMULA DESIGNED FOR COSTCO® MEMBERS

As a membership warehouse club, Costco is dedicated to bringing our members the best possible quality brand name merchandise such as Tide. Costco members look for performance, value and innovation in products.

Tide has always been known for great performance, but now it's gone to the next level with Tide Advanced Power. Tide Advanced Power has added color safe bleach, so you can get extra stain-removal power without worrying about your colors.

GET GREAT LAUNDRY TIPS AT TIDE.COM.

Find Tide® and other P&G products like Olay®, Crest®, Charmin®, and Bounty® at Costco, or visit www.pg.com for more information.

©2006 P&G

Straighten up and file right

THE HOME OFFICE is the space where we want to be our most productive. Often we are anything but. The desk is cluttered with unpaid bills. Files are in a stack on the floor. Someone's schoolwork is front and center.

Whether you're running a business out of your home office or sharing it with various family members, it's important to create a space that works. To help tame the home office chaos, four Costco members who are professional organizers share their tips for keeping things straightened up.

If a cluttered desk is the sign of a cluttered mind, what is the significance of a clean desk?

—Laurence J. Peter

Get into the zone
By Brenda Borenstein, member from North York, Ontario

Organization is a skill that can be learned. The most difficult part is breaking a lifelong habit, such as letting paperwork pile up. The key to getting more organized is to start with one small step and then take others one at a time.

When you have been disorganized for a while, it is difficult to stand back and take an objective look at your surroundings. If you feel overwhelmed, it is hard to know where to begin. Here are some tips to get you started.

Block it out. Address your desk problems in blocks of time. You may be able to straighten out the clutter in a few hours, or you may need a weekend. Sometimes it's better to devote a couple of hours a day to the job until you're done.

Be prepared. Have on hand a trash can, a pen, file folders, labels and other desk organizational aids that suit your needs.

Be clear. Clear the space you want to organize (the desk surface, one of the drawers, etc.). Then make a big pile of all the paper. Evaluate each item, categorize it and put it away (in the desk drawer, in a file, in one of the desk organizers, etc.), throwing out as much as possible.

Keep going. Even when you are feeling overwhelmed, just keep sorting and categorizing. If you devote the necessary time, your desk can be cleared.

Get help. Enlist the help of a partner, a spouse, a secretary, someone who can help you keep going.

Success is at hand
By Tami Reilly, member from North Vancouver, British Columbia

There's more room to think in a tidy office. Often the clutter around you becomes a barrier to moving forward with your ideas.

Start with the obvious. Begin by taking a garbage (or recycling) bag and moving around the office, picking out the obvious things.

Group like things. Start making piles all over the floor to group similar things—for example, unpaid bills, paid bills, customer correspondence, receipts, project ideas, important phone numbers, agonizing pile (see the next tip), etc.

Don't agonize. If you come across papers or things you have no idea what to do with, don't get hung up on them! Make an "agonizing" pile, put them there for now and keep going. Get the bulk of the clutter dealt with now.

Don't get sidetracked. Today is your organizing day only. It can get stalled easily if you allow yourself to start working on tasks as you uncover them within your paperwork piles.

Start on the future. Write down your goals and keep them where you can see them, using your "do it" list as a base. Take one goal that can easily be accomplished by you in a week and accomplish it! Then write another goal for the following week, equally easy, but building on your first accomplished goal.

Going slowly but surely will give you a model of success and the satisfaction of accomplishment. Getting organized is a means to an end: Having a more productive, stress-free work environment means having more time to grow your business!

Sharing a home office
By Donna Lindley, member from Rochester Hills, Michigan

Successfully sharing a home office requires planning and being mindful of the needs of everyone involved. Here are some guidelines to help your household set up a productive home office environment.

Determine activities. What activities occur in this space? Work? Bill payment? Homework? Begin by assessing each individual's home office needs. Make a list of equipment and supplies needed to maximize the efficiency of each activity.

Create zones. Each activity needs a dedicated place, or zone. Use the equipment list to set up the zones. Do multiple zones require use of the copier?

If so, then consider placing the copier between them. Which zones need access to the filing cabinet, phone, etc.? Are people right-handed or left-handed? Questions like these help to determine the best arrangement of furniture and equipment and identify additional needs.

Include ample storage. Determine the quantity and type of storage required. Remember, a place for everything and everything in its place. Bookcases or shelving can store reference materials. File cabinets are the best storage solution for paper files. A closet, not necessarily in the office, can be used for storing additional office supplies and files. Allocate storage space for each person and space for shared supplies.

Label contents of containers, shelves, drawers and cabinets so everyone knows where to find things and where to put them back.

Create a filing system. Because people think differently, they often disagree on file names. Is it "Car"? "Auto"? "Vehicle"? Involve everyone when creating labels for the filing system. If you have more than four drawers of files, consider implementing filing software, such as Kiplinger's The Paper Tiger (*www.thepapertiger.com*), which enables you to use your computer to find both paper and electronic files.

A well-planned, well-organized home office will create an environment that enables everyone involved to accomplish their work more efficiently and with reduced stress.

Filing solutions
By Kathy Vincent, member from Windsor, Ontario

The reason our desks and dining-room tables get piled with papers is because we have no place to put them. We're afraid they are going to get lost. Having a usable filing system will eliminate that worry. Remember, no piece of paper is worth anything if you can't find it.

Follow the FAT Principle. When shuffling papers: File it, Act on it or Toss it. Normally, 60 percent of the papers coming into your office can be tossed immediately.

To move forward, back up. Printing files that should be stored on a hard drive or CD just creates more paper clutter. It is important to maintain hard copies of some materials, but in most cases an electronic backup is sufficient.

File, don't pile. Your desktop should be clear of papers and piles. Creating an effective filing system will allow you to find any file in seconds.
- When creating a filing system, create files with names that you will remember.
- Keep files you reference often in the front of the file cabinet or box for easy access.
- Purge your files regularly to avoid holding on to outdated materials.
- Write a toss date on materials to remind yourself when to get rid of them.
- Keep a recycling container and garbage receptacle nearby.

Eighty percent of filed materials are never referenced again. Before filing a piece of paper, ask yourself: Does that paper deserve to take up valuable storage space? ⁊

Picking the right office chair

By Lynne Meredith Schreiber

LOOKING FOR AN office chair? These versatile pieces of furniture have moved beyond the office to home, school, even places of worship.

With approximately 1.25 million office chairs manufactured in the United States annually (according to the Business and Institutional Furniture Manufacturers Association), office managers aren't the only people picking them up. Everyday folks are buying office chairs for anyplace they need to sit and focus.

Before you go office-chair shopping, keep these simple tips in mind.

Make sure it's adjustable. Look for a chair with easy-to-adjust seat height to allow proper alignment with your desk and computer screen. A knee-tilt adjustment shifts the center of tilt toward the front of the seat to help reduce fatigue.

Plant your feet. When sitting, your backside should meet the chair back and be parallel to your knees or higher, according to Dr. Johnny C. Benjamin, an orthopedic spine surgeon in Vero Beach, Florida. Your feet should be flat on the floor, too. "People get chairs that are too low for them," says Dr. Benjamin. Rule of thumb: Your legs should be bent at 90 degrees, and your chin should be parallel with the middle of your computer screen. Knees should be higher than hips, and your elbows should bend 90 to 120 degrees on short armrests. Pull within 14 inches of the screen for best vision, says Dr. Scott Bautch, past president of the Occupational Health Council for the American Chiropractic Association.

Look for a five-leg base. It allows the chair to move around easily rather than dragging your body weight across the floor.

Think ergonomically. Derived from Greek, "ergonomics" means the science of making the work environment suitable for the worker. Hence, an ergonomic chair is "friendly to the body," says Dr. Bautch. That can mean it provides lumbar support for the lower back, offers adjustability at every level and is easy to move around the desk.

Go for comfort. Materials such as memory foam conform to individual body shapes, personalizing the sitting environment. Memory foam is also temperature sensitive.

Make it match. Office-chair styling has evolved to suit every décor. You'll find round backs and square backs, plus a range of colors and materials to suit any office setting.

Choose material for your climate. For an office with no air conditioning, choose a mesh back, which allows skin and clothing to breathe.

Remember that your chair sends a message. Leather puts an executive stamp on the setting, while faux leather or plastic-backed chairs are the choices of the masses. Upholstered chairs convey fine, high-end design.

Try it out. Spend at least a few minutes sitting in chairs before you buy. Move each one up and down, swivel around and kick your feet back. Try every angle, and make sure it adjusts for your height and weight.

Replace it every four or five years. Given techno-logical advances, new materials and the simple fact that you're wearing out a chair when you sit in it every day, all day long, don't expect to keep your office chair forever.

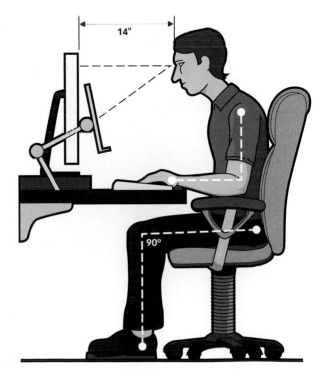

When seated at a computer, your chair should support your back with your arms and legs at a comfortable 90-degree angle.

Sponsored by ***The Print Shop***®

Desktop publishing guide

MARKETING IS ESSENTIAL to achieve business success, whether for a fledgling start-up or for an existing business ready to go to the next profitability level.

Your marketing and communication materials make a powerful statement about you and your business. Having a consistent look and feel across all of your company's communication materials helps to establish brand recognition and encourages customer loyalty.

When tight operating budgets do not allow for professional graphic design help, consider creating your own materials with desktop publishing software.

Desktop publishing software is a versatile tool that allows anyone to create visual communications for professional or desktop printing. Users can easily create page layouts with text, graphics, photos and other visual elements.

Select a distinctive font, layout and graphics and you are on your way to creating polished, professional business cards, letterhead, shipping labels and billing statements that have a consistent and easily recognizable look.

Mail merge and Web page design options in the software provide an easy tool for developing a database to regularly inform your customers about new products, services or promotions.

Desktop publishing software can be helpful for nonbusiness use as well, especially if you're a member of the PTA or a volunteer for civic, community or religious organizations. A multi-page booklet template helps you create exciting projects, including programs, menus, informational pamphlets, brochures and flyers.

These are only some of the many ways that desktop publishing software can help your business grow and your personal projects thrive.

Select the right desktop software

Your desktop publishing program should provide all the tools needed to design and publish professional business materials, multimedia presentations, Web pages, logos and more. Here are some of the features and functions to look for when purchasing desktop publishing software.

- Professionally designed project templates, premium fonts, images and graphics—with quick and easy search capabilities
- Text and layout tools, including spell-check, kerning, letter spacing, text and background effects
- Powerful photo-editing tools that allow you to manipulate images—crop, resize, add special effects and remove red-eye
- Professional printing and sharing tools—borderless printing, saving projects as common file types such as PDF and JPEG, and photo-quality printing
- Web page design tools that let you preview pages, create hot spots, insert hyperlinks and add sound and video
- Calendar and address book features to help you manage appointments and schedules

Create powerful print communications in three easy steps.

Step 1.
Select your layout.

Step 2.
Personalize and customize your project.

Step 3.
Publish your project.

Child and teen Internet safety

Did you know?

For more on keeping kids safe on the Internet, including blogging and social networking sites, check out *www.netsmartz.org/*. The NetSmartz® Workshop is an interactive, educational safety resource from the National Center for Missing & Exploited Children and Boys & Girls Clubs of America for children ages 5 to 17, parents, guardians, educators and law enforcement. The site uses age-appropriate activities to teach children how to stay safer on the Internet.—*Ed.*

KIDS SPEND HOURS ONLINE, and most of the time it's fun and innocent. However, the Internet also has a dangerous side, and it's up to parents to keep their children safe.

From early learners to sociable high schoolers, kids are constantly on the Internet. However, inappropriate Web content abounds, as do online predators. And while it's a challenge, if parents get involved and use the right tools they can minimize the danger to their children and teens.

Predators and pornography

The sad truth is that sexual predators prowl the Internet, and there's no shortage of Web sites with offensive and inappropriate content.

According to the National Center for Missing & Exploited Children

(NCMEC, *www.ncmec.org/*), one in five Americans ages 10 to 17 encountered sexual solicitations online during 1999. That was eight years ago, well before the widespread popularity of blogs, social networking sites and instant messages (IMs). These days kids are constantly chatting, e-mailing and posting personal information and images on Web sites. Regrettably, online predators have become adept at using these technologies to approach children and teens.

Unfortunately, online predators aren't the only problem. The same NCMEC study also found that one in four youngsters happened upon inappropriate sexual images while surfing the Web; only about four in 10 told a parent about it.

Get educated

To protect their children, parents need to educate themselves about their kids' online activities. From IMs and chat rooms to blogs and social networking sites, parents need to learn what these technologies do, how they work and how their kids are using them.

For example, many parents may not know that MySpace.com and other social networking sites have become very popular among teens. These Web sites give kids an easy way to share ideas, images and information about themselves. However, many adults use these sites, too, and it's not uncommon to find lurid content on their pages.

Moreover, according to a recent MSNBC report, predators have recently begun using these sites to approach and sexually assault young teens. Of course, the hosts of these sites put restrictions on content and try to enforce minimum age limits. However, it's simply too difficult to adequately control all the content, given the volume of traffic and information. So, it's up to parents to get involved and take control.

Get involved and take control

Once parents get involved, they can take positive steps to control how their kids use the Internet (see "What parents can do").

Kids do all sorts of things online. They surf, chat, e-mail and even post personal inforamtion. Meanwhile, the Internet is rife with dangers for children and teens, so parents need to get educated and get involved.

What parents can do

If you're a parent, here are some things you can do to protect your children.

Learn what your kids are doing. Ask your kids about their favorite online hangouts and who they meet there. Find out if they have a blog, a personalized Web site, an IM account or e-mail accounts.

Educate your kids. Be very clear about the kinds of personal information your children should never divulge over the Internet, including their name, address and phone number. Just as you would in the real world, teach your kids what to do if a stranger approaches them online. Specifically, tell them to cut off communication with any person they don't know and to notify you immediately.

Set Internet policies. Come up with family policies for e-mail, IMs, blogs and social networking accounts—including the kinds of programs your kids can use and how much time they can spend with each.

Block inappropriate sites. Decide which kinds of Web sites are off-limits to your kids, and use the parental control feature of your Internet security program to block access to restricted sites.

Monitor your kids' accounts. Make sure you know who your children are meeting online. Match the online identity of every person they communicate with to make sure it's someone you know and trust. Regularly check their buddy lists and address books for new and unfamiliar names.

Make the Internet a family activity. Maybe more important than anything else, keep your computers in a central part of the house; that way you can stay involved and keep an eye on what your kids are doing.

Protecting your identity

IDENTITY THEFT CAN sneak into your life in a variety of ways. From online scammers to check-washing thieves, no one is immune to this threat. According to the FBI, 10 million Americans fall victim to identity theft each year, amounting to more than $54 billion in losses for businesses and individuals. A common form of fraud called "check washing" costs individuals in the United States an estimated $815 million annually, according to the National Check Fraud Center (*www.ckfraud.org*). Here are a few hints to help protect your identity.

Monitor your credit report

Sign up to receive a free report from each of the three national credit-reporting companies every 12 months. To order a free annual credit report from each of the three reporting agencies, call toll-free 1-877-322-8228. [See article on page 100.]

Check your charges

Reconcile your credit and checking accounts each month. Make sure your purchases are accounted for.

Sign securely

Use a pen with specially formulated ink when signing checks and credit-card receipts. The ink contains pigments that are absorbed into the paper fibers of a check or receipt. When an individual tries to "wash" the information written on the check or other important documents, the ink is, in effect, "trapped" and cannot be altered. (Look for "HELPS PREVENT CHECK FRAUD" on the pen's packaging.)

Beware of your mailbox

Never leave outgoing bill payments in an unsecured mailbox, especially in front of your residence. The envelopes can be stolen and the checks removed and washed. The thief can then rewrite the check payable to himself or herself, in any amount. Plus, your bill has gone unpaid and you'll be hearing from your creditors. Better yet, pay as many bills online as possible.

Carry only what you need

Keep unessential cards locked up at home.

Surf safely

Make sure the Web sites you are shopping on are secure—look for *https://* in the site URL. Use only one credit card for all of your online purchases; it is easier to track one card versus several. Take the time to create original passwords for your online accounts.

Invest in a shredder

When in doubt, shred. Crosscut shredders are your best bet. ⚡
See page 98 for tips on selecting a shredder.

All inks aren't the same

Dye ink stains the paper, thus changing the color of the fibers. Dye ink can be removed by bleaching or washing the paper, changing it back to its natural color.

Pigment ink does not stain the color of the paper; instead it becomes trapped in the fibers of the paper, making criminal check washing and document forgery virtually impossible. Pigment inks have vibrant colors and excellent fade and water resistance without sacrificing performance.

Sponsored by Fellowes®

When in doubt, shred it

CURRENTLY, IDENTITY THEFT is the fastest-growing crime in America, and this trend shows no sign of slowing down. Many people still aren't aware of how easy it is to have their financial information stolen. And if it is stolen, victims spend an average of $800 and 175 hours of their personal time trying to clear their names!

Misconceptions about identity theft

Myth: Identity theft is not a common crime.
Fact: In the United States, there are 24,000 reported cases every day.

Myth: Senior citizens are the age group most vulnerable to identity theft.
Fact: Eighteen- to 29-year-olds report the largest number of identity-theft incidents.

Myth: Only strangers and hardened criminals steal information.
Fact: Fifteen percent of identity-fraud cases involve family members and friends.

Myth: Identity theft occurs most often on the Internet.
Fact: The majority of identity-theft crimes occur through stolen paperwork or personal items such as credit cards and wallets.

Identity-theft protection tips

How can you fight back against identity theft and corporate espionage?

What to shred

Individuals
ATM receipts
Bank statements
Canceled checks
Credit card statements and receipts
Insurance policies
Investment statements
Junk mail
Pay stubs
Retirement-plan contributions
Tax returns
Wills and other legal documents

Business organizations
Accounts receivable
Client contacts
Financial documents
Insurance records
Medical records
Obsolete legal files
OSHA 300 logs
Payroll records
Personnel files
Trade secrets

Depending on the laws in your area or the nature of your business, there may be privacy, retention and destruction guidelines that you are required to follow.

Be smart with your personal and professional information to ensure that it doesn't end up in the wrong hands. For example, the federal government recommends shredding as one of the most effective ways to destroy confidential information before throwing it away.

Here are some tips to protect yourself from a costly security breach.
- Shred all confidential information before throwing it away.
- Check your credit report annually to track any discrepancies.
- Review your monthly credit-card and bank statements for unauthorized purchases.
- Use a locked mailbox to prevent mail theft.
- Don't keep your Social Security card in your wallet or purse.
- Limit the number of credit cards you carry in your purse or wallet.
- Never give out personal information over the telephone.
- Do not download Internet files, read e-mails or click on hyperlinks sent by strangers.
- Use updated anti-virus, anti-spyware and firewall software on your computer.
- Use a secure, up-to-date Web browser that encrypts your purchasing information.

Selecting the right shredder

How much power do you need?

Because people tend to shred twice as much as they think they will, they often choose an underpowered shredder and end up frustrated by its inability to keep up with their workflow.

Choose a shredder based on sheet capacity, the amount of paper per pass, machine speed per shred and power rating, the amount of paper a machine can shred before the motor needs to rest (one cycle). Though a shredder may have a high sheet capacity per pass, it may not run very long or very fast—which means you get little power or value for your dollar.

Consider a shredder that's powerful enough to destroy credit-card offers, unopened junk mail and even CDs.

What level of security do you need?

Security level is determined by cut type. A strip-cut shredder typically slices paper into quarter-inch-wide strips. While strip cutting is better than hand-tearing, identity thieves can still reassemble and read your information.

Confetti-cut shredders, which cut paper into confetti particles 89 percent smaller than strip-cut shredders do, provide a much higher level of security by making it virtually impossible to reassemble and read your documents.

Do you have any special needs?

Because paper shredders have become more common in businesses and households, concerns have been raised about shredder safety. Look for brands with additional safety features such as automatically stopping if a user comes in contact with the paper opening.

If emptying shredded waste neatly is a problem, choose a shredder with a pull-out bin for hassle-free waste disposal.

Home equity alternatives

IF YOU'RE A HOMEOWNER, you can borrow against the value of your house through either a home equity line of credit (often called a HELOC or a line) or a home equity loan (often called a HEL or loan). Both are essentially a second mortgage.

Generally, a HELOC is a good choice to meet ongoing cash needs, such as college tuition payments or medical bills. A HEL is more suitable when you need money for a specific, one-time purpose, such as buying a car or a major renovation.

Here's a comparison of the two.

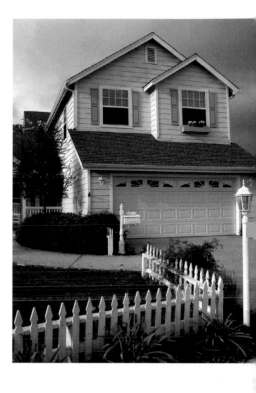

	Home Equity Line of Credit (HELOC)	Home Equity Loan (HEL)
What you get	Revolving credit with a specific credit limit of up to 100 percent of the value of a home (its value minus all debts against it). Some lenders allow borrowing up to 125 percent of the value of a home.	A fixed amount of money up to 100 percent of the equity in a home (its value minus your first-mortgage debt and other debts). Some lenders allow borrowing up to 125 percent of the value of a home.
How to qualify	Provide proof of income, home ownership, mortgage and amount of equity in the home. An appraisal is usually required.	Provide proof of income, home ownership and that at least 20 percent of the value of the home is paid off. An appraisal is usually required.
How you repay it	Minimum payments (as little as interest only) each month; eventually the entire sum borrowed plus interest is repaid.	Fixed payments of interest and principal over a fixed period of time.
How long it lasts	You have a 10- to 20-year period when you can draw on the line (up to the credit limit), after which you have a fixed period to pay off the outstanding balance plus interest.	The term of the mortgage can be as short as a year or as long as 30 years.
Costs and fees	Usually no closing costs, but may have an annual fee.	Closing costs that are lower than for a first mortgage.
How you receive the money	Draw funds as needed using special checks or a credit card.	Receive one up-front lump sum.

Credit basics

DOCTORS SOMETIMES USE X-rays to get a better picture of what's happening with their patients. Similarly, a credit report provides details about your financial life.

Credit reports cover information such as past home addresses; employment history; credit history, including a list of all late payments; and public-record information, such as bankruptcies, court judgments and a list of all inquiries into your file. Because it is often the key component on which another vital record, your credit score, is determined, it is important to make sure the information on your credit report is correct.

1 Your personal information, including your name and address, Social Security number, date of birth and employment information.

2 Any personal statement you added to your report will appear here.

3 List of payment history by five types of accounts:
- Real estate: Primary and secondary home mortgages
- Revolving: Open terms with varying payments such as credit cards
- Installment: Fixed terms with regular payments such as car loans
- Other: Accounts of unknown category such as a 30-day American Express account
- Collection: Seriously past-due accounts

4 Detailed information regarding all credit accounts in your name.

5 Legal matters that affect your credit, such as judgments against you, civil actions, state or federal tax liens or bankruptcies.

6 Lists the date and name of all parties who have made inquiries into your credit history.

Sample Credit Report

CONSUMER INFORMATION
Name: John Doe
Current Address: 1111 Any Street, Any City, Any State
Previous Address: 2222 Any Street, Any City, Any State
Current Employer: Any Employer

CONSUMER STATEMENT
I did not make this purchase on this credit card for $500.00 on 1/1/06.

PAYMENT HISTORY

Type	Count	Balance	Payment	Current	Delinquent	Derogatory
Real Estate	1	$100,500	$1,000	1	0	0
Revolving Acct.	1	$5,000	$100	1	0	0
Installment	0	$0	$0	0	0	0
Other	0	$0	$0	0	0	0
Collection	0	$0	$0	0	0	0

CREDIT ACCOUNT HISTORY

Creditor	Acct.	Date Number	Balance Opened	Pay	Terms Status	Past Due
Any Bank	12345678	01/01/06	$8,000	30 days	360 mos.	$0
Any Bank	910111213	01/01/03	$4,000	30 days	360 mos.	$0
Any Bank	141516171	01/01/00	$300	30 days	360 mos.	$0

PUBLIC RECORDS

Type	Status	Date Filed	Liability	Court
Chapter 7	Filed	01/01/06	$50,000	County

INQUIRY INFORMATION

Creditor	Date of Inquiry	Credit Bureau
Any Bank	01/01/06	Your Credit Bureau

When reviewing your credit, it is best to get a credit report from each of the three main credit-reporting agencies in the United States: Experian, TransUnion and Equifax. Federal legislation requires each of these nationwide consumer reporting agencies to provide you with a free copy of your credit report, at your request, once every 12 months. To comply with this mandate, the three agencies have set up a central Web site, a toll-free number and a mailing address through which you can order your free annual credit report. To order copies of your credit reports, visit *www.annualcreditreport.com*, call 1-877-322-8228 or complete the Annual Credit Report Request Form and mail it to Annual Credit Report Request Service, P.O. Box 105281, Atlanta, GA 30348-5281. You can print the form from the Federal Trade Commission's Web site, *www.ftc.gov/credit*.

It's also important to take a look at your credit score, because most lenders use your credit score to determine the risk they're taking by lending you money when you apply for a credit card, a car loan or a mortgage. Your credit score, often called a FICO score (because it is calculated from a mathematical model developed by Fair Isaac Credit Organization, a leading provider of financial data analysis), is a three-digit number that provides lenders a snapshot of your credit use and your financial standing. Most credit scores fall somewhere between 300 and 850. If credit scores were graded, 300 would be failing while 750 and higher would be an A. Credit scores are available online at Web sites such as *www.myfico.com* for a small fee.

How to read a credit report

Credit reports are divided into four sections: identifying information, credit history, public records and inquiries. When reading through the identifying information section, check it for accuracy. Is your name spelled correctly? Do all of the reports list your Social Security number accurately?

Personal information

Because so much information is listed on your report, you're likely to find errors. Minor mistakes such as misspelled names of employers and incorrect previous addresses are common. However, some mistakes are potentially serious. Make sure your credit reports list all of your current contact information correctly. If your address is incorrect, new credit offers in your name may be sent to the wrong residence, which can easily enable someone to steal your identity.

Use this checklist to determine that important information is correct:
- Name
- Address
- Social Security number
- Date of birth
- All accounts listed are your own
- Credit/charge accounts
- Outstanding balances/limits on the accounts
- Payment histories
- Derogatory credit information has been deleted after seven years (non–Chapter 13 bankruptcies after 10 years)
- Inquiries

Credit account history

This section of a credit report sometimes refers to the individual accounts as "trade lines." Each account will include:

Six steps to better credit

1. Pay your bills on time. Creditors scrutinize your credit history. If you pay your bills on time, this reflects well on you. If you have a record of delinquent payments, you might want to consider credit counseling on how to better manage your finances. Reputable credit-counseling organizations employ counselors who are certified and trained in consumer credit, money and debt management, and budgeting. Organizations that are nonprofit have a legal obligation to provide education and counseling.

But beware—just because an organization says it is "nonprofit" doesn't guarantee that its services are free or affordable, or that its services are legitimate. In fact, some credit-counseling organizations charge high fees, some of which may be hidden, or urge consumers to make "voluntary" contributions that cause them to fall deeper into debt. The Federal Trade Commission provides helpful advice on choosing a credit counselor online at *www.ftc.gov/bcp/conline/pubs/credit/fiscal.htm*.

2. Manage your debt. Your debt/income ratio—the percentage of your income that goes to paying off debt—is another gauge of your financial health. You can calculate this ratio by dividing your monthly minimum debt payments (excluding mortgage) by your monthly take-home income. If your debt payment absorbs: ▶

- Less than 20 percent of your income, you are doing well
- Between 20 percent to 35 percent, consider reducing your overall debt
- More than 35 percent, consider credit counseling or some type of aggressive debt-reduction strategy

3. Don't over-apply for credit. Limit the number of loan applications you submit. Each bid shows up as an inquiry in your credit report. Even if you're just comparison-shopping for the best rate, too many inquiries can be viewed as a desperate bid to obtain credit to get out of financial trouble.

4. Shred your documents. Be sure to destroy any piece of paper with Social Security or credit-card numbers. Thieves often go through garbage and retrieve people's identification so they can use this information to commit fraud.

5. Don't give information away. Be extremely cautious how you use your Social Security number: It is a key personal identification number that is a gateway to your personal identity. If required to provide this information, always ask if there is another option.

6. Check your credit reports on a regular basis. The only way to protect your name and credit is to be proactive. With the rise of identity-theft cases, it is important to review your credit files and to report any inaccuracies to the major credit-reporting agencies.

- The name of the creditor
- Account number (which may be scrambled for protection)
- The date the account was opened
- The type of credit (mortgage, car loan, etc.)
- Whether it's a joint account or in your name only
- Total amount of loan
- How much you owe
- Amount of monthly or fixed payments
- Status of account (open, inactive, closed, paid, "charged off," etc.)

Note: The term "charged off" means that the creditor has written off your account and taken it as a loss. Some reports use numeric payment codes; generally, the lower the number, the better the mark.

Public record

This section lists financial blemishes such as bankruptcies, judgments and tax liens. The goal is to have this section of your report blank.

Inquiries

The final section of the report lists everyone who has asked to see your report. For example, it is increasingly common for insurance companies to review your credit before extending auto or health insurance. Many employers now check credit before they consider you for a position. If you rent, you may have already been through a credit check to determine your worthiness as a renter.

Because your credit history is a critical part of your financial standing, it's important to review your credit reports periodically and follow up with the credit-reporting agencies and your creditors to correct any errors.—*Will Fifield*

Bring harmony to your house.

Make a smarter choice.
AMD LIVE!™ PCs allow you to use your favorite digital devices, including your TV, in ways you never have before. Opening up a whole new world of digital entertainment at home and on the go. **www.amdlive.com**

AMD LIVE! PC
Hi-Fi
Flat Screen TV
Media Player

AMD

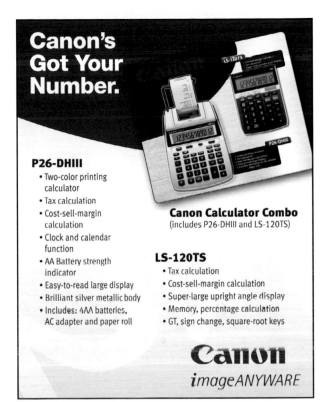

Canon's Got Your Number.

P26-DHIII
- Two-color printing calculator
- Tax calculation
- Cost-sell-margin calculation
- Clock and calendar function
- AA Battery strength indicator
- Easy-to-read large display
- Brilliant silver metallic body
- Includes: 4AA batteries, AC adapter and paper roll

Canon Calculator Combo
(includes P26-DHIII and LS-120TS)

LS-120TS
- Tax calculation
- Cost-sell-margin calculation
- Super-large upright angle display
- Memory, percentage calculation
- GT, sign change, square-root keys

Canon
*image*ANYWARE

DESIGN OPTICS

READING GLASSES
PREMIUM QUALITY

Available In Six Powers:
+125, +150, +175, +200, +250, +300
(New York warehouses carry +275 in place of +300)

Fashion Lifestyle

Design Optics reading glasses are created with the finest optical-grade materials and workmanship available, to provide you with premium quality and exceptional value. Make Design Optics your choice for reading glasses.

FRAME SELECTION

- MONEL SLIM EXECUTIVE
- STAINLESS STEEL FLEX FRAME
- FLEXLITE MEMORY FRAMES
- STAINLESS STEEL SLIM ELITE
- ALUMINUM FEATHERWEIGHTS
- FASHION LIFESTYLE
- MONEL OPTIFLEX

LOOK FOR THIS DISPLAY

Great results begin with Avery

Avery White Ink Jet Address Labels: Smudge-free guarantee, new easy-peel feature and sharper print quality. Avery templates are found in Microsoft Word and other popular software programs. 70 sheets include 2,100 labels. Item #256746

Avery White Laser Address Labels: Jam-free guarantee, new easy-peel feature and sharper print quality. 140 sheets include 4,200 labels. Item #235749

Avery Heavyweight Sheet Protectors 200-Pack: Acid free, easy-load feature, diamond clear for presentation and document protection. Item #248046

Marks-A-Lot Chisel Tip Markers 24-Pack: Permanent, rub and water resistant, nontoxic and low odor. Item #743133

uni-ball®
PERFORMANCE AND DESIGN

SPECIALLY FORMULATED INK
HELPS PREVENT
CHECK FRAUD!

John Smith
1234 E. Erie
Anytown, USA

Date 3/15/0

Pay to the order of THE JERK WHO STOLE YOUR MON

EVERY LAST DIME IN YOUR ACCOU

for

207

C26253 ©2007 Sanford, L.P., Oak Brook, IL 60523 ww.uniball-na.com *A Newell Rubbermaid Company*

SECURE YOUR SIGNATURE™

- Over $815 million is lost annually by Americans to check washing, a form of check fraud.

- The uni-ball® 207™ features a special ink that is trapped in paper, helping prevent criminal check washing and document alteration.

Item #163197

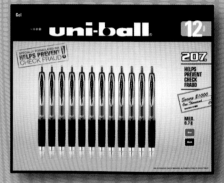

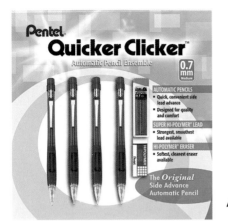

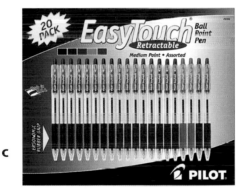

A. Pentel Quicker Clicker™
These automatic pencils are ergonomically designed and quality engineered to ensure years of writing comfort. The unique side-advance system provides precise lead control and performance at the click of a button! Item #213512

B. Scotch Magic Tape 12-Pack
The very best tape for the office. Disappears on paper, won't show on copies and easy to write on. Twelve jumbo length 3/4" x 1500" rolls per pack. Item #133502

C. Pilot EasyTouch Retractable Ball Point Pen 20-Pack
Pilot's EasyTouch pens are retractable, refillable and feature a comfort grip that absorbs most of the pressure associated with extended periods of writing or note taking. The ink is top quality and yields smooth, crisp lines. Item #107700

D. Xerox Premium Multipurpose Paper
This 24-pound, 96 bright paper is perfect for everyday printing in all types of printers, especially inkjet and laser. 800 sheets per pack. Item #428437

A. Lexmark Ink Tank Combo Pack

Ink design is every bit as essential in inkjet quality as printer and cartridge design. Ink formulation is one of Lexmark's most valued and confidential intellectual property assets. Item #642836

B. Kodak Color Cartridge and Photo Paper Kit

Gives you everything you need to easily print real Kodak pictures on your Kodak Printer Dock. Up to 4" x 6" prints are waterproof, stain resistant and will last a lifetime. Item #945712

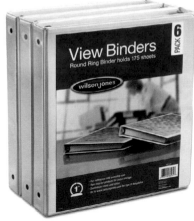

C. Wilson Jones Binders

Wilson Jones binders keep papers in their place. Customize covers and spines for business presentations or for easy project organization. Multi-packs available in 1/2" to 3" sizes. Item #91125

D. Manila File Folders

These 1/3 cut file folders are extra durable, with rounded corners and a scored bottom for easy expansion. Includes 150 per box. Item #217735

 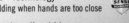

A. Ticonderoga Pencils

Ticonderoga is "The World's Best Pencil"™. Exclusive graphite core and satin-smooth finish allow for excellent performance. Made from premium cedar. PMA certified nontoxic. Item #684756

B. Panasonic Compact Electric Pencil Sharpener

This new sharpener has sturdy suction feet, which allows it to stick to just about any surface. Features include an auto-stop when sharpening is complete, a transparent shaving receptacle and durable steel cutting blades that provide 16-degree perfect pencils. UL listed. Item #11494

C. Neon OPEN Sign

Lightweight, safe, quiet, cool and energy efficient, this 22.25" x 13" x 3.5" sign is visible through tinted glass. Item #44650

D. Sentry®Safe Biometric Safe

Features biometric fingerprint lock with backlit advanced electronic keypad and tubular key. Safe has one-hour UL-classified fire and media protection. Item #110832

E. Power Sentry Experion Surge Protector

Designed for the home office and home theater systems. Experion Plus surge protectors use advanced ClearConnect power conditioning technology so only clean power enters your electronic equipment. The result—equipment remains safe from harmful surges entering through the AC, cable and phone lines. Features include 10 adapter-spaced outlets, three sets of coaxial outlets and a 6' power cord. Item #992836

A

B

C

D

E

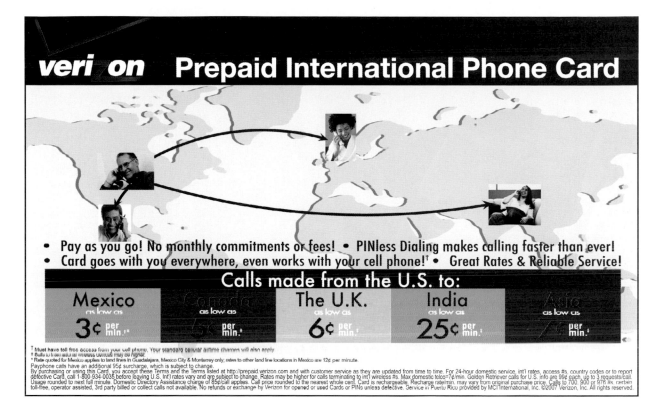

ES Robbins Carpet ChairMAT
The Crystal Edge® design allows for effortless rolling on and off this 45" x 53" mat. Also features removable carry handles and no-crack lifetime guarantee. Item #122164

Small in size, big in features

Optoma's DX625 Projector
is a lightweight, multimedia data projector that features DLP® technology, native XGA resolution and 2,500 lumens of brightness. Weighing only 4.4 pounds, the portable DX625 is HDTV compatible and has a number of connection options for multiple video sources.

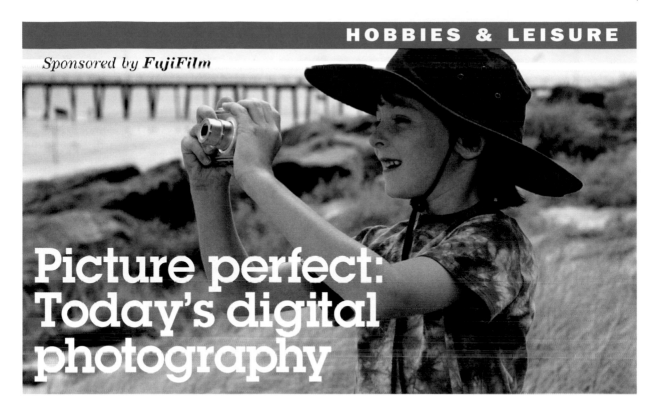

Sponsored by FujiFilm

Picture perfect: Today's digital photography

SOMETIMES WHAT YOU GET in your photos isn't at all what you see as you press the shutter button. What should have been perfect photos of baby's first steps or gorgeous fireworks or the family reunion turn out to be under-exposed, blurry and filled with red-eyed monsters.

Happily, those days are over. New digital cameras have sophisticated technology that automatically corrects the most common causes of flawed photos. And this technology is easy to use, enabling everyone to take amazing images without first devoting years to learning the art and science of traditional photography.

You can further enhance your photos on your computer with easy-to-use image-editing software. You can even transform photos into cool gifts or artistic keepsakes with just a few mouse clicks.

There's really no excuse for ever taking a bad photo again, or for abandoning your photos on your hard drive or in a shoe box.

Saturate yourself with your subject and the camera will all but take you by the hand.
—Margaret Bourke-White

Capturing the image

Take focus, for example. Everyone knows when a photo is in focus and when it's not. But proper focus is much more than just non-blurry images. The focal point—the part of your photo that tells the story—is usually the sharpest part of the photo. If you're photographing your kids, you want the primary point of focus to be their faces, not a section of the wall behind them or the toys in front of them. But unless you're a whiz with depth of field and shutter speed, chances are that some of your photos suffer from misplaced focus.

The introduction of auto-focus was a great advance for photography, and technology is now emerging that lets the camera even better understand where it is you want to focus, then focus for you. Since the majority of photos taken are of people, some new cameras have a great new feature:

face-detection technology. This feature allows a camera to identify up to 10 human faces in a scene and then automatically set the correct focus and exposure to ensure that all of those faces look fabulous.

Even the most active subjects can be photographed perfectly with cameras that offer picture-stabilization technology, which reduces the dreaded "blur" effect caused when hands shake even just a bit. It also adjusts the camera's settings to compensate for the subject's movement, and it works even when you're the one who is moving. For example, if you're shooting out of the window of a moving car, your photos will still be in focus.

Proper focus and understanding light go hand in hand. New digital cameras are much better at capturing images indoors in artificial and low-light conditions without a flash. People look like they do in real life.

When you do need to use a flash, the on-board systems have greatly improved. Intelligent flash systems analyze the scene you're shooting and automatically adjust the flash to capture the image without blasting it with too much light. In case you're not sure if you can get away without using a flash, some cameras even have a feature that takes two photos in quick succession, one with flash and one without, and displays them side by side for comparison.

Film or digital?

Until recently, traditional film offered many benefits that digital could not, but the newer digital cameras have quickly caught up. Traditional film will always have a valued place as a fine-art medium, creating photos with a particular feel and look, but digital cameras in higher megapixel ranges produce results comparable in quality to film.

Of course, you don't have to choose between film and digital—you can use both. If you've decided to invest in a really great digital camera, you can also experiment with the new generation of one-time-use cameras that come preloaded with 1000-speed film. These cameras capture action in sharp focus and brilliant color, and are great to bring along to the pool or beach, or to use in the rain or snow or in any conditions that might damage your primary camera. They are also a great way to introduce children to the joy of photography.

Printing your photos

Digital photographers tend to be lax about making prints, and that's a shame. Sure, you can store your photos on your computer and gather family and friends around the screen when you want to relive your memories. But most people prefer to have printed copies of digital images to flip through and share. Somehow, a photo isn't truly a photo until you can hold it in your hands. And computers aren't the safest home for your digital images; machines malfunction and break, viruses can obliterate files and human error can result in mistakenly deleted or overwritten files.

The best way to make sure your images don't fall victim to some ugly cyber-calamity is to make backups. Digital photos, when printed on good-quality photographic paper, have long life expectancies. Quality prints protected from heat, light, humidity and air pollution (particularly cigarette smoke) will look great for decades. Archival gold CD-Rs also have very long life expectancies when properly stored in their cases.

Your photos shouldn't be allowed to scatter on your computer or you'll soon be wasting way too much time searching for them. Chances are you won't remember that the perfect sunrise photo from last summer's vacation is named "IMG125673GZ." Instead, organize them with image-management software.

You can print your digital images on your home printer or send them to a local photo finisher. Printing at home provides instant gratification, but it can also be time consuming and expensive compared to a photo lab. And unless your computer, monitor and printer are calibrated to exact color settings, the printed image may not match what you see on the computer screen.

You can upload photos via the Internet directly from your computer and pick up your prints at a local photo finisher such as Costco 1-Hour Photo, or have them mailed to you. You can also take photos on a memory card, CD-R or USB flash drive to a local photo finisher to order prints. You can choose among many photo sizes, from wallet-size to poster-size prints; 4 x 6-inch prints remain the convenient and affordable standard.

Create and share

Prints are wonderful, but don't stop there. Creating special keepsakes with your photos is super simple with digital images. You don't need to be a computer whiz, either. All you need to do is click a few buttons to make personalized art and gifts.

For example, you can make your own hardcover book featuring your photos with digital publishing services. Imagine how cool it would be to have your own coffee-table book of vacation memories or family celebrations.

Make note cards, greeting cards, T-shirts, calendars, mouse pads and more. You name it and your photo can probably be put on it.

It's a great time to be a photographer!

Service	1-Hour Photo	costco.com Photo Center
Location	Place orders in warehouse or on costco.com Photo Center; pick up orders in warehouse	Place orders on costco.com Photo Center; pick up orders in any U.S. warehouse or have mailed
Print size (glossy or luster finish)	Wallet size up to 12" x 18"	Wallet size up to 20" x 30"
Digital prints	Kiosk for ordering digital prints from CD-Rs, memory cards or USB flash drives	Upload from any computer with Internet access
Print delivery	Up to 100 digital 4" x 6" prints ready for warehouse pickup in one hour	Pick up orders at any Costco warehouse or via mail; up to 100 digital 4" x 6" prints ready for warehouse pickup in one hour
Archival storage	Gold CD-R	Gold CD-R
Passport photos	Shot at 1-Hour Photo counter; available for pickup in five minutes	NA
Other photo items	Holiday and all-occasion greeting cards	Order holiday and all-occasion cards from home; pick up from local Costco warehouse. Order calendars, mouse pads, mugs, posters and more; delivery by mail
Film developing and printing	One-hour service on 35 mm and APS film	NA
Online image storage	NA	Unlimited photo storage; print ordering required

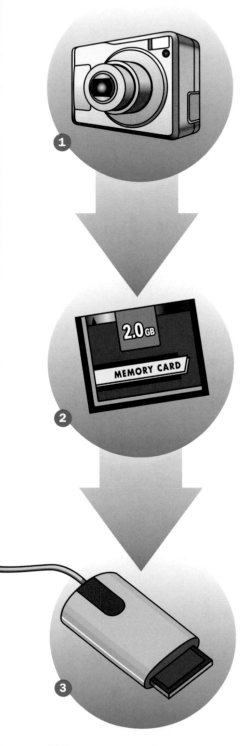

Step-by-step digital photos

1. Buy and shoot

When you buy a digital camera, the biggest consideration—besides the fun you're going to have—is how you will be using the camera. Will you be e-mailing photos or putting images on a Web site, both low-resolution applications, or will you be printing high-resolution photos in a glossy magazine? Your needs are probably somewhere in between those extremes, so look for a camera that offers a range of resolution settings from low to high.

Most digital cameras come with a "quick start" guide. Try the automatic exposure and focusing modes until you feel comfortable with the camera, then experiment with the full range of the controls. You will like the choice of framing each shot in either a viewfinder or on a color LCD (liquid crystal display) on the back of the camera. Click the shutter button, and you've got your first digital image.

2. Store

True, digital cameras don't need film; reusable memory cards, in essence, replace film. Popular memory-card types include Compact Flash, SmartMedia, SD, xD and Memory Stick. The camera determines which card type can be used. These cards are not interchangeable, have slightly different dimensions and come in a range of capacities as high as 16 gigabytes (GB)—1 gigabyte is equal to 1,024 megabytes.

The camera resolution settings determine the amount of storage space you need. The higher the resolution, the bigger the image size in terms of stored information. Most cameras come with a small starter card. If you will be taking many high-resolution shots for detailed 8" x 10" prints, you will need a higher-capacity card. Two-gigabyte cards have become a good value.

It's wise to carry extra memory cards, just as if you were taking along extra rolls of film.

3. Download

Card readers allow you to quickly download the contents of a memory card into the hard drive of your computer via a Universal Serial Bus (USB) connection. On the computer screen, drag and drop image files (photos) into the desired folder, then eject the card. Load the card back into your camera and use the camera setting that reformats the card. Memory-card manufacturers recommend this method of erasing images from the card.

4. Edit

OK, so now the photos are on your computer. What next? The real fun of digital photography begins at this point. You can use the image-editing software that was bundled with your digital camera to enhance, clean up or otherwise manipulate each image. This could be as simple as brightening the exposure to compensate for poor lighting, or as complex as editing a person into or out of an image. There are many desktop publishing applications that will allow you to use your images for designing brochures, ads, invitations, catalogs, posters, greeting cards and presentations.

5. Print

At home, dedicated photo printers and general-use inkjet printers do a good job of printing digital photos. Use special photo paper for best results. Also consider taking advantage of the professional printing quality of Costco's 1-Hour Photo in two ways: Bring digital photos on a memory card, USB flash drive or CD-R into any 1-Hour Photo to place an order through the digital kiosk; or upload your digital photos via the Internet to the Photo Center on costco.com, where you can perform simple image editing such as auto correct, fill flash or remove red eye. Prints ordered online can be picked up at any 1-Hour Photo in the United States, or can be mailed directly to your home.

6. Archive

You probably won't want to devote valuable hard-drive space to storing your photos, and a hard-drive crash could lose everything. Burning images to disc is a cost-effective storage option. (Costco's 1-Hour Photo can copy images onto a gold CD-R with proven archival storage longevity, preferred over the use of regular silver CD-Rs, which could degrade in as few as two years.)

7. E-mail

Most e-mail programs allow you to send images as file attachments. Photos need to be formatted as a JPEG file to keep the size small for speedy transmission and downloading. The image-editing software that comes bundled with your camera will guide you through converting images into the desired size and file type.—*David Wight*

See the glossary of digital photography terms on page 116.

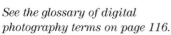

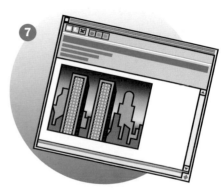

Digital-photo glossary

Automatic exposure (AE). The automatic adjustment of the camera's aperture or shutter speed or both for the proper exposure.

Bracketing. A technique of shooting a number of pictures of the same subject and viewpoint at different levels of exposure; many digital cameras have an automatic setting for bracketing.

CCD. An abbreviation for "charge coupled device," a light-sensitive semi-conductor chip that balances brightness and exposure settings in a digital camera, camcorder or scanner.

Digital zoom. Provides the illusion of an enlarged view by displaying only the central portion of an image, displayed without enhancement at lower resolution.

Download. The transfer of photos from a digital camera to a computer.

FireWire. Also called IEEE 1394; a cross-platform, high-speed standard for transmitting multimedia from peripherals to computers.

Focal length. In digital cameras, the distance between the CCD sensor and the focal point of the lens. This value is usually expressed in millimeters, and indicates how much of a scene will be included and the amount that objects will be magnified.

JPEG compression. A file-format standard for compression of images. Web and e-mail applications require photos to be in this format.

LCD screen. Abbreviation for "liquid crystal display screen," a small color monitor on digital cameras and camcorders used for framing the subject before shooting or reviewing stored images.

Megapixel. An image or image sensor containing more than 1 million picture elements, calculated as the product of the image width times the image height, in pixels.

Optical zoom. The true zoom type, in which the lens controls image enlargement, making the subject look closer or bigger.

Pixel. A picture element; the smallest element of a digitized image; the smallest dot you can see on a computer screen or in a digital image.

Resolution. Refers to the number of pixels, both horizontally and vertically, used to capture an image or display it.

USB. Abbreviation for "Universal Serial Bus," a high-speed connection for interfacing computers with peripheral devices. 🅰

*Sponsored by **Nikon***

Choosing a digital camera

DIGITAL HAS PRETTY MUCH replaced film in every area of photography. The ability to see your picture instantly on a digital camera's built-in color LCD monitor is one of the advantages. Great pictures can be enjoyed right away, and the bad ones can be quickly and easily deleted. The computer has replaced the shoe box for storing images, and easier-to-use software has made it more convenient than ever to add fun and creative touches to pictures you want to e-mail or print.

For most people, capable and compact point-and-shoot-style digital cameras fit their lifestyle perfectly, and the auto-everything nature of point-and-shoot is tremendously appealing. But for an increasing number of people, the substantially enhanced performance capabilities of digital SLR cameras are proving to be the ideal way for them to get the pictures they really want.

The somewhat larger size of a digital SLR means a bigger image sensor, too—the best case for bigger means better ... picture quality, that is.

What makes a digital SLR so good?

Let's start with what an SLR camera is. SLR stands for single-lens reflex, which simply means the camera sees the pictures to be taken, focuses auto-

All about size: Point-and-shoot convenience wins when it needs to slip into a pocket.

matically and determines the precise exposure through the same lens that captures the picture. What's perhaps most important about SLR cameras is the ability to easily change that lens. Typically, digital SLR camera manufacturers offer a wide assortment of lenses, from wide-angle to telephoto, to meet virtually any picture-taking need. This allows you to tailor your digital SLR system to your photographic interests: travel, sports, nature, wildlife, you name it.

Not only lenses, but also powerful flash units and a host of other accessories can be added to your SLR system as you need them.

In the end, SLR cameras offer more precision and versatility than their compact counterparts and, for a number of reasons, have the ability to take visibly higher-quality images.

Megapixels are megapixels, right?

Yes and no. Most people believe that a compact point-and-shoot camera and an SLR with the same megapixel count will have the same picture-taking capacity. This isn't necessarily the case. The imaging sensor in a digital SLR is physically larger and supports higher overall picture quality.

Ready when you are

Almost everyone has experienced the frustration of pressing a compact camera's shutter button, only to have the camera hesitate before taking the picture. Digital SLR cameras react almost instantaneously, virtually eliminating shutter lag. The peak moment of sports action and the perfect portrait expression can be caught as they happen. For many people, this is the most important reason to own a digital SLR.

Any downside to digital SLRs?

Good question. First, even the smallest digital SLR cameras (and some digital SLRs are much smaller than others) are larger than the average compact digital. Most people love the notion of being able to go anywhere with a high-quality camera that fits easily into a pocket or purse—which is why many people who opt for the higher quality of a digital SLR own a compact digital camera as well.

On balance, digital SLR cameras are more expensive than their compact counterparts, though prices have been coming down, making them more affordable than ever.

Finally, digital SLRs have a reputation for being more difficult to use. In some instances, this reputation is well earned, but, in general, manufacturers have made great strides in making their digital SLR cameras easy and intuitive to operate. These new-generation digital SLRs have made high-quality picture taking more accessible and more fun.

Summing up

Compact design has teamed with capability, convenience and lower prices to make digital SLR cameras the right choice for people who want to take great pictures right from the start. For those whose enthusiasm for photography is the starting point, a digital SLR offers practically unlimited potential.

Different tips for different types from Nikon

Share. Kids love digital cameras because they love seeing themselves, so share the view from the LCD. "This is cool, take a look," is what you want to be saying, but *when* you say it is key: Don't stop the action to show them the pictures; wait for natural breaks.

Great outdoors

Vary the view. Wide-angle lenses will take it all in, but the details, patterns and textures of rocks, flowers and trees will add diversity to your collection of outdoor images.

Big stuff. Without a reference point, no one is going to know how large that tree, mountain, boulder, cactus, whatever, really was. Try to include something, like a person, to indicate scale.

Travel

Variety. Record not just monuments and landmarks, but food, architectural details, shop windows, the marketplace.

People. Go gently; go slowly; go with a smile. Don't hide the camera. Make all your settings beforehand; when you've got a person's cooperation, you don't want to be spending time pressing buttons and turning dials.

In general

Almost every photograph can be improved by moving closer. This does not apply, however, to photographs of wild animals.

In most cases, "one subject, clearly defined" is the golden rule. Distracting backgrounds ruin more pictures than camera shake does. Bizarre things happening at the edge of the frame ruin more pictures than distracting backgrounds do.

Sports

Rule 1. Know the game.

Rule 2. Anticipate the action.

Gear up. You can get good overall views and perhaps some interesting closer shots with the long-ranging zoom on your compact camera, but for the details, the expressions and the impact, a digital SLR with a telephoto or telephoto zoom lens is what you need. Consider a lens with a maximum telephoto capacity of at least 200mm.

Kids

Go with the flow. You'll get the best photos of your kids when they're doing the things they love to do. Don't direct them; don't pose them. Keep up, shoot fast— and, whenever you can, shoot from their level; shots of kids taken from the vantage point of a 6-foot adult usually aren't natural looking.

Editing rescues bad photos

Cropping and resizing
Before and after

COMING HOME WITH a set of stunning vacation photos is a great way to relive wonderful memories. But for those of us who aren't professional photographers, taking perfect photos isn't always foolproof even with today's digital cameras. When everyone's eyes in a shot glow bright red or a batch of photos appear to have been washed in yellow dye, the value of being able to alter photos after they've been taken is easy to appreciate.

Thanks to digital photography and photo-editing software, you don't ever have to settle for not-quite-right photos again. While most digital cameras come bundled with very basic editing software, there are affordable software options that give you far more freedom to change your photos, or even re-create them with a new and improved look.

Wish the sun had been shining the day of the big party? With the click of a mouse, you can turn that gray sky blue. The same goes for removing everything from red-eye to wrinkles. Commonly used editing functions include:

- **Color correction.** Applies to everything from removing red-eye to enhancing or altering a background, creating more realistic skin tones, lightening a dim photo or removing shadows.
- **Resize.** Allows you to change the physical dimensions of a photo, which could be useful when using a photo in a layout such as a holiday card, scrapbook or slide show.
- **Crop.** Quickly remove unwanted areas of a photo to remove distractions from the subject.
- **Composite.** Create a photo collage from selected parts of multiple photos.
- **Retouch.** Make a wide range of adjustments to specific areas of a photo.
- **Sharpen edges.** Get crisp-looking images, and even remove blurring caused by low lighting.

Composite
Before and after

In addition to ensuring that your photos are always perfect, some programs allow you to add exciting creative touches, including:

- **Creative layouts.** Incorporate your great-looking photos into one (or several) of the layout options that come with the editing software. This is great for creating photo collages or other creative projects.
- **Creative effects.** Add frame edges; convert color images to dramatic black and whites; create a vintage look with sepia tones; add paintbrush effects, animation, text, sound and more.

Using image-editing software, your photos can come to life through a variety of output options. Now you can share your child's first birthday party with faraway family, with a themed scrapbook or a slide show with text and audio so they, too, can enjoy your child's chocolate-covered face. If you want to delve even deeper into the image-editing process, professional-level applications are also available, giving you nearly endless editing options. The only limit is your imagination. ⚡

Sponsored by CRI2000, LP

Scrapbooking step by step

WHEN STARTING YOUR SCRAPBOOK PAGES, it is good to remember that no two people scrapbook the same way and no two scrapbook pages will turn out exactly the same. Everyone has their own personal style that shines through everything from the use of color and embellishments to the choice of paper and lettering. Scrapbooking is one way to tell your life history, and it allows you to relive the feelings and occasions as if they happened yesterday.

The best way to start your first scrapbook page is to start with your most recent photos. Those photos will be the easiest to find and arrange in an album. You won't feel so overwhelmed by starting way back at the beginning. Seeing your most recent photos organized and nicely displayed in an album will inspire you and give you the motivation and confidence to take on previous years.

Select your scrapbook

With the photo accessories available today, you can do just about anything with what used to be considered a blank scrapbook page. Scrapbooks can be anything from very elegant and simple to elaborate and ornate.

Photo-safe materials. Some albums are made with cardboard, plastic or adhesives that are not archival safe, causing photos to deteriorate. Make sure that any product you use is both acid and lignin free.

Expandability. Be sure to get a scrapbook that has a binding that will fit additional refill pages. It would be disappointing to get to the end of your album with pictures from a special trip that need to be put in another book because you have run out of room.

Page protectors. Top-loading page protectors protect your entire scrapbook page (along with your photos) from fingerprints and accidental spills. The important thing is to protect the creative work you have put together if a lot of people, especially children, will be looking at your albums.

Extras. Look for extras, such as scrapbooks that include CD pockets. Scrapbooks that include pocket pages in addition to full scrapbook pages will be the most flexible.

Choose a theme

Choose a theme or a date to start with for your scrapbook, then carefully organize your photos by page. A birthday, wedding, new baby in the family or a summer vacation are all good theme ideas. The theme of your photos will help determine the style of your album as well as the style of your pages.

Create your page

Selecting photos. When beginning to develop your scrapbook page layout, choose photos that you would like to put together on one to two pages. Be selective when choosing photos for your layouts. There is no rule that every photo you take needs to be in a scrapbook. If some photos are blurry, badly lit or very similar to another, leave them out, give them to friends or family, or let children scrapbook them.

Cropping. Many pictures have space around the focus of the picture that isn't necessary. By cropping or cutting your photos into different shapes, you can include more photos on a page and accentuate the subject of the photo more clearly. Various tools are available to aid in cutting shapes or straight lines. However, don't cut everything, especially photos that have meaning or may be of historical value at some point, or an original print that you don't have negatives for.

Matting. Simply matting a photo on card stock in a complementary color can add to the look of your scrapbook page. When choosing a paper color, be sure that it complements the colors already found within your pictures. Noncomplementary colors or patterned paper that is too busy may detract from the main focus—your pictures.

Page layout

Once you are comfortable with how you have cropped your pictures and have picked a paper color to accentuate them, play with the layout of your photos on the pages. Remember to think about the following:

Balance. Think of your page as a balancing scale: You don't want one side to be heavier than the other.

Focus. Think about what photo you might want as your main focus and highlight it with a special frame or double mat.

Journaling. Be sure to leave ample space for writing in your layout. Words will be as important to telling the story as your pictures. At the very least include the who, what, where and when of your photos. Consider also telling other stories the photos don't capture.

Photo storage basics

Everyone's got them. They're thrown into a drawer or, worse, packed into a cardboard box in a corner of the basement. They, of course, are the photos you promised to organize into albums, but just never got around to. Even though more and more people are doing digital photography these days (which presents its own set of storage issues), most of us still have a signficant stash of photos and negatives that deserve careful treatment.

Your photos are a valued possession, linking you with your past and helping to preserve your favorite memories. They are the record of your family history, of the places you've been and of all the memorable times of your life. And there they wait—getting crumpled, gathering dust, growing mold and fading away.

The key to organizing your photos is to start small—don't try to organize everything at once. Start with the photos you just had printed. Once you develop a system for organizing and preserving your most recent photos, the rest will be easy.

Consider using photo boxes that complement your décor. When photo boxes are stored on shelves like a book collection, it is not only easier to find any given photograph, but removing the clutter of unorganized photos improves the appearance of the entire room.

Here are some simple steps that will extend the life of your photos and create a valuable legacy for you and your family.

Protect and preserve. Take your developed roll of film and negatives out of the envelope they came in when they were processed. These envelopes aren't designed for safe, long-term storage. Instead, transfer your photos to acid- and lignin-free, archival-quality envelopes.

Label. Perhaps the single greatest problem with the long-term storage of photos is the lack of proper identification. If you don't know who is in a picture or when, why or where it was taken, who cares if the photo stands the test of time? Label your photo envelopes, and even the backs of the photos themselves, with names, dates and places as soon as they're printed, using only archival-quality pens or pencils.

Limit light exposure. Light is the number-one enemy of photographs. Although direct sunlight and fluorescent lighting are the most damaging, light levels in an average room can also cause pictures to fade over time. To limit this exposure, store photos in complete darkness, such as in an archival box or photo album specifically designed for long-term photo storage. If you want to display a photograph, make a copy for display and keep the original in storage.

Beware of environmental contaminants. Be sure to handle your photos with care to prevent fingerprints, scratches, folds, stains and other damage. Whenever possible, wash your hands before handling a photo. Storing your photos in archival boxes or photo albums and scrapbooks will also keep them safe from contaminants such as smoke, dust or chemicals from cleaning products, which over time can degrade the quality of your photos.

Protect from heat and humidity. Always store your photos in the main living areas of your house. Upper floors and attics can be too warm, and heat escalates the rate of deterioration of a photo. You will double the life span of a photo for every 10-degree drop in storage temperature. Basements, on the other hand, can be too humid. Excess humidity encourages the growth of microorganisms, which attack the photo emulsion. Changes in temperature and humidity can also cause expansion and contraction, resulting in cracks and flaking.

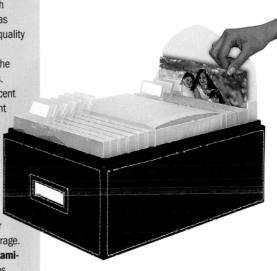

Buying the best binoculars

AMONG THE THINGS no active, well-equipped household should be without is a good pair of binoculars. For birders, sports enthusiasts, campers, whale-watchers, hikers, stargazers, boaters—anyone who wants to get closer to the action—a favorite pair of binoculars will capture the moment with bright, sharp, colorful images and magnify even the smallest detail.

If you are considering a binocular purchase and feel overwhelmed by the myriad choices available, this brief guide may be useful when sorting through all the options, whether in a store or online.

The specs on the package or price sheet can be complicated. Here are the basics.

Magnification. Binocular "sizes" feature two numbers—for example, 10 x 25. The first number refers to the magnification, or the power, of the binoculars. In this example, the viewed object appears to be 10 times closer than it would if seen with the naked eye.

Objective lens size. The second number in the formula, in this case 25, is the diameter of the objective lens—the lens located on the end of the binoculars farthest away from your eye when viewing. The larger the objective lens size, the more light will enter the binoculars and the brighter the viewed image will appear.

Field of view (FOV). This is the side-to-side measurement of the circular viewing field, defined by the width in feet or meters of the visible area viewed from 1,000 yards or meters. Generally, the higher the magnification, the narrower the field of view. So if you are looking at a football field, an FOV of 400 feet means that at a distance of 1,000 yards you will see 400 feet of the field.

Prism system. There are two types of prism systems in binoculars—roof and porro. With roof prisms, the objective, or front, lens lines up directly with the eyepiece, which allows a streamlined shape for less bulk, lighter weight and greater ruggedness. Porro prisms require the objective lens to align slightly offset from the eyepiece, which provides greater depth perception and a wider field of view.

Type of glass. Most optical prisms are made from borosilicate (BK-7) or barium crown (BaK-4) glass. BaK-4 is higher-quality glass, which results in brighter images and high edge-to-edge sharpness.

Coated optics. Lens surface coatings reduce light and glare. There are four types: coated (single layer on at least one lens surface); fully coated (single layer on all air-to-glass surfaces); multi-coated (multiple layers on at least one lens surface); and fully multi-coated (multiple layers on all air-to-glass surfaces).

Exit pupil. This reflects the size of the circle of light visible at the eyepiece. The larger the exit pupil, the brighter the image. To determine the size, divide the objective lens diameter by the power (a 10 x 25 model has an exit pupil of 2.5mm).

Eye relief. This is the distance the binoculars can be held away from the eye and still present the full field of view. Extended or long eye relief reduces eyestrain and is ideal for eyeglass wearers.

Waterproof/fogproof. Some binoculars are sealed with O-rings and nitrogen purged to make them completely waterproof and fogproof. They can withstand total immersion in water, staying dry inside, and their interior optical surfaces won't fog due to rapid temperature change or humidity.

How to select the right binoculars

1. Determine how you will use the binoculars. There is a wide variety of sizes, magnifying powers and features for all kinds of applications or preferences.

- Small, compact binoculars that fit in your pocket are perfect for hiking, camping and sporting events.
- Digital binoculars, which combine a digital camera with the binoculars, can capture that special moment.
- Giant binoculars work for amateur astronomers or avid stargazers.
- Binoculars with night vision appeal to hunters, hikers and birders.

2. Buy the best. You get what you pay for, so pay for the features you want. The grade of glass, quality of the prisms and barrel construction make all the difference in the binoculars' performance and durability. BaK-4 prisms are superior to BK-7.

3. Try before you buy. Binoculars that are perfect for your spouse may not be the ones for you. If possible, test them at the store; if that's not an option, or if you're buying them online, make sure you can return them. Don't struggle or strain when testing—you should be able to see through the binoculars quickly and easily. If you can't, try another pair.

With high-quality binoculars, you should not even be aware of them when they're in use. Your attention should be on what you're viewing, not the binoculars. Good binoculars make you feel as if you're seeing through your own eyes, only everything seems closer. If the optics are inferior, your eyes will feel a slight sense of relief when you stop looking through the binoculars.

How to start and run a book club

"READING IS TO the mind what exercise is to the body," wrote Joseph Addison in the early 1700s. The staying power of the need for mental fitness that Addison addresses is evident in the recent popularity of reading groups. If you're in need of the kind of mental workout a reading group provides, visit your public library or a local bookstore; they often sponsor reading groups or have a bulletin board where newly formed reading groups advertise for new members.

If you can't find a reading group, you might want to start your own reading club. To get your group up and running, you'll need to consider the following factors.

Members

How many members will you have? Most sources recommend eight to 12 people. Too many members can lead to a chaotic meeting, and too few members can affect the number of opinions and ideas shared. You need enough members to account for the fact that some people won't speak up and others will not be able to attend every meeting.

It's important to make sure that you get people who are serious about joining and will be open to reading all kinds of books. If not, you will have to keep rescheduling to meet people's schedules and you'll have people attend who won't read the book.

Meetings

Set a meeting day and time and stick to it. A good meeting schedule is once a month to once every six weeks. The person who selects the current pick can also select the location—if the group doesn't have a fixed spot. Reading groups tend to meet in libraries, a member's home or coffee shops.

Discussion of the book should last anywhere from 45 minutes to two hours. Every group needs to decide on a schedule that works best for them. The group should also designate a specific time for socializing, including a snack or even a full meal, either before or after talk of the book. The schedule will help to keep the discussion on track.

Books

Choosing a book can be the most difficult part of running a reading club. The members of most reading groups share a love of reading, but chances are they don't love reading the same kinds of books. Some groups have members take turns selecting a title, some throw suggestions in a hat and draw a title at random.

If you're looking for suggestions, *The Reading Group Handbook* by Rachel W. Jacobsohn (Hyperion, 1998) suggests hundreds of books, from Pulitzer Prize winners to historical fiction and banned books.

Discussion

Now that your group has a book selection, what do you talk about? Characters, plot, emotional response and author's purpose are all good subjects for a discussion. *Talking About Books: A Step-by-Step Guide for Participating in a Book Discussion Group* by Marcia Fineman, Ph.D. (Talking About Books, 1997), includes questions to generate discussions.

Resources

For additional inspiration, turn to the online reading guides published by Vintage Books (*www.randomhouse.com*) and Penguin Putnam Inc. (*www.penguinputnam.com*), among others. The Web site *www.Reading GroupGuides.com* has nearly 2,000 reading guides posted online and searchable by title, author and subject. Guides often provide summaries along with a list of discussion questions.

The reading guides may also include biographical information about and interviews with the author. Use library resources such as *Current Biography* and *Something About the Author* for additional information. Check with bookstores or the public library to find out which authors are speaking in your area.

For added depth in a book discussion, members can conduct background research, prepare a dinner related to the book or plan a field trip to either the book's setting or the author's hometown.

With determination and a dash of creativity, you and your group members will be flexing your cerebral muscles in no time.—*Stephanie E. Ponder*

Discuss books online

A major obstacle for people who want to join a book group is finding a group that meets at a time and place that suits their schedule. If you find yourself in a similar situation, consider joining an online reading group. Instead of sharing ideas with people who may only be coming from across town, you can share thoughts and opinions with people from across the country or across the world.

One place to begin looking for an online book club is the Book Browser Web site at *www.Book-Clubs-Resource.com*. Choose "Online Book Clubs" and then browse the list of clubs organized by the format of the discussion they use.

You will see nearly a dozen online reading groups, along with additional resources for having a successful reading group.—*SEP*

Great greetings— it's in the cards!

By Robyn Freedman Spizman

ROBYN FREEDMAN SPIZMAN (www.robynspizman.com) *is a television and radio personality and one of the foremost gift experts in the country. A prolific author, she has written several books, including* Make It Memorable: An A–Z Guide to Making Any Event, Gift or Occasion ... Dazzling!*;* The Giftionary: An A–Z Reference Guide for Solving Your Gift-Giving Dilemmas ... Forever!*;* When Words Matter Most: Thoughtful Deeds and Kind Words for Every Occasion*; and* The Thank You Book.

FOR GENERATIONS, GREETING CARDS have helped people express a world of sentiments for every possible occasion. From birthdays, congratulations and anniversaries to sympathy and get-well wishes, a simple greeting card has the power to cheer someone up and make his or her day.

They can also help you sum up your innermost feelings as you sign your name, seal it and add a stamp. A greeting card is a tried-and-true way to express your thoughts, but when you add a signature touch, you can transform a generic greeting into a meaningful gesture.

With a spark of creativity, a greeting card becomes a special way to share your heartfelt feelings. Here are some innovative ways to add your personal touch and make it memorable.

Add the element of surprise! Place a greeting card under someone's pillow for a good-night greeting. It's a fun way to end the day with a word of praise or a romantic sentiment.

Keep those cards flowing! Send a get-well card every week until the patient's health improves. The weekly card will be something your friend or family member looks forward to, and your wishes will be greatly appreciated for years to come.

Create a community greeting-card campaign. If you know someone who is really sick, ask friends and family to contribute a greeting card to your get-well campaign. Decorate a gift box in colorful wrapping paper, then fill the box with an outpouring of greeting cards. Accompany this big box of wishes with a card that says, "Read one a day and get well soon!"

Celebrate half birthdays! Think of fun and festive ways to commemorate special days by sending a greeting card on a child's half birthday or your half anniversary. Write half of a greeting, such as "Hap Birt"! The recipient is certain to get the full picture and have a good laugh!

For no reason at all. Make up fun days, like Best Friend Day or Most Lovable Daughter Day, and send a card declaring that special person as the winner! Make it an annual occasion and add some pizzazz.

Give a gift in a gift. Send a greeting card with movie tickets inside, or even a special photograph of the two of you. Or how about inserting a homemade coupon for baby-sitting? You're bound to get a thank-you card in return!

Create a unique signature. Be creative with your closing remarks when signing a greeting card. Instead of writing "Love, so-and-so," wake up your words with phrases such as "Hugs and kisses to the Mr. and Mrs." or "I'll shout it to the moon, Get well soon!"

Enclose words of inspiration. When giving a graduate a gift, consider including a check along with a letter of recommendation addressed "To Whom It May Concern," recommending the young man or woman for any job! Or tell someone special how much you love them and why.

Add your stamp of approval. Select a box of gift cards and add a postage stamp to each envelope. Select a variety of colorful stamps or stamps with a particular theme for a special touch that will transform this gift into a time-saving surprise.

Greeting cards are clearly one of the most thoughtful resources you can instantly give, so stock up on them and always have some on hand. And when in doubt of what to say or do, you can always insert a bill that has a picture of Abraham Lincoln or Andrew Jackson on it—guaranteed to satisfy even the most difficult to please! ⚑

All wrapped up

GIVING PRESENTS is always an enjoyable experience, and a gift that's beautifully wrapped heightens the recipient's anticipation and makes an event even more special.

There is an art to good gift-wrapping—and it is easy to master. The wrapping need not be complicated, just well executed. Follow these simple, illustrated step-by-step guides to achieve a stunning effect every time.

Pleated bow

1. Fold a sheet of paper in a basic fan shape, keeping each fold equal in width.
2. Attach tape around the center of the bow to hold it together.
3. Attach the bow to the gift with tape.

Basic fan

1. Fold a sheet of paper in a basic fan shape, keeping each fold equal in width.
2. Attach tape around the center of the bow to hold it together.
3. Open the fan as shown and attach to the gift with tape.

Fanfare

1. Starting at the corner of a sheet of paper, softly fold each pleat (remember, no sharp creasing). Always aim toward the opposite end of the paper.
2. Use tape to fasten the center of the fan.
3. Tape a small strip of paper around the bow to form a loop; attach to gift.

Shooting star

1. Fold a sheet of paper into a basic fan shape.
2. Hold the fan approximately 2½ inches from the top and staple to hold it together.
3. Make a diagonal cut above the small stapled section as shown.
4. Open up the small edge of the fan to form a star, and open up fan.
5. Attach to the gift with tape.

Trumpets

1. Softly fold a sheet of paper to form a tube.
2. Hold in the center of the tube and gently pull from the middle of the trumpet to form a layered effect.
3. While holding the trumpet, attach tape along the outside to hold in place.
4. Repeat numerous times to form multiple trumpets.
5. Attach trumpets to the gift with tape. Place trumpets on top of each other to give a layered effect, as shown.

Curly swirls

1. Cut paper into strips of equal width.
2. Gently pull the edge of a scissors blade along the length of the paper strip, forming a curl. Repeat with each strip.
3. Attach each curly swirl to the gift with tape to form a mass of curls.

Reversible wraps

The recent introduction of reversible gift wrap means that a single piece of paper offers several benefits:

- An element of surprise when opening the gift
- The convenience of storing only one roll but having the options of two different designs
- The opportunity to wrap more than one gift in coordinating designs
- Value for your money

Consider an HDD camcorder

IF YOU THINK a camcorder is something you take from the closet shelf once or twice a year, the new hard-disk-drive (HDD) camcorders will likely change your mind. Do you own an MP3 player or an iPod? The reasons you love them are the very same reasons you will love HDD camcorders: storage capacity, computer connectivity and ease of use. What's more, these camcorders are small and, at about one pound, lightweight.

The first advantage is long recording capacity

Some models allow you to record more than seven hours in the highest-quality recording mode, providing image quality comparable to that of a Hollywood DVD movie. You can also record for more than 37 hours at Internet quality.

Second, you can record without interruption

Whether you're recording a soccer tournament, baseball game or your family's entire vacation, HDD camcorders allow you to do this without the need to keep changing discs or tapes. Besides uninterrupted recording, ridding yourself of tapes and discs offers another benefit: cost savings.

Third, it's easy to delete unwanted scenes

If you record something you don't want, you can delete it at the touch of a button, just as with a digital still camera. With an HDD camcorder, there's no need to limit yourself. Record it all.

When you want to play back a particular scene, navigate to the desired thumbnail image that identifies the scene, and push "Play." There's no rewinding or fast-forwarding. View exactly what you want, when you want it.

Every time you record on an HDD camcorder a new independent file is created. That makes it easy to find what you want, and it makes it impossible to record over a previously recorded memory. Also, because an independent file is created, you can edit within the camcorder by rearranging scenes in any order you desire. Plus, you can create custom play lists by grouping scenes.

Some HDD camcorders offer technology to protect the camera's built-in hard disk drive. One example is a "floating suspension" that operates on the same concept as a car's shock absorbers. This suspension system effectively dampens vibrations and allows active camcorder use. Another safeguard technology is drop detection (gravity sensor system), which senses sudden acceleration. If you should accidentally drop the camera, its power is turned off and the writing head is disengaged to avoid disk damage.

Have you ever tried to download and edit video on your computer? Tape-format cameras download in real time. This means a one-hour video will take at least one hour or more just to transfer into your computer. HDD camcorders record your video footage as a computer file, which means that transferring to a computer and editing is easier and faster than ever. A one-hour video recorded at the highest quality typically takes up about 4 GB of memory, and will download in 10 minutes or less on average.

Most HDD camcorders include easy-to-use software that enables you to edit your videos; add titles, scene transitions, music and/or narration; and then burn your finished video to a DVD.

The no-tape, no-disc approach is the future of home video, because it means that you're always ready to capture every special moment. So keep recording, and have fun sharing the results with that special someone next to you or halfway around the world.

Tips for home movie success

Avoid zoom controls. Zooming in and out while shooting is extremely distracting to viewers. If you must zoom—first put the camcorder on pause, zoom in, turn the camcorder on, and turn it off again when you switch to another scene.

Pan in sloooow motion. New videographers are tempted to pan because they now have a 360-degree view of the room, rather than a limited still-picture format. But they tend to pan much too quickly. If you must pan—go at a pace 10 times slower than you think normal.

Eliminate "shaky camera syndrome." Use your body like a tripod, and use two hands to keep the camcorder steady. Otherwise, your home movies will look as if you shot them during an earthquake.

Keep track of the audio track. You'll have good audio if you're never more than two to three feet away from your subject. Don't talk while you're shooting, as your voice will be much too loud for the microphone on the video camera. Be sure to get in closer to Grandma Mildred so you capture her voice perfectly.

Create a story. Set up what's called an "establishing shot" before you launch into the main activity. Show the family members arriving and coming up the walkway Christmas morning. Shoot your main footage, then end with a powerful "coda," such as the guests leaving or the kids sleeping peacefully in their beds after a long day.

Catch people in action. The beauty of video is that it adds two things that still pictures cannot: motion and sound. The best home videos show family members engaged in self-absorbing activity. Save the artificial posing for the still camera.

Keep it short. Don't focus on any one activity or subject for more than 10 minutes. All you need of the kids opening presents is 30 to 60 seconds at most—viewing that simple short clip later will resurrect in your mind the entire morning. Capture the essence of the experience by filming in short bursts.

Remember the rule of thirds. Professional cinematographers divide a screen into three vertical columns. Rather than putting your subject dead center in your viewing screen every shot, mix it up. Have the subject in one of the left or right thirds. This adds character and variety to your shots.

Watch your home movies right away. If you watch your footage immediately, you can catch and correct your bad habits.

Share what you've shot. With the power of digital media, now everyone can enjoy the footage, whether it's Uncle Bob in Boston or Aunt Cathy in California. So make it memorable.

Source: iMemories

Tips for traveling with your dog

TAKING YOUR PET ALONG on your travels can enhance your trip or turn it into trouble. More and more hotels, motels and entertainment venues are catering to pet owners. But it's still important to be prepared. Here are a few reminders to make your trip a success.

Weather. When traveling with pets in extremely hot weather, make sure the air conditioning functions properly before you hit the road. And be careful about leaving your animal unattended in a car with the windows closed. Several states now have laws that will prosecute pet owners who do this.

Food and water. Bring your pet's favorite food, but consider cutting back on the quantity just a bit to prevent too many pit stops.

Towels. Your pet will likely get into something she shouldn't. Use the towels to wipe her feet at the door; if she is the active sort, bring plenty of towels. You can also wipe your feet at the door. Extra sheets draped over the furniture and bed will protect them from a rambunctious canine and keep you from paying a damage deposit.

Health records. In case you want to board your dog, or need to make an unexpected vet visit, having his health record is essential. And remember the first-aid kit.

Pet sitters or day care. Check ahead for day care and pet sitters before you travel. You might want to take in an event where Rover is not permitted. Don't leave him in the room alone unless he is kenneled. Even then, it's probably not a good idea unless he sleeps all day and you know he won't bark his head off. A strange place can bring out strange behavior, and many hotels will not allow you to leave your pet unattended for any reason, kenneled or not.

Activities. If your pooch is a couch potato at home, don't expect her to hike to the tallest peak on your vacation. Work up to any extra activity before the trip. Start taking her out more often for extended walks and hikes before the big vacation so it's not a shock to her system and her paws.

Safety restraints. Do not let your best friend ride in the back of a pickup. Road debris can fly up and harm him, and in case of an accident he will have no protection. When traveling by car, use a special safety restraint or place him in a kennel that is secured. There are many sad stories of pets becoming projectiles during a car accident.

Airlines. All airlines differ in their policy of transporting pets. Be sure to check the policy before planning your trip. Remember, you will probably have to fly your dog as cargo, and the weather may dictate what time of year you fly. Be sure to ask the airline if their cargo area is heated or air-conditioned. Temperatures can be extreme. Some airlines prohibit transporting pets during certain times of the year.

Familiar items. Bring along lots of toys and chewies, a dog bed or blanket, and, most of all, lots of hugs and kisses. Happy travels! /A\

Tips courtesy Costco member Fido Friendly, The Travel Magazine for You and Your Dog, www.fidofriendly.com.

Order Prints from Home

Go to COSTCO.COM and click on PHOTO CENTER.

Get high-quality prints from your digital camera in as little as 1 hour.

- Convenient – pick up prints at Costco.
- Enhanced editing options such as cropping and red-eye reduction.
- Choice of glossy or lustre prints.
- Create greeting cards, gifts and more.
- Share your photo albums with friends online.
- Download free software to manage, edit and print your pictures.

HELPFUL TIP:

Most digital photos do not fit the "standard" 4" x 6" print size. As a result, you may lose $1/4$" on the top and the bottom edge, as shown above.

To avoid this:
- Check to see if your digital camera has 3:2 aspect ratio setting; or
- Make sure you leave room at the top and bottom by taking one or two steps back after setting up the shot.

This will allow you to capture the correct image for printing and provide the room to make the print you desire.

FOR ALL YOUR TREASURED MEMORIES!

2 PK

MemoryStor®
SCRAPBOOKS
- 30 pages
- 12" x 12" sheet protectors
- Top-loading pages
- Easily expandable
- Archival safe

Item #897259

2 PK

OLD TOWN
DESIGNER SERIES
PICTURE FRAMES
- Solid wood, walnut finish
- 8" x 10" (5" x 7" mat) or 11" x 14" (8" x 10" mat)
- Factory installed hinged hangers

8" x 10" – Item #946738
11" x 14" – Item #766907

OLD TOWN®
PHOTO ALBUMS
- Bonded leather
- 600 photo capacity
- Holds up to 4" x 6" or panoramic photos
- CD & storage pockets
- Archival safe

Item #101757

2 PK

CUTTING**EDGE**®
ULTRA-GRIP SCISSORS
- 9 ½", 8 ½" & 5" micro-serrated
- Stainless steel throughout
- Cushioned grip
- Bi-directional sharpener
- Lifetime warranty

Item #787189

MemoryStor®, Old Town® & CuttingEdge® are registered trademarks of **Combined Resources International**
Colors & styles may vary by location ▪ *Satisfaction Guaranteed* ▪ © 2006 CRI2000, L.P.

For more great products, visit us at www.cri2k.com

Incredibly advanced,
Remarkably simple.

EOS Digital Rebel XTi features a 10.1 megapixel CMOS sensor, DiG!C II Image Processor plus a host of new features, including a 2.5-inch LCD monitor, the EOS Integrated Cleaning System, shoots up to 3 frames per second and Canon Picture Style technology. It's fully compatible with over 50 EF and EF-S lenses and a wide range of EOS System accessories. Item #137652

A. Crayola® Twist 'N Color
Gives you more than 100 crayons for endless coloring possibilities. Create with classic, rainbow and neon colors! Item #924106

B. Pentax Optio M30 Digital Camera
Features include a 7.1 megapixel CCD, 3x optical zoom, 2.5" LCD, shake reduction, rechargeable lithium-ion battery and face-recognition technology for perfect portraits. Item #178015

C. Fiskars Rotary Trimmer
This 12" rotary trimmer cuts up to 10 sheets of paper and features a 45 mm rotary blade, aluminum grid measuring surface and a magnetic clip holder. Item #416356

D. SwissGear® by Wenger 2-Piece Business Set
This spacious wheeled case is constructed from durable Cordura ballistic nylon, can hold a 17" wide-screen computer and features a removable notebook case that can hold a 15.4" wide-screen computer. Item #117754

E. Ricardo Beverly Hills Travel and Sport Utility Duffle
Lightweight and rugged, Ricardo Beverly Hills' bestselling duffle offers plenty of room and versatility, with eight compartments/pockets and multiple transport options (wheeled, handle or backpack) for travel ease. Item #158480

F. Samsonite 3-Piece Ballistic Nylon Luggage Set
This refined luggage features leather handles, rugged ballistic nylon, lightweight honeycomb frames and spinner technology that allows each case to roll upright so there is no weight on your arm. Item #146315

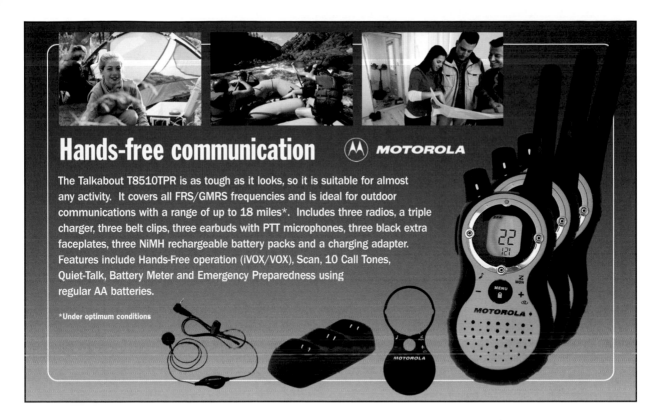

Hands-free communication

The Talkabout T8510TPR is as tough as it looks, so it is suitable for almost any activity. It covers all FRS/GMRS frequencies and is ideal for outdoor communications with a range of up to 18 miles*. Includes three radios, a triple charger, three belt clips, three earbuds with PTT microphones, three black extra faceplates, three NiMH rechargeable battery packs and a charging adapter. Features include Hands-Free operation (iVOX/VOX), Scan, 10 Call Tones, Quiet-Talk, Battery Meter and Emergency Preparedness using regular AA batteries.

*Under optimum conditions

Incredible pictures, push-button ease.

Nikon® makes incredible pictures easier for everyone. From the fast-handling, intuitive D40x™ digital SLR to the sleek and stylish COOLPIX® S200, you'll find innovative technology, state-of-the-art features and legendary Nikkor® optics that make it easier to capture the pictures you really want.

Item #187756

Nikon's smallest digital SLR ever!

COOLPIX. STYLE
brilliance made beautiful

Item #187737

D40x™ 2-Zoom Family Sports and Action Outfit
Incredible pictures, even easier!

Get the pictures you really want. From family memories and beautiful portraits to youth sports, the D40x™ captures them all perfectly. With 10.2 effective megapixel picture detail, ultra-fast start-up, instant shutter response and world-famous Nikkor lenses, you'll be amazed at how easy it is to get the pictures you've always dreamed of. This special outfit includes the D40x™ digital SLR camera, 18-55 mm and 55-200 mm Zoom-Nikkor lenses, a 1 GB SD memory card, versatile system case and two special Nikon School DVDs that make getting great pictures easier and more fun.

All Nikon products include Nikon Inc. USA limited warranty. ©2007 Nikon Inc.

Nikon™

At the heart of the image™

COOLPIX. S200 Outfit
Smart, stylish all-metal design

For casual photographers who want great pictures from an easy-to-use camera, the COOLPIX® S200 is ideal. It's small enough to fit into a shirt pocket, but has impressively powerful features. Capture crisp, clear details with 7.1 effective megapixels, 3x optical zoom Nikkor® lens and a large, bright 2.5" LCD. Vibration Reduction/Image Stabilization reduces the effects of camera shake, and high ISO (1,000) lets you take incredible pictures, even in low light. This special outfit comes complete with a stylish and convenient leather carrying case.

www.nikondigital.com

Stocking your kitchen

YOU DON'T NEED A large number of bowls, utensils and small appliances to cook well, but you do need the correct tools for the task. Well-made equipment will last for years, even a lifetime. Although small appliances don't have the longevity of quality knives and cookware, they can provide years of trouble-free service if you buy high-quality items and follow the warranties.

Here is a primer on basics you should have for a starter kitchen, a more advanced kitchen, a busy family kitchen and a kitchen for entertaining.

Starter kitchen

Note the difference between baking pans and baking dishes. A baking pan refers to a metal pan, and a baking dish refers to an oven-safe glass or ceramic container. When you use glass or ceramic cookware in the oven, reduce the recommended baking temperature by about 25 degrees for the best results. An easy way to begin setting up a kitchen is to buy one piece of cookware, a preparation tool or a necessary small appliance every payday. If you have a shortage of helpful gadgets, pick up one or two with your weekly grocery shopping or when you shop at discount stores.

Small appliances: Coffee maker, handheld portable electric mixer, two-slice toaster

Range-top cookware: 1-quart covered saucepan, 2-quart covered saucepan, 4- or 6-quart Dutch oven, 10-inch ovenproof skillet with cover, 8- or 10-inch sauté pan

Bakeware: 2-quart rectangular baking dish (12 x 7½ x 2-inch), 2-quart square baking dish (8 x 8 x 2-inch), 15 x 10 x 1-inch baking (jelly roll) pan, 8 x 1½-inch round baking pan, baking sheet (two), 8 x 4 x 2-inch loaf pan or dish

Preparation and cooking gadgets: Bottle opener, can opener, chef's knife, clear glass measuring cup (for liquids), colander, corkscrew, instant-read thermometer (for meat), kitchen timer, ladle, long-handled fork, pancake turner, paring knife, pasta server, polypropylene cutting board, potato masher,

> There is no love sincerer than the love of food.
> —George Bernard Shaw

rubber spatulas, serrated knife, set of dry measuring cups, set of measuring spoons, set of mixing bowls, knife sharpener, slotted spoon, tongs, utility knife, vegetable peeler, wire cooling racks, wooden spoons

Starter kitchen with extras

As you discover new recipes and techniques, you'll acquire more small appliances, cookware and convenience tools. Time-crunched households often rely on crockery cookers and microwave ovens.

Small appliances: Blender, 3½- to 4-quart crockery cooker, small basic countertop microwave oven, steamer

Range-top cookware: 3-quart covered saucepan, 6- or 8-inch skillet, double boiler

Bakeware: Muffin pan, 9-inch pie plate, pizza pan, 9 x 9 x 2-inch baking pan, roasting pan with rack

Preparation and cooking gadgets: Basting brush, flexible metal spatulas, grater, kitchen shears, pizza cutter, oven thermometer, rolling pin, small and large strainers, wood cutting board

Busy family kitchen

Rely on small appliances to prepare food while the family is at work or school. Appliances and cookware such as bread machines, crockery cookers, Dutch ovens and roasting pans will help you get meals on the table quickly.

Small appliances: Bread machine, food processor, four-slice toaster, 6-quart crockery cooker, microwave oven, mixer with stand, pressure cooker, programmable coffee maker

Range-top cookware: Griddle

Bakeware: Large Dutch oven or stockpot, 3-quart rectangular baking dish (13 x 9 x 2-inch), 9 x 1½-inch round baking pans, fluted cake pan, various sizes of casserole dishes, 6-ounce custard cups, 9 x 5 x 3-inch loaf pan or dish, 10-inch tube pan

Preparation and cooking gadgets: Additional vegetable peelers, extra utility and paring knives, cutter shapes, four-egg poacher, hand juicer, pastry blender, meat mallet, rotary eggbeater, ruler (to measure dough thickness, width and length), sifter, whisk

Kitchen for entertaining

Add a few small appliances and gadgets to set up your kitchen for entertaining.

Small appliances: 12-cup coffee maker or urn, deep fryer, electric wok, 12-cup food processor, tabletop grill, rice steamer

Range-top cookware: Grill pan, wok

Bakeware: Mini-muffin pans, quiche plates, soufflé dishes, tart pans

Preparation and cooking gadgets: 12-cup carafe, cookie press, cheese slicer, garlic press, bulb baster, pastry bag and tips, pastry blender, pepper grinder, salt grinder ⚡

Baking pan basics

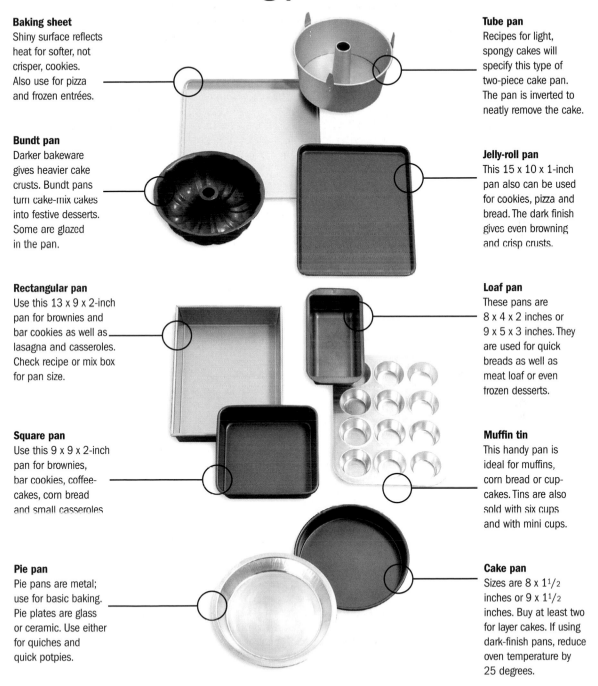

Baking sheet
Shiny surface reflects heat for softer, not crisper, cookies. Also use for pizza and frozen entrées.

Bundt pan
Darker bakeware gives heavier cake crusts. Bundt pans turn cake-mix cakes into festive desserts. Some are glazed in the pan.

Rectangular pan
Use this 13 x 9 x 2-inch pan for brownies and bar cookies as well as lasagna and casseroles. Check recipe or mix box for pan size.

Square pan
Use this 9 x 9 x 2-inch pan for brownies, bar cookies, coffee-cakes, corn bread and small casseroles

Pie pan
Pie pans are metal; use for basic baking. Pie plates are glass or ceramic. Use either for quiches and quick potpies.

Tube pan
Recipes for light, spongy cakes will specify this type of two-piece cake pan. The pan is inverted to neatly remove the cake.

Jelly-roll pan
This 15 x 10 x 1-inch pan also can be used for cookies, pizza and bread. The dark finish gives even browning and crisp crusts.

Loaf pan
These pans are 8 x 4 x 2 inches or 9 x 5 x 3 inches. They are used for quick breads as well as meat loaf or even frozen desserts.

Muffin tin
This handy pan is ideal for muffins, corn bread or cup-cakes. Tins are also sold with six cups and with mini cups.

Cake pan
Sizes are 8 x 1$^1/_2$ inches or 9 x 1$^1/_2$ inches. Buy at least two for layer cakes. If using dark-finish pans, reduce oven temperature by 25 degrees.

Source: Adapted from Better Homes and Gardens' Making a Home: Housekeeping for Real Life. *For more information, visit* www.bhg.com.

Time for your kitchen to shine

Keeping your kitchen springtime fresh

Now that your kitchen is spot-on perfect, how do you keep it that way? Here are some great techniques and new products for quick cleanups and little touch-ups.

- A multipurpose spray cleaner for hard surfaces can be great for spot-cleaning floors, walls and ceilings. Always have a bottle handy.
- Replace germy sponges with a container of disinfecting wipes. Pre-moistened and easy to use anywhere and anytime, wipes can kill germs that can make your family sick. (Use as directed.)
- A pen with gel bleach will help you to stay on top of grout. The sooner you treat a stain, the faster it comes out.

THERE'S NOTHING QUITE as fresh as spring's blue skies, gentle breezes and brilliant sunshine. So throw open the windows, pull back the curtains and let spring into your kitchen.

Unfortunately, all that sunshine just might throw a big spotlight on winter's grease, grime and clutter. Well, that's why they call it spring-cleaning! Here are some great hints, tips and suggestions on how to bring sparkle, organization and shine back to your kitchen.

Start at the beginning—make a to-do list

It's true: The first step to getting organized is to get organized. Take a look at your kitchen and decide what you want to accomplish. Do you need to do a super-deep cleaning in which all of the walls and cabinets are washed? Or is it a question of reorganizing and de-cluttering? Or is it both?

Once you've decided what needs to be done, prioritize your list. Look at it logically. For example, you wouldn't want to wash the floors and then clean the countertops. You might accidentally brush or drip something from the countertop onto your nice, clean floor. Making a list of what you want to do ahead of time will save you time in the long run.

Check your cleaning supplies

The right tools make any job easier, and spring-cleaning your kitchen is no exception. Make sure your cleaning caddy includes a multipurpose cleaner that is effective on hard surfaces such as your stove, sink, countertops and backsplash. (It will come in handy later for quick cleanups, too!) By checking your supplies ahead of time, you can avoid making trips to the store in the middle of cleaning. (Nothing kills momentum like having to run out to pick up more bleach.) Have whatever you need on hand and you're good to go.

Set the mood for good, cleaning fun

Do you have favorite tunes that just won't let you sit still? That's perfect cleaning music! Play your "can't stop moving" music and get energized. It will make cleaning more fun and make the time fly by. Your TV might work as good background noise, but if it proves to be a distraction, turn it off.

Dress for success

Cleaning can be fun, but you're not going to a party. Wear comfortable loose clothing that allows a wide range of movement—you're going to be reaching and stretching to get into tight places. And make sure that anything you wear is something that you don't mind getting stained or dirty. Cleaning can be a very messy job, so this is no time for fashion—it's time for function.

Now you're ready to go. You've got your list. You've got your supplies. You've got your tunes. You're looking like someone who's going to do some serious cleaning. So what are you waiting for? Get shining.

Keeping your kitchen healthy all year round

It's a scary fact, but, according to the American Society for Microbiology, about 36 percent of food-borne illness in the home results from cross contamination. That means cutting boards, counters or utensils are not properly disinfected or sanitized before they are used to prepare foods that are eaten raw, such as fruits or vegetables.

Cleaning with soap and water isn't good enough. Soap and water remove some germs from surfaces, but they can't kill those germs. In fact, they may spread them around. Even though a surface looks clean, that doesn't mean it's clean from a health standpoint. Only a disinfectant can kill a broad spectrum of harmful bacteria and viruses.

The good news is that you can help kill nasty bacteria that can cause food-borne illness by following simple sanitizing and disinfecting routines when preparing your family's meals.

Counters, tabletops and highchairs

After each use, spray a disinfecting cleaner on surfaces until thoroughly wet. Let stand for 30 seconds, then rinse or wipe clean. For nonporous countertop surfaces, use a disinfecting wipe for one-step cleaning and disinfecting.

Wooden cutting boards

Use approximately 3 tablespoons of bleach per gallon of water to create a sanitizing solution. Wash, wipe or rinse items with dishwashing detergent and water, then apply solution. Let stand two minutes, then rinse all surfaces with a solution of 1 tablespoon of bleach per gallon of water. Do not let soak overnight.

Always read and follow precautions and usage directions before using cleaning products. Always store cleaning products out of reach of children.

Refrigerators, freezers, plastic cutting boards, stainless utensils, dishes, glassware, counters, pots and pans*

Wash or rinse with detergent and water, then soak in a solution using 1 tablespoon of bleach per gallon of water. Let stand two minutes, then air-dry.

These kitchen sanitizing routines might take a little more effort, but your family's health is worth it. Just remember that good healthy food always comes from a good healthy kitchen.

* Do not use on steel, aluminum, silver or chipped enamel items.

▶

More kitchen cleaning tips

Things have probably changed quite a bit since your mom (or dad) first taught you how to clean. There are all kinds of new products that will make your life easier and your cleaning go much faster. So here are some great tips that will help you get your kitchen spring-cleaning done right.

Clear out the kitchen clutter

Put little-used appliances away so they're out of your way. Store dry goods in bins, on racks or in a convenient rolling cart. Remember, the fewer things you have sitting out, the fewer things you'll have to clean next year.

Make your kitchen work better

Organize specific areas inside your cupboards for specific items. Make a baking center. Keep all your canned goods together. Have a snack cupboard. Then everything will be easy for everyone to find.

Use disposable containers to round up small, loose items such as cupcake liners, birthday candles and cookie decorations. That way they're less likely to fall over and spill out, and they're conveniently located in one place.

Clear out your refrigerator. Then spray the shelves and drawers with a hard-surface sanitizing spray that kills 99.9 percent of bacteria. (Some pre-cleaning may be necessary first.)

Store veggies and meats in your fridge in disposable containers, food storage bags and sealable wrap to keep them fresher longer.

Make it cleaner than clean

Bright white dish towels and curtains make a kitchen look fresh and clean. Wash all bleachable kitchen linens with detergent and a good bleach to get them their brightest and whitest.

Use a soft toothbrush for small, hard-to-reach spaces. But first, be sure the surface isn't easily scratched.

Use a bleach spray to disinfect, deodorize and remove tough stains and greasy messes on hard, nonporous kitchen surfaces. It will cut through and get the job done in no time.

Clean from the top down. That way you can avoid drips on already clean surfaces.

Don't forget to look up—check for cobwebs in corners and on light fixtures.

Wear rubber gloves to protect your skin. To keep water and cleaning solutions from running down your arm when you're reaching up, wear exercise sweatbands around your wrists.

If you're cleaning above your head, always wear eye protection too.

Don't forget to look inside your microwave. Spatters, boil-overs and crumbs can really cake on and build up. This is a spot where that multipurpose, hard-surface cleaner might come in very handy. (Always follow the manufacturer's instructions for cleaning any appliance.)

If you have stains on your tile grout, use a pen with a gel bleach to target the spots and get the stain right out.

Good job. Now relax

Hopefully these helpful tips will make your kitchen spring-cleaning go by with a minimum of effort and time. When you're done, move a chair to the middle of the kitchen, sit down with a nice cup of tea, take a look around and savor your sense of accomplishment. (It's OK to open up a cupboard or two and take a peek to enjoy how neat, organized and tidy they are!) Be proud—you've earned it.

Cold-storage guidelines

IF YOU'RE FREQUENTLY UNCERTAIN about how long to save that casserole or whether month-old hot dogs are a safe meal, this simple guide to food cold-storage times will prove valuable, time and time again.

Food	Refrigerator (40°F)	Freezer (0°F)
Bacon (opened package)	7 days	1 month
Butter	1 to 3 months	6 to 9 months
Cheese, hard	6 months, unopened; 3 to 4 weeks, opened	6 months
Cheese, soft (e.g., Brie)	7 days	6 months
Chicken leftovers (casseroles)	3 to 4 days	4 to 6 months
Chicken or turkey (fresh)	1 to 2 days	9 to 12 months
Cooked fish	3 to 4 days	4 to 6 months
Cooked shellfish	3 to 4 days	3 months
Corned beef (in pouch)	5 to 7 days	Drained, 1 month
Cream cheese	14 days	Doesn't freeze well
Fresh eggs	3 to 5 weeks	Don't freeze
Fried chicken	3 to 4 days	4 months
Fruit beverages (juice or drinks in cartons)	3 weeks, unopened; 7 to 10 days, opened	8 to 12 months
Ground beef and stew meat	1 to 2 days	3 to 4 months
Ham, canned (open)	3 to 5 days	1 to 2 months
Ham, whole (fully cooked)	7 days	1 to 2 months
Hot dogs (open package)	7 days	1 to 2 months
Luncheon meat (opened package)	3 to 5 days	1 to 2 months
Margarine	4 to 5 months	12 months
Mayonnaise (opened jar)	2 months	Doesn't freeze
Meat leftovers	3 to 4 days	2 to 3 months
Milk	7 days	3 months
Pizza	3 to 4 days	1 to 2 months
Roasts	3 to 5 days	4 to 12 months
Shrimp, scallops, shucked clams or oysters	1 to 2 days	3 to 6 months
Smoked fish	14 days, or date on package	2 months in package
Soups and stews, veggies or meat added	3 to 4 days	2 to 3 months
Sour cream	7 to 21 days	Doesn't freeze
Steaks	3 to 5 days	6 to 12 months
Yogurt	7 to 14 days	1 to 2 months

Source: USDA Food Safety, www.foodsafety.gov

Reviving food

Dry vanilla beans: Place dry vanilla beans in a sealed container with a slice of fresh bread for two days.

Hard almond paste: Place a fresh slice of bread in a sealed plastic bag with the almond paste overnight.

Hard brown sugar: Place about a cup of the hard brown sugar in a glass pie plate, cover with a small piece of waxed paper and top with a slice of fresh bread. Loosely cover with plastic wrap and microwave on high until softened (about 30 seconds).

Rescuing crystallized honey: Heat the jar of honey with the lid removed on high in microwave for 10-second increments, stirring between each increment, until crystals have dissolved.

Reviving slightly burned cookies: Grate the burned bottoms gently with a microplane food grater.

Saving overripe fruit for bread: Instead of discarding it, freeze overripe fruit in a zipper bag; add fruit to the bag until enough is accumulated to make bread. Thaw at room temperature until softened.

Separating bacon slices stuck together in a shrink-wrap package: Roll the package lengthwise into a cylinder and then flatten it out.

Stale bread: Individual slices can be revived by steam: Place slice on a splatter screen and hold over a pan of simmering water for a minute or two.

A full loaf can be revived by putting it in a paper bag, sealing, dampening the outside of the bag with water and placing it on a baking sheet in a 350°F oven for 5 minutes.

Stale chips or crackers: Place 2 cups of chips or crackers in a Pyrex pie plate, microwave on high for 1 minute, then place while hot on double thickness of paper towels until chips or crackers reach room temperature.

Source: Kitchen Quick Tips, *by the editors of* Cook's Illustrated

Things you never thought you could do with vinegar

WE AT COSTCO KNOW that the 128-ounce jug of white vinegar we sell in our warehouses may be a lot to swallow. That's why *Household Almanac* editors were thrilled when we came across these helpful hints from writer Earl W. Proulx in the 1989 edition of *The Old Farmer's Almanac*.

Air freshener. Set out a shallow dish of white vinegar.

Aluminum pans. Remove dark stains by boiling water containing 1 tablespoon white vinegar for each quart of water.

Aluminum screens. For corrosion, apply white vinegar, let stand a few minutes, then scrub off.

Chrome fixtures. Clean off soap and stains with a mixture of 1 teaspoon salt dissolved in 2 tablespoons white vinegar.

Clogged drains. Pour 1/2 cup baking soda down the drain, then 1/2 cup vinegar. Close the drain and let work for a while, then open the drain and let hot water pour through for 3 or 4 minutes.

Clogged shower head. To unclog, soak in diluted white vinegar overnight, or put some vinegar in a plastic bag, tie it around the shower head and leave in place overnight.

Garbage disposal. If the rubber shield smells after much use, remove it and soak it in a pan of white vinegar.

Hair care. After washing, rinse hair well with 1 cup water containing 1 tablespoon white vinegar. This removes soapy film.

Itching relief. White vinegar is a time-honored remedy for wasp stings, bruises, chapped hands, sunburn and hives. It relieves the itching of mosquito and other insect bites. Apply full strength unless area is raw.

Oven. Dampen a cleaning rag in vinegar and water, and wipe out the interior. This will prevent grease buildup.

Pest fighter. A teaspoon of vinegar for each quart of drinking water helps keep your pet free of fleas and ticks. (This ratio is for a 40-pound animal.)

Plastic antistatic. Add a tablespoon of white vinegar to each gallon of rinse water when washing plastic curtains. Vinegar cuts down on the attraction of dust. Plastic upholstery also can be wiped clean with a damp cloth wrung out from a water-and-vinegar solution.

Plastic shower curtains. Wash them in the washing machine with a bath towel. Add 1 cup of white vinegar to the rinse cycle. Briefly tumble dry.

Stainless steel. White hard-water stains can be removed by rubbing with white vinegar.

Wood paneling. To clean, mix 1 ounce olive oil with 2 ounces white vinegar and 1 quart warm water. Dampen a soft cloth with this and wipe the paneling; then wipe with a dry soft cloth.

Cask for making vinegar

Vinegar in it

Tips for using vinegar are one of the oldest of standbys for almanac editors. Here are two we found in a classic called *Household Discoveries and Mrs. Curtiss' Cook Book, An Encyclopedia of Practical Recipes and Processes*, written by Sidney Morse and published in 1908 by the optimistically named Success Company.

Moist hands. If the hands are constantly moist from too much perspiration, bathe them frequently either in salt water, which acts as a stimulant or tonic, or in a solution of vinegar or lemon juice, which acts as an astringent.

Lamp wicks. Wicks should be changed occasionally and may be cleansed by boiling them with vinegar and afterwards drying thoroughly before using.

Lemons are for more than cooking!

WHEN LIFE HANDS YOU A LEMON, make lemonade out of it ... or maybe a bleach for cleaning rolling pins. That's just one of many home-spun alternate uses for this yellow fruit, as suggested by our good friends at *The Old Farmer's Almanac*.

- To remove scratches from wooden furniture, mix equal amounts of lemon juice and salad oil. Apply with a soft cloth and rub until the scratches disappear.

- Make your own furniture polish by mixing lemon juice with two parts olive oil or vegetable oil.

- To renew the sparkle and brightness inside a glass decanter, shake a small piece of freshly cut lemon and a little water inside. Rub cloudy glasses with cut lemon or soak them in lemon juice and water, and dry with a lint-free towel.

- When the finish on bathtubs and sinks looks dull, rub them with half a lemon dipped in borax to regain the shine.

- Polish copper and brass with lemon juice. For heavy corrosion, use a paste of lemon juice and salt. Rub, wash with clear water and dry.

- To clean ivory (including piano keys), rub with half a lemon or with a paste made of salt and lemon juice. Wipe with a clean, wet cloth.

- Bleach pastry boards and rolling pins clean by occasionally rubbing them with half a lemon.

- If you slop paint on the glass when you're painting windows, let the paint dry. Then rub gently with hot lemon juice. Leave until almost dry and wipe off.

- Bring hardened paintbrushes back to life by dipping them in boiling lemon juice in an enamel or stainless steel saucepan. Lower the heat immediately and leave the brush in the hot juice for 15 minutes, then wash in soapy water.

- After washing woodwork, rinse it with the juice of one lemon to a quart of water to maintain the gloss. (This will also work on any painted or enameled surface or linoleum.)

- Use lemon juice in the rinse water to remove soap film from the interiors of ovens and refrigerators.

- Remove spots from kitchen and bathroom faucets by rubbing them with lemon peel. Then wash and dry with a soft cloth to restore their shine.

- Use full-strength lemon juice on white washable fabrics to remove lipstick stains; use diluted juice on colors.

- Take wine stains out of washable fabrics with a paste of salt and lemon juice. Rinse, then wash in soapy water.

- A drop of lemon juice rubbed on insect bites or stings instantly relieves the irritation.

- Mulch rosebushes with used lemon peel and pulp.

- Gargle with lemon juice and warm water two to three times daily for fresh, sweet breath. (Lemon is a local antiseptic and internal alkalizer.)

- Add lemon juice to a few teaspoons of alfalfa tea to relieve headaches from hangovers or other causes.

- To alleviate coughs, roast lemons until they crack open. Mix their juice with brown sugar and fresh pineapple juice and drink it. The pineapple juice adds its powerful digestive enzymes to those of the lemon to help disintegrate mucus in the throat.

- If you want to stop smoking or chewing tobacco, carry a lemon with a hole in its tip, wrapped in wax paper. When you have the urge to smoke or chew, suck a mouthful of lemon juice. You may need several lemons to kick your habit.

Source: Sunskist Inc. and Sunkist Growers Inc., courtesy of
The Old Farmer's Almanac Hearth & Home Companion, 1994

Filtered water– a healthy choice

DID YOU KNOW that you can start leading a healthier life with something as simple as a glass of filtered water? From getting better-tasting water to lowering your monthly drinking-water costs, there are many benefits to drinking filtered water.

In many communities the water supply contains sediments such as dirt, rust and sand. Contaminants such as lead, mercury, chlorine and asbestos may also be present. Luckily, some water filtration systems can easily reduce many of these contaminants, as well as remove 99.9 percent of parasites that can cause gastrointestinal illness. (To learn more about your city's water supply, ask your local public water utility for a copy of its annual consumer confidence report; see sidebar.)

Water filtration systems provide healthy, delicious water at one-tenth the cost of bottled water, which could save your family as much as $600 or more a year versus buying bottled water.

It's important to note that just because water is bottled, it is not necessarily the best choice. The Food and Drug Administration does not require bottled water to be of any higher quality than tap water. Many bottled waters originate from municipal tap water, and not the glaciers and waterfalls that their labels might suggest.

There are two main types of point-of-use home water filtration systems: faucet-mount filters and pitchers. Both are effective, but they offer different benefits.

Faucet-mount filters
- Have clearly marked on/off buttons to change water from filtered to unfiltered
- Are easy to install on all standard faucets
- Allow for an endless supply of clean water for all beverage and cooking needs
- Offer a space-saving design and easy shut-off that allows access to the sink and unfiltered water for washing dishes
- Do not filter out fluoride, which is important for the development and maintenance of healthy teeth
- Fit right onto faucets, saving precious refrigerator space
- Are available in a variety of colors to match any décor

Water-filtration pitchers
- Fit in the refrigerator to keep water cold
- Are easy to lift and carry
- Are offered in a variety of shapes and sizes to best match a family's water-drinking habits
- Are convenient for entertaining or for having lots of refreshing, chilled water available
- Do not filter out fluoride, which is important for the development and maintenance of healthy teeth

Regardless of which method you choose, keep these factors in mind

Buy a filter that does not remove fluoride from tap water. The American Dental Association endorses community water fluoridation as a safe, beneficial and cost-effective public-health measure for preventing tooth decay.

Look for certification by NSF® International, an independent agency that certifies that products have passed a series of stringent product performance tests.

For maximum effectiveness, look for the filtration system with the highest level of contaminant reduction.

Some faucet-mounted filters offer additional features, such as three-stage water filter technology to best reduce contaminants and provide the best-tasting water, and a reminder light that electronically monitors filter life, shutting off water flow when the filter needs replacing.

The most important thing to keep in mind when shopping for a filtration system is to pick the faucet-mount filter or walter filtration pitcher that works best for your family. And whether it's to filter out contaminants, keep your costs down or make your water taste better, filtered water could be the most effective and easiest way to keep your family healthy.

Learn what's in your water

You should receive a report on the water quality in your community from your local public water treatment plant. This consumer confidence report usually comes with your water bill, or you can also get a copy from your water company, local library or the Environmental Protection Agency Web site (*www.epa.gov*). Click on "water" and then "drinking water." Also, ask your water company if it has found any contaminants, even those not required to be tested for by the federal Safe Drinking Water Act. You might be surprised by the results of your research.

Stay healthy by drinking water

Drinking water has a number of benefits. Staying hydrated will help you to:

Reduce your risk of a heart attack. Researchers at Loma Linda University in California studied more than 20,000 healthy men and women and found that people who drink more than five glasses of water a day were less likely to die from a heart attack or heart disease than those who drank fewer than two glasses a day.

Get energized and be alert. On average, most adults lose about 10 cups of fluid a day through sweating, exhaling, urinating and bowel movements. Even minor dehydration can cause impaired concentration, headaches, irritability and fatigue.

Reduce your risk of disease and infection. Water can help prevent kidney stones and reduce your chances of getting bladder, kidney and urinary tract infections. A study published in the *International Nursing Review* in 2005 found that the risk of colon cancer for women who drank more than five glasses of water a day was 45 percent lower than for those who drank two or fewer glasses a day.

Control your weight. Increased water consumption can help you lose weight by preventing you from confusing hunger with thirst. Water will also keep your body systems, including metabolism and digestion, working properly and give you the energy (and hydration) necessary for exercise.

Flush toxins. By helping to flush toxins, appropriate water intake lessens the burden on your kidneys and liver.

Keep your joints and muscles healthy. Water makes up a large part of the fluid that lubricates and cushions your joints and muscles. Drinking water before, during and after exercise can also help reduce muscle cramping and premature fatigue.

Stay regular. Water helps prevent constipation by adding fluid throughout the body, making bowel movements easier.

Regulate your body temperature. Perspiration is your body's natural mechanism to control body temperature. You also need plenty of water to sweat.

Get healthy skin. Drinking water moisturizes your skin from the inside out. Water is essential to maintaining elasticity and suppleness, and helps to prevent dryness.

Get well. The traditional recommendation to "drink plenty of fluids" when you're sick still holds strong. Water can help control a fever, replace lost fluids and thin mucus.

Good water is good for your life

YOU'VE HEARD THE advice: Drink eight 8-ounce glasses of water a day. But do you know why your body needs eight glasses of water a day? What does water do for you that nothing else can do?

The answer is simple: Around 70 percent of your body is made up of water, so your entire body, from your skin to your brain, relies on water to keep functioning properly.

Water

- Helps feed and cushion your brain
- Regulates body temperature
- Aids in digestion
- Keeps skin clear and healthy
- Cushions and lubricates bones and joints
- Maintains muscle tone
- Helps metabolize fat
- Lubricates organs
- Transports nutrients throughout your body

• Helps remove toxins and waste

Essentially, water helps you do all the things you need to do throughout your day. Walking, eating, breathing, laughing … every aspect of your life is touched by water.

Everybody's body is different

There are times in your life when your body's need for water might change. It's important to be able to identify those times and to respond accordingly.

Pregnancy. It may be a cliché, but you really are drinking water for two. Your baby needs water to grow and to get a good start in life. For instance, fluoride is very important to a developing fetus. It helps bones and teeth grow. (Be aware that not all bottled waters contain the proper amount of fluoride.) Even after your baby is born, you can help proper bone and tooth development through the fluoride in your breast milk.

If you're suffering from morning sickness, dehydration can be a real concern for you and the baby you're carrying. So keep drinking a lot of water—both of you need it.

Childhood. Running, playing, jumping and just plain being a kid is a lot of activity. Children can lose 1 to 2 quarts of water in just one day, water that they need to grow big and strong. Help your child develop healthy habits by making water a part of his or her diet.

Senior years. As you age, your body doesn't keep you as well informed as it used to—it may even not tell you when you're not getting enough water. So make a point of remembering to drink plenty of water. Water can offer many health benefits, including helping to prevent kidney stones, helping to ease constipation, improving the condition of your skin, improving mental sharpness, aiding in digestion and helping circulation.

Cold and flu season. Germs and viruses are out there, and even if you do everything you can to avoid them, they may still find you. If you find yourself starting to feel under the weather, turn to a glass of water for help. Hydration will give you energy and will also help your body to fight illness. And because dehydration is a side effect of many illnesses, be aware of the symptoms (see below) and keep drinking at least eight 8-ounce glasses of water a day.

A thirsty body needs attention

Water is so important that when you don't get enough of it your entire system can break down. Dehydration can happen more often when you're exercising, if you have an intestinal illness or during hot summer months. Even eight glasses a day might not be enough, so it's important to be aware of the signs and symptoms of dehydration.

When you're mildly dehydrated you'll feel thirsty and your lips and mouth

might be dry. Moderate dehydration symptoms include a lack of skin elasticity and sunken eyes. Severe dehydration symptoms include all of the symptoms of mild and moderate dehydration, plus a rapid, weak pulse, cold extremities, rapid breathing, confusion and lethargy.

Listen to what your body is telling you. When you feel the symptoms of dehydration coming on, drink water. Consult a doctor immediately if you experience the signs of severe dehydration, or if you have any questions at all.

Water, water everywhere. Which one should I drink?

Now you know why water is good for you. And you know how much water you should be drinking. But you might be asking, What kind of water should I be drinking? There are a lot of possibilities out there; tap water isn't the only way to go.

One of the most popular ways to get good healthy water is by using a water filtration system. Such systems are easy, they're convenient and they turn ordinary tap water into healthier water that tastes better.

All filtration systems are not alike

Once you've made the decision to purchase a water filtration system, how can you be sure that you're getting the one that's right for you?

Consider the following four key points when you're deciding on a water filtration system. Select a water filtration system that will:

- Reduce harmful impurities such as lead, zinc, benzene, cadmium, copper and mercury. Over time, these contaminants can cause certain health problems. Not all tap water contains all these contaminants. A good way to find out what your tap water does contain is to contact your local water utility. Municipal water is tested for quality, so if you would like more information, just make a request to see the report.
- Reduce chlorine so that your water tastes better as well as being better for you. Better-tasting water means better-tasting coffee and tea, powdered drinks and even ice cubes.
- Leave fluoride in your water. Fluoride is good for you—that's why it's put in tap water. The right filtration system will leave a beneficial amount of fluoride in your drinking water.
- Be well designed so that it's easy to use and pleasing to the eye. In other words, style and function are both important. After all, if water is going to be a big part of your healthy lifestyle, your water filtration system should be designed to fit perfectly into that lifestyle.

Once you have the right water filtration system at home or at work, you will always have healthier, better-tasting water at hand. And drinking eight glasses a day will be something that you want to do, not just something you have to do!

So remember: Healthier water will make a healthier you. And that will help you do all the things you want to do in life.

Seven steps to food safety

THE GOVERNMENT AND MANY RETAILERS have adopted programs to help keep fresh food as safe as possible. Just as important are the steps that consumers take in food preparation. Here's a look at commonsense practices for the safe handling of food—whether you're a home cook or a small-business owner involved in food service.

There are two basics to food safety: Keep foods, such as raw meat and vegetables, separate from each other; and maintain proper temperatures—during storage and cooking.

The purchase. It all starts with reading the labels on all fresh and frozen foods. These contain all the critical safety information: proper storage techniques, safe cooking temperatures and "best before" dates.

Keep ready-to-eat foods separate from raw foods in your shopping cart to avoid cross contamination. It's also smart to make grocery shopping your last errand so that perishable foods can be placed in the refrigerator or freezer as soon as possible. If you can't refrigerate these foods immediately, keep them in coolers with ice.

Handling meats. The key is proper refrigeration—at all times, including the period from the store to your home. Most raw meats will keep for about three days under proper refrigeration, and they should be cooked within that time. Refrigerators with a special "meat keeper" compartment may safely lengthen the storage time by two or three days.

There should be little or no discernible odor to fresh meat. Spoiled meat may turn brown, green or rainbow-colored, develop spots or have a slimy coating.

The safety rule for frozen meats is simple: Keep them thoroughly frozen. Frozen raw meats that have been thawed must be cooked thoroughly before they can be safely refrozen.

Storing foods. Perishables must be kept at temperatures of 40°F or colder. And frozen products must be held at 32°F or below. Check your refrigerator with a thermometer to make sure it is accurate and working at these levels.

Keep raw meats separate from other foods in the refrigerator: Don't allow meat to contaminate other foods by touching or dripping on them. It's a good idea to store these items on a low shelf in containers that will not leak onto other foods.

The thawing process. Frozen foods are best thawed in the refrigerator. This may take two days and even longer for large roasts and turkeys. Safe thawing alternatives are using a microwave or running cool water over the item while it's tightly wrapped in plastic, followed by immediate cooking.

Never thaw frozen meats at room temperature. Bacteria can multiply rapidly on the warmer surfaces of thawing foods that are still frozen inside.

Preparing the food. Continue keeping foods separate to prevent contamination. Don't cut vegetables on the same surface that you cut meat on—and wash these surfaces when switching tasks. Likewise, use separate knives and utensils while preparing your foods. And wash your hands with hot, soapy water to make sure you don't pass bacteria.

Don't taste raw cake or cookie batter, or any other food that contains uncooked eggs. And marinate foods in the refrigerator—not on the counter.

Cooking tips. One of the best kitchen investments is a metal probe thermometer. Always clean the thermometer in hot, soapy water before you use it. When inserting the thermometer, make sure it doesn't touch the bone, which will make the reading inaccurate. Also, don't leave the thermometer in the meat while it's cooking—it can pick up the temperature of the air in the oven, making your reading inaccurate.

The best guide to proper cooking temperatures is usually right on the product labels. Follow these instructions, and use your thermometer to make sure the food has been cooked to the right temperature.

Handling leftovers. Refrigerated leftovers should be used within three days. Make sure leftovers are reheated quickly to 170°F. Reheat only the amount you plan to eat and leave the rest refrigerated.—*Tim Talevich*

For more information on food safety, see www.foodsafety.gov.

Tips for safe grilling

Summer is the season for picnics and barbecues, but it brings some food-safety risks. Food transported without proper refrigeration or left in the sun at a picnic won't stay safe for long. Here are helpful food-preparation hints for a picnic or barbecue.

- Keep the cooler in the shade. Keep the lid closed and avoid repeated openings. Replenish the ice if it melts.
- Use a separate cooler for drinks so the one containing perishable food won't be constantly opened and closed.
- Except when being served, the food should be stored in a cooler.
- When handling raw meat, remove from the cooler only the amount that will fit on the grill. The U.S. Department of Agriculture recommends against eating raw or undercooked ground beef because harmful bacteria could be present.
- Cook hamburgers and ribs to 160°F (71°C). Cook ground poultry to 165°F (74°C) and poultry parts to 180°F (82°C). Reheat precooked meats until steaming hot.
- Do not partially grill extra hamburgers to use later. Once you begin cooking hamburgers by any method, cook them until they're completely done.
- When taking food off the grill, put it on a clean plate. Don't put the cooked items on the same platter that held the raw meat.
- Place leftover foods in the cooler promptly after grilling or serving. Any left outside for more than an hour should be discarded. There should still be ice in the cooler when you get home to keep the food cold enough.

—*TT*

Setting up and stocking a place for your wines

THE PROBLEM WITH being a wine lover is that sooner or later we all have to face the same question: Where do I keep my wine? Fortunately, there are many solutions available to suit a wide range of pocketbooks and floor plans, from custom-built rooms to a cupboard under the stairs.

The word "cellar" sounds terribly grand, but should be interpreted loosely. All you really need is somewhere cool, dark and free from vibration; that's why on top of the fridge usually isn't a good idea. Ideal cellar temperature is around 55° F, but it's more important to find a place where the temperature doesn't fluctuate too much day to day or throughout the year. Better a constant 65 degrees than 45 one day and 75 the next.

If your cool, dark place is also relatively humid, so much the better, as this will help prevent corks from drying out. A dry cork contracts, which allows in air, spoiling the wine. A dry cork also lets wine leak out, which is why wines are stored lying down, keeping the corks wet.

An option that is becoming increasingly popular is the temperature-controlled storage unit. These cellars, which can hold anywhere from a couple dozen to several hundred bottles, are a great instant, all-in-one solution for properly storing wine. The upper-end units are attractive enough to serve as furniture pieces.

Having a wine cellar adds a world of versatility to your culinary offerings. While the vast majority of wines are meant to be drunk within a year or so of purchase, a small percentage of the world's top wines need anywhere from three or four years to three or four decades to reach their peak of maturity. The problem is, by the time these wines are ready you won't be able to find (or afford) them. Hence the need for a cellar.

Meanwhile, a cellar is also an excellent place to store your pantry wines. These may be your two or three favorite reds and whites that you drink on a regular basis. Stock up on them while they are available and your cellar will keep them in tiptop condition, whether you keep them for a week or a year. Warning: When you start a cellar, you will inevitably start to drink better wine, and you might just look at that walk-in closet in a different light.—*Tim Talevich*

No cellar should be without ...

What you put in your cellar is very much a matter of personal taste, but my ideal starter cellar would need representation from among the following.

Reds

- **Barolo.** Traditionally made Italian Barolos can be tannic and acidic when young. Give them 10 years plus. If you can't wait that long, stock up on Barbaresco, Brunello di Montalcino, Chianti Classico or Super Tuscans.
- **Bordeaux.** The top wines from good vintages will improve for 10 to 15 years and live for decades more.
- **Burgundy.** Often underwhelming in youth, Burgundy can blossom into ethereal beauties in maturity.
- **California and Washington Cabernet Sauvignons or Bordeaux blends.** The top wines often sell out quickly upon release, so cellaring is the way to go.
- **Northern Rhône.** No cellar is complete without a smattering of noble Syrahs from Hermitage or Côte Rôtie.
- **Rioja and Ribera del Duero.** From Spain, both can begin to taste remarkably like Bordeaux after 15 years or so.

Whites

Most white wines are made to be drunk young and fresh, but there are notable exceptions. Indeed, the world's best white wines are often drunk far too soon, before they have had a chance to show the complexity of which they are capable.

- **Loire Valley Chenin Blanc.** Savennières, for example, having great acidity, hits its stride at about 10 years and can keep going for many more.
- **Riesling.** The top wines of Germany and Alsace are a constant source of amazement as they mature.
- **White Burgundy.** Puligny-Montrachet and Meursault are a couple of the greats and fine examples of the ubiquitous Chardonnay grape.

The others

Vintage port can take 20 or more years to reach early maturity and go on for decades more, while Madeira can outlast us all. Sauternes only gets richer and more exquisite as the decades pass. And Champagne, noted for its freshness and finesse in youth, can develop a wonderful nutty richness in middle age.—*TT*

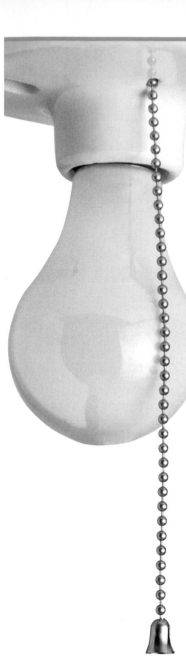

When you've exhausted all the good ideas ...

Our resident parodist just couldn't resist ...

ALRIGHTY, SO WE'VE ALREADY told you more than you ever thought you could know (or want to, perhaps) about the zillion and one different uses for lemons and vinegar. I guess this is the essence of an almanac, or at least one of its grand traditions—to show you the extraordinary in the ordinary.

On the other hand, if you really think about it, it's sort of silly. I mean, you can find an alternate use for just about anything, if you're willing to stretch. (Whipped cream: It's a floor wax! No, it's a dessert topping!)

For instance, if we were to put together *The A to Z Almanac of Alternate Uses for Any Random Product You Find at Costco*, it might go like this.

Water. When you're done with those multi-packs of Kirkland Signature water, set the bottles up for your own street "carny" booth. "Get the Ping-Pong ball in the bottle, win a prize." Your secret: Ping-Pong balls won't fit; the bottle necks are too small. You are laughing all the way to the bank.

I admit, I cheated; this is not really an alternate use for water. But, hey, you were all set to rook a bunch of unsuspecting kids out of their paper-delivery money. Give me a break!

Steel wool. It's not just an (extreme) emergency toilet tissue on extended camping trips, it's a group loofah for masochists!

Cat litter. Want to quit hosting parties? These 400-pound bags of gravel (you are paying for rocks, people) will fill an ample supply of popularity-thwarting snack bowls.

DVDs. Mobiles. You've watched the Adam Sandler extended-edition collection 4,000 times. Give Adam a rest and create something beautiful out of those worn-out DVDs. (Hint: Your "Best of the Big Hair Bands" CD retrospective box set and "The Smurfs Sing Four Decades of Johnny Cash Favorites" multi-disc collection will work just dandy too.)

Brussels sprouts. Skeet-shooting targets. Oversized marble competition. *Anything* is an improvement over actually eating these things, at least the way my Mom overcooked those mini-cabbages from hell.

Olive oil. With this 5-gallon drum, you're just a Twister® board and a box of Rice Krispies away from an evening of slip 'n' slide, snap, crackle and pop party fun!

And the list goes on. Toilet tissue: These 32-roll packages can be used as modular furniture. Soy sauce: an exotic bath soak. Fiber supplements: If it keeps *you* regular, shouldn't it work on your home's plumbing, too? Anyway, you get the idea. Use your imagination. Think outside the Big Box. Toss away convention and put your gray cells to work.

And keep your hands out of the snack bowl.—*T. Foster Jones*

Seal it!

With its two easy-to-close zippers, the new Ziploc Double Zipper seal creates our tightest seal ever. The Double Zipper seal is now available on Ziploc freezer bags. With their tough, durable plastic, Ziploc freezer bags are specially designed for the harsh freezer environment. Costco has a full range of Ziploc items, including the EZ Zipper and handy sandwich bags.

Fill your life... with BRITA

Water is essential to every aspect of your life. So fill your glass with refreshing, better-tasting water... Brita® water.

- **NEW!** Sleek, contemporary pitcher design
- Our largest-capacity pitcher—10 cups
- Flip-top for easy refilling
- Filter-change indicator

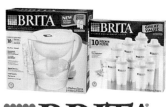

BRITA

A. The Griddler™ by Cuisinart™
With four separate cooking options, the Griddler can handle everything from pancakes to sausages to grilled cheese to steaks, hamburgers and panini. Simply change the cooking plates and adjust the floating hinge to use the unit as a contact grill, a panini press or your choice of an open grill or griddle. Item #921289

B

B. Sharp R-306LW Microwave Oven
This 1.0-cubic-foot, 1,100-watt oven features 16 automatic cook, reheat and defrost settings plus popcorn and Minute Plus™ buttons for perfect results every time. Item #103223

C

C. Panasonic Stainless Steel Microwave
This 1.2 cubic foot unit features a 13.5" turntable, 1300 watts, pop-out dial for easy operation, 4-digit display programming, and Sensor/Inverter technology for outstanding cooking results. Item #102100, 172047

D. Sanyo Mini Refrigerator
Mixing style and functionality, this compact fridge is a fit for any room or environment, with a stainless steel door and stylish Eclipse™ series black interior. Item #776960

D

A

B

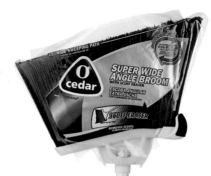

C

A. Litter Purrfect
This all-natural cat litter is made from 100% natural clay and clumps harder and faster for quick, easy waste removal. Also features all-new natural lemongrass essence and baking soda to keep your litter box fresh, clean and virtually odor free. Item #133890

B. OxiClean
Color safe and chlorine free, this super-oxygenated formula features powerful, fast-acting bubbles that tackle more than 101 stains around your home or business. Use it on clothing, carpets, blinds, shower curtains, decks, linens, garbage cans, boats, outdoor furniture and more. Item #111299

C. O Cedar Super Wide Angle Broom
This broom offers an easier way to get floors dirt and scuff free. The scuff-eraser pad on the end of the broom safely removes scuff marks during sweeping. Item #947528

D. Libman Extra-Wide-Angle Broom
Featuring a thick steel handle and a hanger hole for easy storage, this broom has a 14"-wide sweeping surface that is perfect for indoor and outdoor use. Item #699124

D

Everyday convenience

Hefty Super Weight Foam Plates
These plates and hinged-lid trays feature a strong, soakproof design and are perfect for parties, holiday events or everyday use. Not available in all locations. 200-ct. Item #265999, 175-ct. Item #229444, hinged tray Item #39401

Simple Solutions...

...for your household cleaning and personal care!

LYSOL® Disinfectant Spray
Kills 99.9% of nasty odor- and illness-causing germs on hard nonporous surfaces.

LYSOL® Sanitizing Wipes
Kill germs on surfaces quickly by using disinfecting products such as **LYSOL®** Sanitizing Wipes in kitchens and bathrooms.

WOOLITE® Fabric Wash
Care for all your favorite clothes with **WOOLITE®**; It won't cause shrinking, stretching or fading.

SPRAY 'N WASH® Laundry Stain Remover
Just what you'd expect from the stain-removal experts! Unsurpassed stain-removal formula is safe for all colorfast washables and works in all temperatures.

ELECTRASOL® 3 in 1 Tabs with Jet-Dry Rinse Agent Keeps your dishes sparkling clean with **ELECTRASOL®** Automatic Dishwashing Detergent and Jet-Dry® rinse agent.

AIRWICK® Scented Oils
Freshen your home with **AIRWICK®** Scented Oil to add a warm and consistent long-lasting fragrance.

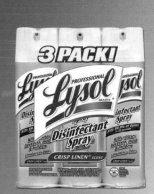

The Georgia-Pacific Quality Line of Products

Dixie's New Plate Design

Vanity Fair's Best

New Improved Kirkland Signature Products

Seasonal maintenance checklist

IT'S SO EASY to put off, or just forget about, those essential home maintenance tasks. This handy checklist, courtesy of the DIY Network, will help you protect your property—and your family.

Spring

- ☐ Clean windows and repair screens
- ☐ Unclog and secure gutters and downspouts
- ☐ Regrade around foundation
- ☐ Test sump pump
- ☐ Clean air-conditioning system
- ☐ Inspect and maintain laundry room
- ☐ Check attic fan
- ☐ Test GFCI (ground fault circuit interrupter) outlets
- ☐ Change furnace filters
- ☐ Change batteries in carbon monoxide and smoke detectors

Summer

- ☐ Clean and care for deck
- ☐ Clean siding

Laughing at our mistakes can lengthen our own life. Laughing at someone else's can shorten it.

—Cullen Hightower

☐ Check crawl space
☐ Maintain yard growth
☐ Test and lubricate garage door
☐ Remove rust on railings
☐ Check skylights
☐ Clean shower heads
☐ Change furnace filters
☐ Test carbon monoxide and smoke detectors

Fall

☐ Check and seal windows
☐ Reprogram thermostat
☐ Check and clean humidifier
☐ Close critter entrances
☐ Shut off hose bibs
☐ Check and maintain dishwasher
☐ Clean out gutters
☐ Clean outdoor drains
☐ Check toilets
☐ Clear out sink drains
☐ Change furnace filters
☐ Test carbon monoxide and smoke detectors

Winter

☐ Check and upgrade insulation
☐ Check and maintain furnaces
☐ Vacuum air registers
☐ Check and flush water heater
☐ Recaulk bathtub
☐ Maintain fireplace and chimney
☐ Check crawl space
☐ Replenish flashlight batteries
☐ Check gutters for ice
☐ Change furnace filters
☐ Test carbon monoxide and smoke detectors

Periodic

☐ Weatherpoof doors
☐ Pressure-wash deck
☐ Pressure-wash siding
☐ Check and maintain roof shingles
☐ Check and recaulk flashing
☐ Repair and reseal driveway
☐ Check life expectancy of appliances
☐ Lubricate door hinges and hardware
☐ Vacuum out-of-the-way spots

Reprinted with permission from DIY Network/DIYnetwork.com
© Copyright 2005

*Sponsored by **Dust-Off***

No fuss, no dust

OFTEN THE SIMPLEST things in life are the most useful. Duct tape comes to mind. Everyone has it around the house, but not everyone uses it for the same purpose.

Similarly, a can of compressed-gas duster sits on the shelf ready to clean the computer, but its uses are limited only by the imagination.

Introduced in the 1970s, the compressed-gas duster was designed to aid photographers in cleaning their photographic negatives. At the time, accidentally touching a negative could result in finger smudges on the finished print. With the compressed-gas duster, photographers could direct a pressurized blast at any dust or lint that may have collected on negatives without needing to touch them, resulting in perfect prints.

In the mid-1980s, the compressed-gas duster found another application—computers. Early computers were considerably more expensive than they are today, and preventive maintenance was an important consideration. Keeping the air vents clean on the central processing unit helped prevent unnecessary crashes. A weekly blast between the keyboard keys could keep cookie crumbs from collecting and keys from sticking.

To this day the compressed-gas duster remains a staple for computer technicians and home PC users. However, this simple technology has evolved into a multipurpose tool found in everyone's home or garage.

People use compressed-gas dusters for:

General household cleaning. Compressed-gas dusters can be used to clean mini-blinds, dust a lampshade or dust a bookcase without removing the books, trophies or figurines. Use it to clean smoke detectors or vacuum-cleaner filters. Wiping off silk flower arrangements with a cloth is time consuming; a compressed-gas duster makes easy work of this task.

Hobbies. Model builders use compressed-gas dusters to blast dust and lint from the surface of a model they are about to paint. Once on display, many of a model's parts might be too delicate for a dust rag—the compressed-gas duster to the rescue. Woodworkers also use the duster to clean out small cracks, holes or grooves in their projects. It's also great for cleaning dust and lint off slides or off glass while framing pictures.

Car detailing. A compressed-gas duster is ideal for blasting dust from those tiny nooks and crannies inside a car, such as the dashboard vents, instrument panel, center console, air vents, steering column, seat rails and more.

These are just a few of the hundreds of home and office applications for this simple technology.

If you have an unusual use, let us know. For each idea we use in our next Household Almanac, *we'll pay $50. See page xi for details.*

Safety first

Because the compressed-gas duster is an aerosol product, the contents can be hazardous if used improperly. An extremely distasteful bittering agent added to the compressed gas is intended to discourage inhalant abuse.

Read the caution label on the can and get familiar with the product's characteristics before undertaking any cleaning task. These dusters should not be used near potential ignition sources, such as open flames, hot surfaces or spark-producing equipment (such as paper shredders).

Do not tilt the container too much before or during use. This can cause liquid contents to be emitted, which can freeze or discolor computer components or any other plastic.

Hiring a home-improvement contractor: a quiz

MORE HOMEOWNERS are deciding to remodel and renovate rather than move. Whether you're planning to add a powder room or a master bedroom with a fireplace and vaulted ceilings, checking out your contractor is the first step to a successful project. Before you sign a contract or make the first payment, take this simple test developed by the Federal Trade Commission. It will give you a better idea of what you can expect from your contractor and the home-improvement process. You'll find the answers on page 174.

1. An advertisement in the "Home Improvement" section of the Yellow Pages is your assurance that a contractor is licensed and reputable.
  ☐ True ☐ False

2. All states require home-improvement contractors to be licensed.
  ☐ True ☐ False

3. Your state licensing agency can verify that the contractor you're considering has the appropriate licenses, if required, and that they're current.
  ☐ True ☐ False

4. Contractors should carry what type of insurance?
  ☐ **A.** personal liability
  ☐ **B.** workers' compensation
  ☐ **C.** property damage
  ☐ **D.** all of the above

5. Comparison shopping should be based on:
  ☐ **A.** reputation and price
  ☐ **B.** reliability and experience
  ☐ **C.** price only
  ☐ **D.** A and B

6. When comparing estimates, make sure each one is based on:
   ☐ **A.** the same set of plans
   ☐ **B.** the same set of specifications
   ☐ **C.** the same scope of work
   ☐ **D.** all of the above

7. You should expect to pay for a written estimate for your project.
   ☐ True   ☐ False

8. A well-written contract should include the contractor's name, address, phone number and license number, if required. It also should specify:
   ☐ **A.** the payment schedule for the contractor, subcontractors and suppliers
   ☐ **B.** an estimated start and completion date
   ☐ **C.** the cancellation policy
   ☐ **D.** how change orders will be handled
   ☐ **E.** all of the above

9. A change order is a written agreement to change the work described in the original contract. It could affect the project's cost and schedule.
   ☐ True   ☐ False

10. In most circumstances, oral contracts are as enforceable as written agreements. Oral contracts related to real property are an exception to this rule.
   ☐ True   ☐ False

11. If you sign the contract in your home or at a location that is not the seller's permanent place of business, you have three business days to cancel the deal.
   ☐ True   ☐ False

12. You should expect to make payments when you:
   ☐ **A.** sign the contract
   ☐ **B.** get a regular invoice weekly, monthly or at milestones
   ☐ **C.** sign a change order
   ☐ **D.** order a custom-made item
   ☐ **E.** all of the above

13. You should avoid making the final payment or signing an affidavit of final release until you are satisfied with the work and have proof that subcontractors and suppliers have been paid.
   ☐ True   ☐ False

14. If you get a loan for your home-improvement project, you should have the lender make out the check to the contractor.
   ☐ True   ☐ False

15. If you use your home as security for a home-improvement loan and you don't repay the loan as agreed, you could lose your home.
   ☐ True   ☐ False

Hiring a home-improvement contractor: the answers

1. False. Anyone can advertise in the Yellow Pages. An ad should not be considered as an indication of the quality of a contractor's work. It's still best to get recommendations from friends, neighbors and co-workers who have had remodeling work done. Contractors who are required to be licensed often list their license number in their ads. Check out the contractor with the Better Business Bureau and with state and local consumer-protection officials. They can tell you if there are unresolved consumer complaints on file. One caveat: No record of complaints against a particular remodeler doesn't necessarily mean no previous consumer problems. It may be that problems exist but have not been reported, or that the contractor is doing business under several names.

2. False. Thirty-six states require home-improvement contractors to be licensed; 14 states do not. Check with your state licensing agency or consumer-protection officials to find out about licensing requirements in your area.

3. True. You also can check with local building inspectors.

4. D. All of the above. Avoid doing business with contractors who don't carry the appropriate insurance. Otherwise, you'll be held liable for any injuries and damages that occur during the project.

5. D. Reputation, price, reliability and experience are the keys to a quality home-improvement project. Price alone is never an indication of a remodeler's competence or ability to complete your project.

6. D. All of the above. If your remodeler suggests deviations, ask that they be presented as options.

7. True. Most remodelers will charge for the time they spend preparing a detailed written estimate. The cost of the estimate will vary depending on the scope and complexity of the project.

8. E. All of the above. The contract also should spell out what will and will not be performed.

9. True. Remodelers often require payment for change orders before the work begins.

10. True. Therefore, it's always best to get verbal agreements added to your written contract.

11. True. The Federal Trade Commission's Cooling-Off Rule gives you three days to cancel the contract. During the sales transaction, the salesperson (contractor) must give you two copies of a cancellation form (one to keep and one to send back to the company) and a copy of your contract or receipt. The contract or receipt must be dated, show the name and address of the seller and explain your right to cancel.

12. E. All of the above.

13. True. Lien laws in your state may allow unpaid subcontractors and suppliers to "attach" your home through a "mechanic's lien." That means the subcontractors and suppliers could go to court to force you to sell your home to satisfy their unpaid bills from your project. Protect yourself by asking the contractor, and every subcontractor and supplier, for a lien release or lien waiver.

14. False. The check should be made out to you. Otherwise, you lose control of the funds.

15. True. The lender can take your home and sell it, using the proceeds to pay off the loan and any foreclosure costs. 〽

Source: Federal Trade Commission

Before you start a remodeling project

The Federal Trade Commission (*www.ftc.gov/ftc/consumer.htm*) has several helpful guides to planning a remodeling project and hiring and overseeing contractors. Another good source is the National Association of the Remodeling Industry (NARI) (*www.nari.org/level2/homeowners/*). They offer a free brochure to homeowners called "How to Select a Remodeling Professional." Contact the NARI toll-free at 1-800-611-NARI (6274) to request a copy.

*Sponsored by Jasco Products Company, maker of **GE SteelBEAM**™ **Lantern***

Prepare an at-home emergency kit

PREPARE YOUR FAMILY for emergency disasters such as blackouts, earthquakes, fires, floods, hurricanes, tornadoes and winter storms by taking a few minutes to put together an at-home emergency kit. By keeping these American Red Cross–recommended items in an easy-to-carry container, you can have the security of knowing that your family will be ready for almost any emergency.

Food and water

Keep a three-day supply of food and water per family member. Calculate at least one gallon of water per person each day. Water can easily be stored in plastic soft-drink bottles. Make sure food items are nonperishable. Include canned meats, fruits and vegetables that require little to no preparation. Don't forget a nonelectric can opener.

First-aid kit

A well-stocked first-aid kit is a must for your disaster kit. Include adhesive bandages, gauze pads, hand sanitizer, antiseptic wipes, adhesive tape, antibacterial ointment, cold packs, scissors and tweezers. Pain relievers and other over-the-counter medicines are also smart to stock in your kit. Make sure to store extra prescription medicine for family members with specific health concerns such as asthma or diabetes.

Battery-operated lights and radios

A battery-operated lantern or flashlight can shine a little light on any emergency situation. Consider lanterns with energy-efficient compact fluorescent bulbs, which provide a bright ambient light sure to comfort those scared of the dark. Battery-operated radios allow you to easily tune in to the latest emergency information for your community. And pack plenty of extra batteries.

Necessities

Toilet paper, soap, plastic bags and household disinfectants allow you to keep conditions sanitary, and extra clothing and bedding will keep you comfortable and warm. Other helpful items include basic tools (wrench, pliers, utility knife), compass, whistle, signal flare, area map and fire extinguisher. ⒜

Essential safety tips

Make a plan. Communication is key. Get together with family members and outline evacuation routes and communication plans to stay connected during an emergency. Practice makes perfect; routinely revisit these skills to stay sharp.

Get a kit. Prepare a comprehensive emergency kit for your home as well as a small kit for each of your family vehicles. Don't forget to check your kit every six months to refresh supplies and replace batteries.

Be informed. Read up on community-specific emergency action plans and keep a list of local emergency contacts. Contact your local American Red Cross branch to request informational materials and learn about first aid and CPR training.

Source: American Red Cross

Create an at-home emergency kit by gathering common household items such as water, nonperishable food, battery-operated lights and other supplies in a convenient, portable duffel bag.

Mold FAQs

What are molds?

Molds, one of the major forms of fungi, are found everywhere in the environment, both indoors and outdoors. Most of the time, they are found in association with decaying organic materials such as leaves and food. Molds make their living by helping break down these organic materials so they can be recycled and reused by other living things in the great circle of life. Thus, molds are very important to the world's ecology.

How do molds get into my house?

Molds travel about as microscopic spores. Spores are like seeds, but much smaller, so they are easily blown great distances through the air. Because of this, mold spores are found literally everywhere. For example, it is not unusual for a cubic meter of outside air to contain 500 to 1,000 mold spores.

Should I be concerned?

Yes and no. For the most part, molds don't find people, pets or houses to be inviting places to live. Humans' nasal passages and lungs are designed to handle those spores that we do inhale. While mold spores may be present in the air, they cause trouble only if they are permitted to grow. However, if significant mold overgrowth occurs in the home, it can damage the home's structure and trigger allergies in its occupants.

Is mildew the same as mold?

Yes. Mildew is a common term for mold overgrowth.

What do molds need for growth?

Only two things: food and moisture. There are molds that specialize in eating just about every possible type of organic material. When provided with suitable food (for example, a ceiling tile or some drywall) and moisture (in the form of very high humidity, condensation or water from a leaking pipe), some fungi will gladly set up housekeeping and begin to grow.

How do I look for molds in my home?

The keys are your eyes and nose. If you smell a moldy, musty or earthy odor, a fungus may be present. Or if you see a dark discoloration that is fuzzy and expanding, it is likely produced by mold growth. Look especially closely at areas that have been damaged by water. Molds can be many different colors, but most are green to black. Once you have found a spot of mold on the floor, wall or ceiling, keep in mind that there may well be mold growth that you can't see. Molds often grow behind walls, under floor tiles or on the top (back) of ceiling tiles.

Should I have my home tested for molds?

Professionals can culture your air and walls for fungi. However, this may not be necessary. First, these cultures will always be positive. Molds are simply everywhere, and, short of very specialized and highly filtered cleanroom environments, it is not possible to eliminate them. Second, molds are a problem only if you can see or smell them.

OK, I've got mold here. How do I clean it up?

Even before cleaning it up, you need to think about why it got there to begin with. The key is always moisture: Where did it come from? While the steps listed in the sidebar will get rid of your current mold infestation, mold will absolutely return if you don't eliminate the source(s) of moisture.

How do I keep mold from coming back?

Again, moisture is the key. As long as the moisture content is low, the fungus can't grow. Fix the leak and keep things dry. You also want to keep the indoor relative humidity at 30 to 60 percent or (even better) 30 to 50 percent.

If you are dealing with surfaces that are consistently moist due to condensation, you might want to try two approaches. First, try to eliminate the condensation. Second, consider treating the surface with paint containing inhibitors to prevent mold growth.

Source: Courtesy www.doctorfungus.org © *2007*

Cleaning up small areas of mold

1. Wear gloves and a good-quality mask rated N95 or better.

2. Dried molds are easily scattered, whereas wet molds are sticky and will stay put. This may mean that, yes, you are going to remoisten at least the surface of the contaminated material with water or disinfectant; the fungal spores will be spread less easily if they are dampened before being wiped away.

3. Truly porous materials (drywall, ceiling tiles) will have fungus that has deeply penetrated their surfaces. These materials must be discarded. Cloth-covered furniture can sometimes be cleaned using a high-efficiency vacuum process (referred to as HEPA vacuuming), but this is expensive, and simply discarding the furniture may make more sense. Semi-porous materials (concrete, wood) may have varying levels of fungal penetration. These can sometimes (but not always) be cleaned. Non-porous materials (plastics) usually have only surface contamination and are readily cleaned.

4. Bag and discard grossly infested materials such as drywall. It is often suggested that you remove a 12-inch rim of clean, unaffected material beyond the damaged area. Contaminated carpet is almost impossible to clean, and discarding it is the easiest solution.

5. Allow the area to dry.

6. Clean the surface with a standard detergent.

7. Your surface(s) should now be clean, dry and free of mold. You might want to check back later on to be sure the cleaned area is still mold free and that no moisture is accumulating.

For extensive contamination, hire a professional firm that specializes in dealing with this problem.

*Sponsored by **Graber** Window Coverings*

Easy steps to custom window coverings

WHEN YOU'RE REDECORATING a room, building a new home or noticing that cold draft coming through a window, it's time to think about window coverings. Here are a few things to consider to make your custom window-covering purchase easy and fun.

How do you use the room? Do you need extra privacy? Are you concerned about energy efficiency? What's your personal style?

Window coverings can drastically affect the mood and ambience within a room, depending on how they affect incoming light. On one end of the spectrum, they filter light so it is gently diffused throughout a room; on the other end, they block light completely for privacy and darkness.

Window coverings complement any style—casual or elegant, traditional or modern. They're made with soft, sheer fabrics or strong, durable materials. Whatever your need, there's a window covering that's right for you.

Here's a look at some of the options

Wood blinds make homes warmer in winter and cooler in summer, keeping ever-rising energy costs down. They're available in a variety of rich stains and contemporary paint colors to complement other finishes or furnishings in your home.

Concerned about the environment? Insist on wood blinds made from 100 percent North American hardwoods, a sustainable and renewable resource.

Composite blinds, with their authentic wood-grain appearance, are the perfect alternative to wood blinds. Choose these when the room's function calls for an alternative to real wood. Where room-darkening wood blinds are appropriate for the bedroom or dining room, composite blinds are more suitable for the bath or kitchen as they do not absorb moisture. Composite blinds, or "faux wood" blinds, are made of synthetic materials and are typically more economical than wood, yet as substantial and durable.

Cellular shades present a softer look at the window, yet provide the highest level of insulation of any window covering. Their construction forms pockets of air to keep out winter cold or summer heat. Wider fabrics effectively, and beautifully, cover the larger windows that are so popular in today's newer homes. Fabrics are available in three opacity levels (light filtering, room darkening or blackout) and in a color palette that ranges from neutral to vibrant.

Want even more choices? Consider sleek, contemporary fabric or vinyl vertical blinds. Many vertical styles coordinate with timeless Roman shades and classic pleated shades. For more casual décor, choose natural shades in woven bamboo, jute, reed or straw. Consider solar shades for the exceptional ultraviolet light protection they provide. And don't forget about colorful and affordable 1-inch aluminum mini-blinds.

Look for smooth, quiet controls that are designed for years of trouble-free operation. Several options are available in addition to the standard cord or chain.

- Continuous loop control makes lifting larger, heavier treatments easier.
- Cordless systems help keep young children and pets safe.
- Bottom-up/top-down options provide privacy while allowing light through the top of the window.
- Cordless bottom-up/top-down shades combine the benefits of two popular options into one.

Once you've chosen a custom window-covering solution, it's time to measure, order, install and enjoy!

Easy three-step measuring*

Determine whether you want an inside or outside mount. An inside mount is installed within the window casing, while an outside mount is installed outside the window casing, covering an area larger than the window itself.

Using a steel tape measure (a cloth one may stretch, giving you inaccurate results), follow these three simple steps to ensure a perfect fit all around.

1. Width. Measure in three places, from left to right; use the smallest measurement.

2. Height. Measure in three places, from top to bottom; use the smallest measurement.

3. Diagonal. Measure in two places, from top left to bottom right and top right to bottom left. If diagonal measurements are not equal the window opening is not square, and you may want to consider an outside mount for optimal light control and aesthetics.

*Depending on the type of window treatment you choose, the manufacturer may specify additional measurement requirements. Go to *www.memberblinds.com* or the specific manufacturer's Web site for complete measuring instructions for each window-treatment type.

Do-it-yourself installation

When you receive your custom window coverings, you'll find everything you need to install them yourself, including all brackets and mounting hardware, as well as easy-to-follow instructions.

Enjoy the view

Now it's time to sit back, enjoy the fruits of your labor and revel in the rave reviews you'll receive from family and friends.

By following these simple guidelines, you'll be sure to have a rewarding experience with every window-covering purchase you make.

Window coverings at Costco

Select the color and fabric for your window coverings by viewing and feeling an actual swatch of the materials. You can check out a sample book at your local Costco warehouse to take home, view the fabrics in the warehouse display or request fabric swatches on *www.memberblinds.com*. A checkout fee will be refunded to you when you return the sample book.

Measure your windows following the how-to-measure instructions for the product you have selected (see "Easy three-step measuring," at left). For convenience, the Web site listed above has a work sheet for you to use. Print it out and fill in your measurements.

Fill out the purchase form. The form can be completed at your local Costco warehouse, or you can take the form home to complete. For step-by-step ordering assistance, call toll-free 1-800-538-9419.

Pay for your order at the warehouse by bringing the completed form to a cashier.

Mail the green copy using the postage-paid envelope provided on the purchase-order form. (These can also be faxed.) Your order will not be manufactured until a confirming green copy of the order is received.

The blinds you have ordered will be shipped directly to the address specified on the purchase-order form. Install and enjoy your new window coverings.

—Steve Fisher

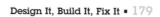

Buying carpet the smart way

Do the "value math"

Value is the relation of price to quality. A carpet that costs $3 per square foot and lasts five years has less value than one that costs $5 per square foot and lasts 10 years. Knowing how long you need the carpet to last will help you determine how much you want to spend.

To learn more about carpet performance ratings, visit the Carpet and Rug Institute at *www.carpet-rug.org*; click on "Selecting Carpet & Rugs," scroll to "Residential" and then "Performance Rating."

"It has been said that a beautiful floor is the foundation of a beautiful room. Just as your shoes can make or break an outfit, what's on the floor can change the look and feel of a room."
—*Julia E. Lewis*, Southern Accents *magazine*

NEW COLORS, textures, styles and patterns have made carpet a fashion statement and changed perceptions about what it can do for a room. Many interior designers now use carpet as a focal point, drawing inspiration from the colors and textures to coordinate the look for the rest of the room. Whether you want a fresh new look or just need to replace an ugly old carpet, here are some pointers to help you make a smart choice.

Start with your needs

When you start to think about carpeting a room, consider how the room is used as well as its décor. What does the carpet need to do? Wear well in a

high-traffic area? Look elegant in a formal living room? Stand up to kids and pets? Some carpet styles work better than others in given situations. A loop carpet—with its ability to resist matting and crushing—is a good choice for a room with lots of activity, while the soft, elegant look of a velvety plush carpet would complement a formal living room.

Color follows style

Today's carpets offer unprecedented color choices, from bold shades that define a room to neutrals that serve as the backdrop to furniture, art and other décor. Neutrals used to mean shades of beige, but today they can include khaki, taupe, gray, green, blue and terra-cotta. Other color trends include dark, rich browns, steely blues and deep charcoals. Two points about color: Dark colors make a room feel more intimate; light colors make a room seem larger.

Make your own personal fashion statement

Look for a color and style solution that is uniquely yours (see "What's your style?"). Consider talking to a professional designer, who can help with design advice as well as product information. A good designer can also open up your thinking to new ideas about color and texture that you may not have considered.

See the carpet in your home for best results

Viewing carpet in a fluorescent lit showroom is a poor indicator of how it will look in your home. Instead, take samples home so you can see them under your own lighting conditions, with your furniture and décor. Be sure to view them at various times of day: Evening light will impart a different hue than daylight.

For best value, buy quality

Start with the fiber. Nylon is superior to other synthetics in its durability and comfort. Look for branded fibers, such as Stainmaster, Anso or Wear-Dated, that have a reputation for quality. Or consider wool, a natural and renewable alternative to synthetics.

Next, check the performance. Most carpets are rated by the industry for wearability. A carpet with a rating of 3.5 or more (on a scale of 1 to 5) is considered premium grade; these generally represent the best value. Performance ratings are shown on the label on the backside of the carpet sample.

Look at the carpet's density and twist: Thick yarns packed closely together resist wear better. Don't be deceived by carpet weight; a poor-quality carpet

What's your style?

Here's a simple way to match your carpet style with your personal style and décor.

Traditional

Do you like formal lines and elegant dinner parties? Rich, velvety plush carpets impart a stately touch. One of the new patterns with tone-on-tone florals, vines and swirls would also be appropriate.

Casual

Do you exude warmth and a welcome feeling to all who enter your home? Look at textured, twist and shag carpets as well as carpets with level or patterned loops.

Contemporary

Do you prefer a polished style with clean lines and an urban feel? Consider patterned or textured carpets with a geometric design.

Eclectic

Are you an independent thinker whose style ranges across many categories. Do your own thing with prints, patterns and colors that pop. Mix and match different styles in each room while staying in the same color family.

Here's how to order from Costco

- Call the Costco in-home design service toll-free at 1-888-992-2773 to schedule a complimentary in-home appointment with a designer.
- A designer will come to your home with carpet samples to review.
- You select the style and color and the designer will measure your floor and provide a quote for the job to cover the carpet and installation.
- You approve the quote and the designer writes up the contract.
- Your order is placed and managed through client services.

with high pile height will weigh more than a good-quality carpet with low pile height.

Two final points. Most carpets come with some kind of treatment to inhibit staining and soiling. Look for a branded treatment such as Stainmaster. And be sure the carpet has an anti-static treatment, preferably filaments embedded within the fibers.

Don't ignore what's underneath your carpet

A carpet is only as good as the cushion or pad underneath it. Why? Because a quality cushion reduces matting and crushing, which decreases pile height and causes that worn-out look. Be sure to follow the carpet manufacturer's recommendation when purchasing a pad.

Know the seller

Where you buy a carpet can be as important as what you purchase. Look for a reputable source that stands behind both the product and the installation and will handle the entire job from start to finish. The seller should offer professional guidance to enable you to achieve a solution just right for your situation. Look for a dealer that sells only premium-grade carpet—from a quality mill, such as Shaw Industries—that will last as long as you need it to.

Get professional help

Buying carpet is a significant investment, so do it right. Work with a professional designer who knows about carpet and design. Look for someone who can help you make the right selection based upon your color, style and functional needs, and who will give you the confidence to go for a look that's all your own: your personal fashion statement. Ask for an in-home consultation to look at samples and get help with the selection. This is often complimentary, and is well worth the time. Carpet buying is a complex process worthy of professional guidance. It's a sure-fire way to gain all the confidence you need to make the right carpet choice. ▲

Sticky solutions

YOU BOUGHT A ROLL of that porous, spongy shelf liner, lined all your shelves and drawers, and you still have half a roll left over. You could stash it in the garage for three years, or come up with some unique ways to use it up.

This stuff is sticky, so it would come in handy to:
- Hold area rugs in place
- Keep chair pads from slipping
- Line a tackle or tool box
- Put under your CDs to keep the stack from sliding over
- Use as a disposable bathtub mat
- Line the trunk of your car to keep stuff from sliding around
- Wrap your steering wheel
- Grip a jar lid to open
- Put under a cutting board to keep it from slipping

It's cushiony, so you could use it to:
- Put between plates for storage
- Wrap Christmas ornaments
- Protect jewelry and other small items when traveling
- Wad up and stuff inside packages for mailing
- Cut to fit inside your shoes as an insole cushion
- Line a glasses case
- Pad furniture to protect the floor

It has holes in it, so it could be useful:
- For sponge painting
- As a sink strainer
- To line a hanging basket
- To protect the floor under boots and shoes

These are just a few of the hundreds of home and office applications for this innovative product.

If you have an unusual use, let us know. For each idea we use in our next Household Almanac, we'll pay $50. See page xi for details.

Still more uses

Bookmark
Car floor mat
Car seat cover
Car window shade
Coaster
Cutouts for card making
Dashboard cover
Fun tablecloth or individual placemats
 cut out in great shapes
Game-table cover
Gentle dish scrubber
Jewelry-case liner
Liner between mattress and box spring
Picture-frame backing
Protect floor under wood at fireplace
Put under furniture for balance
Vacuum-cleaner edge padding
Window covering
Yoga mat

Saving energy at home

KEEPING ENERGY COSTS DOWN at home is a smart move for a couple of reasons: It saves you money, and it's good for the environment. The good news is that many energy-saving steps don't require significant expenditures: They can be as small as changing light bulbs or adding insulation strips around doors. And in many cases, saving energy is simply a matter of changing habits.

Here are some energy-smart tips for the home from Energy Star, a government-backed program that promotes energy conservation.

Seal your home

If you add up all the hidden air leaks in your home, they can equal a hole the size of an open window—and can lead to higher energy bills by allowing heat or cool air to escape. Sealing air leaks and adding insulation—paying special attention to the attic and basement, where the biggest gaps and cracks are often found—will keep air inside where it belongs and help your equipment perform more efficiently. For more information, get the Environmental Protection Agency's (EPA) "Guide to Energy-Efficient Heating and Cooling" and "A DIY Guide to ENERGY STAR Home Sealing" at *www.energystar.gov*.

Maintain your equipment

Dirt and neglect are the No. 1 causes of heating- and cooling-system failure. Schedule a fall checkup of your heating system with a licensed contractor. Also, clean or change your system's air filter once a month to prevent increased energy costs and system failure. You'll recoup the costs of maintenance through lower energy bills.

Use a thermostat

Using a programmable thermostat to regulate your home's temperature saves energy by offering convenient, preprogrammed temperature settings that scale temperatures down when you are away and up when you return. This can save as much as $150 every year in energy costs.

Use a ceiling fan

Even in winter a ceiling fan can help improve comfort. Most fans have a switch that allows you to reverse the motor and operate the ceiling fan at low speed in the clockwise direction. This produces a gentle updraft, which forces warm air near the ceiling down into the occupied space. For the summer, fans cool people by creating a wind-chill effect against their skin. So there's no reason to leave the fan on when nobody is in the room.

Change your lights

Replacing traditional light bulbs with new compact fluorescent lights (CFLs) can significantly reduce your energy usage. CFLs provide the same amount of light while requiring less energy than older lights.—*Tim Talevich*

It's in the label

Equipment such as computers, printers, refrigerators, fans and air conditioners that meet Energy Star requirements use less energy. They do this by smart design and by "sleep" functions that turn down the machines when they're not in use. The Energy Star label can now be found on some 50 types of products.

There's an added bonus to adopting energy-saving tips and appliances. They help protect the environment. Expect to save about 20 percent annually on total energy costs—while being a good environmental citizen.

Energy Star, a joint program of the EPA and the U.S. Department of Energy, offers more energy-saving tips for homes on its Web site, *www.energy star.gov/home*. Energy Star also offers an interactive feature on its Web site for information about your particular home setting. Click on "Home Energy Yardstick" to access this feature.

ALL GREAT GATHERINGS START AT THE TABLE.

© 2007 Lifetime Products, Inc.

A

B

C

A. Feit Electric Conserv-Energy Compact Fluorescent Reflector Lamps
These bulbs save energy and last four times longer than standard incandescent bulbs. Available for indoor and outdoor use. Item #877533, 877397, 877748

B. Kawasaki Cordless Drill/Driver Set
Featuring 19.2 volts of power, this combo unit features 24 torque settings, various titanium drill bits, two one-hour rechargeable batteries and a built-in light. Item #148476

C. Angelus Manufacturing Hand Truck
This convertible hand truck easily hauls 850 pounds upright and 750 pounds in platform mode. Handle adjusts from 47" to 56". Also features 10" pneumatic tires, 9" x 18" toe plate, and plastic frame runners and fenders for added protection. Item #535167

D. Samsonite Padded Folding Chair
Featuring an extra-wide 16" x 16" solid steel seat that adds strength, safety and comfort, this folding chair also features a tubular steel Y frame, triple-welded leg braces, powder-coat finish and plastic leg caps. Made in the USA. Item #253029

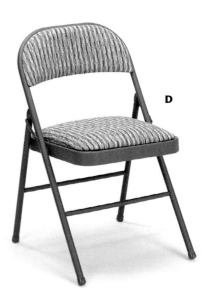

D

E

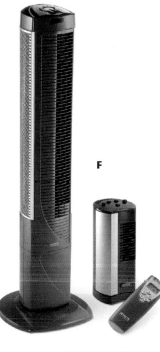

F

E. A. Joffe Bookcase

Featuring a warm cherry finish with tempered glass shelves and wood-veneer shelves. A three-way light and touch dimmer switch included. Dimensions: 84.78" H x 52.58" W x 15.18" D. Item #951639

F. Seville Classics UltraSlimline Fan Pack

This combo-pack features one 40" floor fan and one 12" personal fan, each perfect for your home, office, commercial space or anyplace there is need for a breeze. Item #142661

G. Safety First Multi-use Ladder System

This 21' two-story extension ladder features an exclusive platform step, slip-resistant footing, positive locking hinges and dual climbing surfaces. Designed for indoor and outdoor use. Item #986532

G

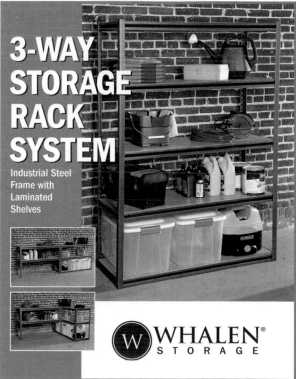

3-WAY STORAGE RACK SYSTEM

Industrial Steel Frame with Laminated Shelves

W WHALEN® STORAGE

Clean House!

The simple and easy way to keep your house, home office and work spaces clean and dust free!

Home Offices

Craft and Work Areas

For more cleaning tips and products, visit us online at:
www.dust-off.com.

Available in a 4-Pack

Item #126555

Palm Key™ Ceiling Fan
- Cocoa Finish
- 5 Antique Halifax Plank Blades
- Amber Scavo Light Bowl with Resin Trim Ring

Island Breeze™ Patio Fan
- New Bronze Finish
- 5 Dark Plastic Bacara Blades
- Includes Accessory Table and Accessory Light Kit

Item #126587

Legendary Hemingway style comes home!

ERNEST HEMINGWAY® COLLECTION FANS

The bold style and adventurous spirit of Ernest Hemingway live on in two new Ernest Hemingway® collection fans from Hunter. Each is a unique blend of the straightforward and the sophisticated, as crisp, clean lines combine with exotic touches worthy of a world traveler.

Ernest Hemingway®

The Ernest Hemingway® collection is a trademark of Hemingway Ltd. and under exclusive license through Fashion Licensing of America, Inc. 212-370-0770.

© 2007 Hunter Fan Company

Reclaim your garage

AT THE BEGINNING OF THE last century, homes began being built with garages to accommodate an exciting new invention called the horseless carriage. Today, according to the National Association of Home Builders, 82 percent of homes have a garage that holds two or more cars—yet, ironically, only 15 percent of people park their cars in them. Why? In many cases, the garage is a catchall, storing everything from garden tools to exercise equipment to discarded appliances, leaving no room for cars.

The good news is that if you organize your garage you will gain a storage center, the ability to find things easily—and covered parking.

Before you start

Before you tackle the task of cleaning your garage, take a look at what's in it. Note items that are stored properly and those that are lying around. A few shelving units, inexpensive overhead cabinets and a tool caddy or two may be all you need to organize the area.

One of the simplest and most affordable ways to take advantage of the potential storage your open wall space offers is to install Pegboard. This old-school hardware staple can be screwed right into the open studs of your garage walls (assuming wallboard doesn't prevent this), and with the various hooks available for Pegboard you can hang a myriad of useful items on your wall.

If you like being able to change things easily, a modular garage system allows you to add, move or remove cabinets as needed. This type of system consists of slotted panels that are attached to garage walls. Cabinets, shelves

To have little is to possess. To have plenty is to be perplexed.

—Lao-tzu

and organizers slip right into the slotted panels but are not fixed permanently.

After considering how you might optimize your garage, think about how you'd like to use it as well. You might want to designate a special area for hobbies such as woodworking, playing music, sewing or even tinkering with cars in the free space that will open up in your soon-to-be-organized garage.

Before buying what you need to outfit your garage, consider the floor. You can improve traction, facilitate cleaning and improve the appearance of your garage by installing garage flooring or having it professionally installed. Popular garage flooring options include interlocking tiles and textured flooring that rolls out like vinyl, but epoxy paint is an affordable alternative.

Six steps to an organized garage

The following strategy will help with the hands-on work of cleaning and organizing your garage.

1. **Make a date.** If your garage has become really disorganized, it could take an entire weekend to bring order to the chaos. Plan your cleaning party on a dry weekend, as you'll most likely be pulling all kinds of things out of their shelter temporarily.

2. **Get some help.** Hire or recruit a team of workers to help you tackle this project or you may end up getting overwhelmed. If you ask family and friends, be sure to have an organized plan to direct your helpers from start to finish.

3. **The big reckoning.** Take a look at everything that's currently in your garage. Ask yourself if you really want each item to stay in the garage, or could it go somewhere else? For instance, could seasonal gear go in the attic? Would it make sense to store some of the gardening tools and supplies in a garden shed?

4. **Get into it.** Once you've scheduled a date, made arrangements to get help and decided what to do with the items in your garage, it's time to begin pulling every item out of your garage and grouping them in areas: one for items that will go back in the garage, one for items that will be taken to the dump and one that will be donated to Goodwill, the Salvation Army or another local thrift shop.

5. **Resettle the space.** Install the garage accouterments you purchased and put all the temporarily displaced items in their new homes.

6. **Reap the reward.** Once everything is back in its place, slowly pull your car into its new spot. Turn the engine off and take a deep breath. Sit a moment and bask in the tranquillity your newly organized garage affords you.—*Will Fifield*

Gadgets to go

WHILE MANY MODERN vehicles feature all sorts of electronic and mechanical gadgetry for creature comfort and safety, there are plenty of add-ons on the market for those who are driving older models or who found the manufacturer's options a bit too pricey. The criteria for the items described here are that they have to be usable out of the box or easily installed. In some cases, they are also meant for relatively late-model automobiles. (Items listed are not necessarily endorsed by Costco.)

GPS devices

GPS stands for Global Positioning System and covers a range of products that give you real-time navigation assistance. While women may believe it was created to help men avoid the embarrassment of asking for directions, it was originally developed by the U.S. Department of Defense for military purposes.

Aided by a network of 24 satellites in Earth orbit, GPS systems calculate a vehicle's position and can provide directions to a given location accurate to within an average of approximately 15 meters, or a little more than 49 feet.

GPS systems can be ordered as installed options in new vehicles or purchased separately. Manufacturers such as Garmin, JVC and Magellan offer portable models that work right out of the box and can be carried in a briefcase for the mobile worker who frequently changes vehicles. Many models even offer entertainment capabilities, such as satellite radio, MP3 players and photo viewers. Just don't forget to watch the road.

On-board entertainment

Numerous devices are available to keep you and your passengers from crying, "Are we there yet?"

Satellite radio. Proponents of satellite radio proclaim it the answer to all broadcast woes. It offers crystal-clear reception, little or no advertising, a wide variety of programming and no censorship. The current major program providers, Sirius and XM, offer more than 100 channels of music, talk, news, weather and sports.

DVD players. While some cars may already include an on-board DVD player as an option, there's no need to go without if your vehicle didn't come with one. Overhead entertainment units are available from costco.com, some with installation included. Portable, handheld DVD players can be purchased at costco.com and in the warehouse, with no installation required.

Radar detectors

The term "radar detector" is used as an umbrella category for devices that sense when signals are being aimed at your vehicle. There are varying technologies today, radar being only one of them, but the name has become part of the vernacular.

There is a wide range of detectors using different technologies and features, depending on price. Some are designed to detect any type of signal, while others are dedicated to one technology or another. Some offer audio as well as visual alerts. Some include additional tools, such as a compass or a memo voice recorder. Some make claims that don't hold up upon testing. It is wise to do a little research before buying.

While the primary intent of these devices is to alert the driver that law enforcement is monitoring the speed of passing traffic, they are legal in most of the United States, except Virginia and Washington, D.C. Restrictions on the types of detectors that are acceptable exist in several states. Because the technology used by police is keeping pace with the technology available to drivers, you might want to be aware of any restrictions to be sure you're not caught breaking the law in more ways than one. Of course, the easiest way to avoid a speeding ticket is to not go over the speed limit.

Remote entry

Many cars today offer keyless remote entry as a standard feature. However, if you have an older model and would like this feature but aren't ready to buy a new car, check out the range of kits on the market. If you have mechanical automotive expertise, you may be able to install one yourself. If not, your neighborhood mechanic may be able to do the task in as little as one to two hours. Your car should have power door locks in order for this to work.

Keyless entry systems come in different varieties. Some merely open the doors. Others are tied to alarm systems, anti-theft engine cutoff and remote starters. What will work in any particular car is tied to the functionality of the vehicle. For instance, remote trunk-opening capability cannot be used with cars that have mechanical trunk openers as opposed to electronic openers.

Portable power supply

There's nothing worse than jumping in your car to go somewhere, turning the key and having nothing happen. The battery is dead. Even if you have jumper cables, there's no guarantee a willing jumper will be available. If you belong to an automotive association, you can call for roadside assistance, then wait an hour for a repair truck to arrive.

Rather than leave your fate in the hands of random strangers, rechargeable portable power units are available for anywhere from around $50 up to stow in the trunk for such an emergency. These units all allow you to jump-start your car. Many offer additional capabilities, such as air compressors, which allow you to pump your tires and sports equipment; emergency lights; and radios. The units may be recharged at home or in your auto.

If you're an avid camper, portable units usually can also power other devices, such as televisions, camcorders, laptops and cell phones. No need to completely rough it!

Refrigerator/warmer

When going on a long road trip, the experienced traveler often packs bottles of beverages and snacks to avoid having to stop any more than necessary. Keeping them cold or warm is another story and frequently involves carrying a cooler packed with ice, which might begin to leak or collect condensation over the course of the trip. This may lead to wet seats, and potential hernias from trying to remove the water-sodden unit at the end of the trip.

Thanks to modern ingenuity, portable storage devices that plug into your car power source and can hold multiple cans of beverages, as well as other perishable items, are available. Many may also be used in the home or dorm. Some offer additional features, such as radios, CD/DVD storage and pockets to hold corkscrews, can openers or other utensils.

Car chips

If you'd like to know how well your car is functioning without racking up an expensive mechanic bill or are curious as to how your teenager is handling the family auto while out with friends, the technology is here today. Computer chips are on the market that easily plug into a car and report back to a computer, allowing you to:

- Record key trip information, with departure times, distances traveled and speeds recorded every five seconds
- Discern between business and personal usage, facilitating easy expense reports
- Check engine function, including rpm, engine load, fuel pressure, battery voltage, timing advance, airflow rate and more
- Calculate gas mileage and test emissions
- Monitor a kid's or employee's driving habits

The chips even act as "black boxes" in the event of an accident, recording the final 20 seconds before impact, which may help your insurance claim. The cost is modest; the chips retail for less than $200, including software and USB cable.

Car-seat massage/heat cushions

One of the options in some cars is heated seats, but you don't have to up your monthly payment by opting for this add-on. Cushions are available that slip over existing seat cushions and plug into your auto's power source.

Some models offer heat only, promising to ease tension and relax sore, aching muscles. Others also offer vibrating massage, and some provide vibrating massage, soothing heat and magnetic therapy. All can be found for less than $100.

Of course, if all these options are confusing you, simply contact the Costco Auto Buying Program and start shopping for a new car, fully loaded.

—Steve Fisher

Car maintenance for the automotively challenged

THERE ARE THINGS the mechanically unschooled can do to keep a car running smoothly and efficiently as long as possible. (Consult your owner's manual for specific recommendations from your car's manufacturer.)

Engine oil

Check your oil monthly when the car is cool and parked on a level surface. Remove the dipstick, wipe it with a paper towel or rag and note the markings, usually "FULL" or "ADD." Insert it again, then remove and recheck. If it is below "ADD," remove the engine cap and add oil according to the manufacturer's recommendations. Never fill past the "FULL" mark. If the oil is dark, change it promptly. Oil should be changed approximately every 3,000 miles. Engine oil should never be white or foamy or smell like gasoline. With newer cars, not changing oil on schedule may void the warranty.

Transmission fluid

Check your transmission fluid monthly or if the transmission is not functioning well. Transmission fluid should be checked while the car is running, or at least warmed up. Some cars may be different. To be sure, consult your owner's manual. Locate the automatic transmission fluid (ATF) dipstick toward the rear of the engine and remove it. Wipe with a paper towel or rag, then reinsert. Check the level again. Some ATF dipsticks have two sets of markings — one for "WARM," one for "COLD." The fluid should be pink or red and have the consistency of cough syrup. If your vehicle is low on fluid, that's often a sign there's a leak. See a certified mechanic.

Brake fluid

Locate the brake master cylinder at the rear of the engine. Late-model cars may use clear cylinders. Older cars may have metal containers with a clamp on the top, which could require a screwdriver to pop off. The cap may have the words "USE ONLY DOT 3 OR 4 BRAKE FLUID." It is normal for the brake-fluid level to ebb as your brake pads wear. If fluid is needed, use fluid from a sealed container only and open the reservoir for only the time needed to replace it. Brake fluid must keep a high boiling point; air in the reservoir adds moisture and decreases it. The fluid is highly toxic, so keep it away from your hands, eyes and the automobile's paint. Do not allow it to spill on the ground. Dispose of used containers by depositing in a hazardous-waste container.

Power steering fluid

When you check the fluid level, it should not deviate from the "NORMAL" mark. If you find you have to add fluid more than once or twice a year, have the system checked for leaks. As with the transmission system, driving with a subnormal fluid level can easily damage the steering system. If you hear a buzzing or wheezing noise when you turn the wheel, that's a sign of low fluid.

Battery

Many car batteries claim to be maintenance free, meaning you don't need to check the water. But you should check your battery to be sure it is clean and dry, and corrosion free around the terminals. If corrosion is present, use a wire brush with a solution of baking soda and water to remove it. If moisture and corrosion are always present, have a mechanic check it.

Coolant (antifreeze) level

If you must open the radiator cap to check the coolant level, be sure the car is cool. The contents of the radiator are under extremely high pressure and, if hot, could erupt like a geyser, with the liquid exceeding the temperature of boiling water. Check the reserve tank first. It is usually a translucent container near the radiator and will have two markings—"FULL" and "LOW." The fluid level should be somewhere in between. If the reserve tank is empty, add coolant and water (in a 50-50 ratio) directly into the radiator. If the level continuously falls to "LOW" or below, you should have the system checked by a mechanic.

Belts and hoses

You can tell a lot about belts and hoses just by looking at them. With the car cool, try to squeeze the radiator hose. It, and the belts, should be free from cracks and brittleness and should feel firm to the pinch. Visibly inspect for any ballooning. Check the belts for proper tension, as well as cracks and wear.

Tires

All tires should be inflated according to manufacturer guidelines and free from extreme wear. Do the penny test to determine tread health. Insert a penny into the tread with Lincoln's head pointing into the tread. If you can see the top of the head, it's time for new tires. If you are putting air in a tire frequently, there is probably a leak. Tires should wear evenly, across all four tires. If one tire, or one side of tires, appears to be wearing disproportionately to the others, you may need a wheel alignment.—*Steve Fisher*

Sources: www.familycar.com; *How to Do Just About Everything, Simon & Schuster (2000)*

Servicing guidelines

If your vehicle does not have its own list of when to go for a checkup and what to have checked, use these guidelines.

7,500 miles. Get a lubrication, change oil and oil filter, rotate tires, check brakes and perform a complete safety check.

11,250 miles. Change oil and oil filter.

15,000 miles. Get a lubrication, change oil and oil filter, rotate tires, check brakes, check transmission, clean air filter and perform a complete safety check.

18,750 miles. Change oil and oil filter.

22,500 miles. Get a lubrication, change oil and oil filter, rotate tires, check brakes and perform a complete safety check.

26,250 miles. Change oil and oil filter.

30,000 miles. Get a lubrication, change oil and oil filter, rotate tires, check brakes, replace air filter, replace spark plugs, adjust valves (unless hydraulic), check timing, flush brake fluid, change transmission fluid, flush cooling system and perform a complete safety check.—*SF*
Source: Autowcb

Generator safety

BACKUP GENERATORS can literally and figuratively save your bacon when storms or rolling blackouts temporarily knock out electrical service to your home. But when you buy a generator, be sure to get one that will deliver enough power for your needs.

To determine the wattage you will need, look at the labels on lighting, appliances and equipment you plan on powering with the generator. The data plates on these appliances will usually specify the number of volts and amps they require. Multiply volts by amps to get the wattage. Many appliances list both "run wattage" and "surge wattage." As the term suggests, run wattage is the amount of electricity required to continuously run appliances. Surge wattage is the higher amount of electricity required to start electric engines. Choose a generator that produces more power than you will actually use because of the big draw when these devices are initially turned on. If you get stumped, ask an electrician to determine how many watts your generator should deliver.

While generators can be lifesavers when your utility power is out, improperly operating a generator can result in carbon monoxide poisoning, shock or electrocution and fire. The following tips can help you avoid these hazards.

To avoid carbon monoxide poisoning
- Always use the generator outdoors, away from doors, windows and vents.
- Follow the manufacturer's instructions.
- Install battery-operated or plug-in (with battery backup) carbon monoxide alarms in your home; follow the manufacturer's instructions.
- Frequently test carbon monoxide alarms and replace batteries when needed.

To avoid electrical hazards
- Keep the generator dry and operate on a dry surface under an open canopy-like structure.
- Dry your hands before touching the generator.
- Plug appliances directly into the generator or use a heavy-duty outdoor-rated extension cord. Make sure the entire extension cord is free of cuts and tears and that the plug has all three prongs, especially the grounding pin.
- Never plug the generator into a wall outlet. This practice, known as backfeeding, can create an electrocution risk to utility workers and others served by the same utility transformer.

To avoid fire hazards
- Before refueling the generator, turn it off and let it cool. Fuel spilled on hot engine parts can ignite.
- Store fuel outside in properly labeled, non-glass containers and away from any fuel-burning appliance, such as a natural-gas water heater in a garage. Local laws may restrict the amount of fuel you can store and/or where you store it.—*Will Fifield*

For more information about backup generator safety, visit the following sources

- The United States Fire Administration, *www.usfa.dhs.gov/safety/co/ generators.htm*; (301) 447-1000

- The American Red Cross, *www.red cross.org/services/disaster/ 0,1082,0_565_,00.html*

- The Consumer Product Safety Commission, *www.cpsc.gov/ CPSCPUB/PUBS/portgen.pdf*

Make sure your gourmet salmon and bulk paper towels always get home safe and sound.

Costco prices aren't the only thing that puts your mind at ease. Michelin® tires give you confidence on the road. Ask a Michelin certified tire technician at Costco about HydroEdge® tires for your car, LTX® tires for your truck, or Cross Terrain® tires for your SUV. These tires are all engineered to give you great grip and handling for a long, long time.

DURACELL ®

ARE YOU READY?

Stock Up Today!

USE & CARE TIPS

Use the correct size and type of battery specified by the manufacturer of your device.

Keep battery contact surfaces and battery compartment contacts clean by rubbing them with a clean pencil eraser or a rough cloth each time you replace batteries.

Remove batteries from a device when it is not expected to be in use for several months. Remove batteries from equipment while it is being powered by household (AC) current.

Make sure that you insert batteries into your device properly, with the (+) and (-) terminals aligned correctly. CAUTION: Some equipment using more than 3 batteries may appear to work properly even if one battery is inserted incorrectly. Store batteries in a dry place at normal room temperature. Do not refrigerate DURACELL Batteries.This will not make them last longer. Most DURACELL Batteries will provide dependable long life even after 5 years of storage in these conditions. Extreme temperatures reduce battery performance. Avoid putting battery-powered devices in very warm places.

TRUSTED EVERYWHERE®

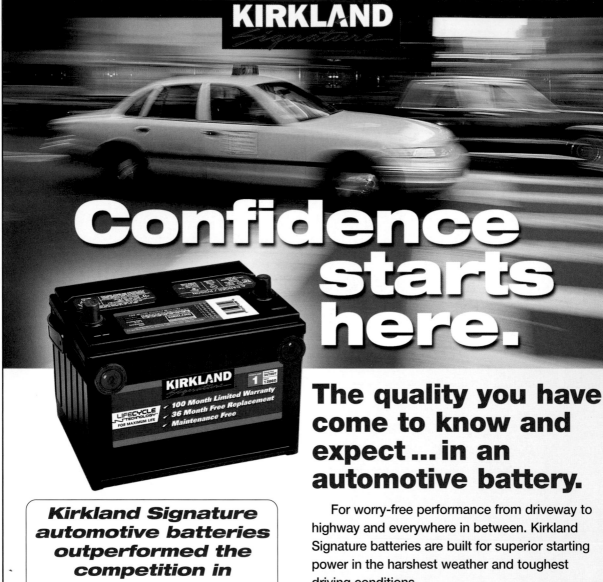

KIRKLAND
Signature

Confidence starts here.

KIRKLAND *Signature*
- 100 Month Limited Warranty
- 36 Month Free Replacement
- Maintenance Free

LIFECYCLE TECHNOLOGY
FOR MAXIMUM LIFE

The quality you have come to know and expect ... in an automotive battery.

For worry-free performance from driveway to highway and everywhere in between. Kirkland Signature batteries are built for superior starting power in the harshest weather and toughest driving conditions.

And because heat is the enemy of batteries, we tested our batteries in the brutal heat of Las Vegas—in hard-running taxicabs. One hundred million starts later, Kirkland Signature batteries have been proven to easily outlast the competition.

Kirkland Signature batteries also feature patented Lifecycle™ technology for maximum power. Turn the key with confidence. Guaranteed to meet or beat the standards of leading national brands.

Kirkland Signature automotive batteries outperformed the competition in real-life testing!

Tested in Taxicab Fleet

MILEAGE INDEX

Kirkland Signature	**100%**
Competitor A	**87%**
Competitor B	**42%**

2004 Competitive Fleet: Grp 65 (Sequence 130) Installation April 2004 Las Vegas

Kirkland Signature automotive batteries are available exclusively at Costco.

Vehicle Care Technology for Improved Protection and Performance

PRO-GARD FIC

PRO-GARD® Fuel Injector Cleaner utilizes Techron® technology to remove deposits from fuel injectors that can cause hesitation or loss of power. It also can help to remove water to fight gas line freeze and restores clogged fuel injectors to like-new cleanliness in one tankful. It is safe for use every 1,000 miles/1,600 km or as needed to keep fuel injectors clean.

ATF MD-3

Chevron ATF MD-3 is formulated with ISO-SYN™ base oil stocks for extra oxidation protection. Additionally, robust additives ensure excellent oxidation stability, optimal frictional properties and long service life.

Havoline

Havoline® Motor Oils with new Deposit Shield™ formula are designed to provide extra deposit protection for a cleaner, smoother running engine. While all grades meet API-SM requirements, multi-grades, SAE 5W-20, 5W-30 and 10W-30 meet API energy conserving and ILSAC G-4 standards for improved fuel economy. The new Deposit Shield formula provides advanced deposit control, patented antioxidant technology and superior viscosity control.
(Available in select Costco stores.)

Supreme 10W-30

Chevron Supreme Motor Oils are superior quality automotive engine oil. While all grades meet API-SM requirements, multi-grades, SAE 5W-20, 5W-30 and 10W-30 meet ILSAC G-4 standards for improved fuel economy. They are formulated with ISOSYN™ base oil for extra oxidation protection. Chevron Supreme offers excellent viscosity control, oxidation stability and deposit control that promotes long engine life.

Chevron Delo® 400 LE

Chevron Delo 400 LE is an industry-leading, premium-quality heavy duty motor oil that exceeds industry and engine manufacturers' performance requirements. Chevron Delo 400 LE can be used in both new low emission engines with ULSD (2007 engines and beyond) and pre-2007 engines. It is backward compatible with prior engine oil categories and suitable for top-off. Chevron Delo 400 LE helps reduce maintenance costs through exceptional soot dispersancy and wear control. It helps keep your diesel engines running smoothly by controlling piston deposits.

Chevron

Our Family of Brands

OIL, EVIDENTLY, IS NOT JUST OIL.

Mercedes-Benz AMG recommends Mobil 1

Mitsubishi Lancer Evolution recommends Mobil 1

Viper recommends Mobil 1

Corvette recommends Mobil 1

Aston Martin recommends Mobil 1

Cadillac XLR recommends Mobil 1

Mobil 1 is original equipment in many of the world's finest automobiles and recommended by their makers for good reason. Mobil 1 is a leader in anti-wear technology— we prove it every day on the track and on the road. And Mobil 1 with SuperSyn is the most advanced Mobil 1 engine protection ever. For more information, call 1-800-ASK-MOBIL or log on to www.mobiloil.com.

THE MORE YOU KNOW ABOUT MOBIL 1, THE BETTER IT IS FOR YOUR CAR.

COSTCO WHOLESALE

Official Motor Oil of ///// NASCAR.

Mobil 1

Multi-Season Protection

Protect your vehicle with our heavy-duty, four-piece, all-weather rubber floor-mat set

- Traps and contains moisture, dirt and debris
- Patented raised rib design
- Raised border for protection
- Anti-skid nib backing
- Fits domestic and import vehicles
- Available in tan or gray

KRACO
SINCE 1954

Turtle Wax ICE Car Wash
Turtle Wax ICE Car Wash delivers thick, rich suds that gently wash away dirt, road grime and dust, leaving behind an incredible sparkling-clean shine.
Item #156553

Turtle Wax ICE Liquid and Detailer Combo Pack
Turtle Wax ICE is formulated to deliver a brilliant, mirror-like shine and long-lasting durability to your car's surface without leaving white residue.
Item #131364

The ideal driving companion from the first name in GPS™

Have you ever found yourself stumped while looking for an address in an unfamiliar part of town or in a new city? Have you ever had the meeting location changed on you — and your printed directions were to get to the original address? Magellan has many solutions for you.

Maestro Series

Magellan® RoadMate™ Series

Only on Magellan

Why buy a Magellan GPS?
- The easiest to use – just turn it on and go!™
- Pre-loaded database of ATMs, gas stations, restaurants, hotels...
- No monthly fees
- Hands free calling with compatible Bluetooth® phones*
- Pre-loaded with maps of the US and Canada*
- Live Traffic Services can reroute you around highway problems*[1]
- Maesto™ series is the only vehicle navigation GPS with built-in AAA TourBook® travel information and Roadside Assistance details[2]

MAGELLAN®

magellanGPS.com

DO ALL YOU CAN TO HELP PROTECT YOUR FAMILY.

*Did you know that **a home fire can double in size every 30 seconds***? And that **carbon monoxide is the #1 cause of accidental poisoning death** in America**?*

Smoke alarms help provide early warning of smoke or fire. According to the NFPA, they should be placed on every level of a home and in every bedroom for maximum protection. The sooner you know about a fire, the sooner you can get your family outside!

3-Pack of Battery Operated Smoke Alarms with silence button; Item #290541

It's easy to use a fire extinguisher! Just remember to P.A.S.S.: Pull the pin, Aim low, Squeeze the lever, Sweep across the base of the fire.

2-Pack of First Alert 1-A:10-B:C rated Multi-Purpose Household Fire Extinguisher; Item #540002

3-A:40-B:C rated Heavy Duty Commercial Fire Extinguisher suitable for businesses; Item #540003

Carbon monoxide (CO) is an invisible, odorless gas and can hurt or kill you before you know it's there. It can be produced by common household appliances like a furnace, clothes dryer, stove or water heater, and also by a running car. When not vented properly, it can build up and cause problems. For maximum protection, CO alarms should be placed on every level of your home and inside each bedroom.

Plug-in Carbon Monoxide Alarm with Battery Back-up and Digital Display; Item #155016

*Source: National Fire Protection Association
**Source: Journal of American Medical Association
©2006 BRK Brands, Inc. A Subsidiary of Jarden Corporation. Aurora, IL 60542
First Alert® is registered trademark of the First Alert Trust. All rights reserved.

First Alert®

3M Company, *105*
3M Center
St. Paul, MN 55144
800-3M-HELPS
www.3m.com

A Joffe Furniture, *187*
2100 East Slauson Avenue
Huntington Park, CA 90255
800-765-9035
www.ajoffe.com

ACCO Brands Corporation, *106*
300 Tower Parkway
Lincolnshire, IL 60069-3640
800-541-0094
www.acco.com

Adobe Systems Inc., *120*
345 Park Avenue
San Jose, CA 95110-2704
408-536-6000
www.adobe.com

Advanced Micro Devices, *103*
One AMD Place
Sunnyvale, CA 94088-3453
408-749-4000
www.amd.com

AgroLabs Inc., *50, 63*
225 Long Avenue
Hillside, NJ 07205
817-410-2140
www.agrolabs.com

Alltrade Tools LLC, *186*
1431 Via Plata
Long Beach, CA 90810-1462
800-368-6653
www.alltradetools.com

Angelus Mfg., *186*
5431 Brooks Street
Montclair, CA 91763
800-748-7779

**Aveeno, Johnson & Johnson
Group of Consumer
Companies,** *67*
199 Grandview Road
Skillman, NJ 08558
www.aveeno.com

Avenues Inc., *138*
750 Hope Road
Tinton Falls, NJ 07724
732-935-1700
www.avenuesusa.com

**Avery Dennison Consumer
Service Center,** *104*
P.O. Box 129
Brea, CA 92822
800-GO-AVERY
www.avery.com

**Band-Aid, Johnson & Johnson
Group of Consumer
Companies,** *35*
199 Grandview Road
Skillman, NJ 08558
www.band-aid.com

Beiersdorf Inc., *68*
187 Danbury Road
Wilton, CT 06897
203-563-5800
www.niveausa.com

Belkin Inc., *21*
501 West Walnut Street
Compton, CA 90220
800-223-5546
www.belkin.com

Body Choice Inc., *52, 66*
1802 N. Carson Street, Suite 212
Carson City, NV 89701
866-956-7546
www.bodychoicenutrition.net

Borghese, *60*
10 East 34th Street, 3rd Floor
New York, NY 10016
800-409-0091
www.borghese.com

Bushnell Outdoor Products, *124*
9200 Cody
Overland Park, KS 66214
800-423-3537
www.bushnell.com

Canon U.S.A. Inc., *103, 136*
One Canon Plaza
Lake Success, NY 11042
800-OK-CANON
www.usa.canon.com

Chevron Corporation, *201*
6101 Bollinger Canyon Road
Building BR1
San Ramon, CA 94583-5177
925-842-1000
www.chevron.com

CIBAVision Corporation, *38*
11460 Johns Creek Parkway
Duluth, GA 30097
678-415-3937
www.cibavision.com

Vendor Listing

The Clorox Company, *144, 155, 163, 165*
1221 Broadway Street
Oakland, CA 94612
800-227-1860
www.thecloroxcompany.com

Colgate-Palmolive Company, *44*
300 Park Avenue
New York, NY 10022
800-468-6502
www.colgate.com

Combined Resources International, *121, 137*
www.cri2k.com

Conair Corporation, *82*
1 Cummings Point Road
Stamford, CT 06902
800-726-6247
www.conair.com

Cosco Home and Office Products, *187*
2525 State Street
Columbus, IN 47201
800-457-5276
www.coscoproducts.com

Crayola LLC, *138*
800-CRAYOLA
www.crayola.com

Custom Decorators, *180*
12006 SW Garden Place
Portland, OR 97223
888-992-2773
www.customdecorators.com

Design Optics, *103*
1331 S. State College Boulevard
Fullerton, CA 92831
800-824-4143
www.personaloptics.com

DIRECTV, *19*
2230 E. Imperial Highway
El Segundo, CA 90245
800-531-5000
www.directv.com

Divatex Home Fashions Inc., *82*
295 Fifth Avenue, Suite 515
New York, NY 10016
212-252-0802
www.divatex.com

DiversaFile Everett LLC, *106*
2216 36th Street
Everett, WA 98201
888-387-8723
www.dfellc.com

Dixon Ticonderoga Co., *108*
195 International Parkway
Heathrow, FL 32746
800-824-9430
www.dixonusa.com

DWI Holdings Inc., *80*
2100 Riveredge Pkwy NW, #300
Sandy Springs, GA 30328
800-768-4800
www.dwiholdings.com

Eastman Kodak Company, *106*
343 State Street
Rochester, NY 14650
800-23-KODAK
www.kodak.com

Encore Inc., *92*
999 N. Sepulveda Boulevard
Suite 700
El Segundo, CA 90245
310-768-1800
www.encore.com

E.S. Robbins Corp., *109*
2802 East Avalon Avenue
Muscle Shoals, AL 35661-3748
800-633-3325
www.esrobbins.com

Everbrite GHN Neon, *108*
7472 Chapman Avenue
Garden Grove, CA 92841
714-620-7440
www.neoncentral.com

ExxonMobil, *202*
3225 Gallows Road
Fairfax, VA 22037
800-662-4525
www.mobiloil.com

Falcon Safety Products Inc., *171, 188*
25 Imclone Drive
Branchburg, NJ 08876
908-707-4900
www.falconsafety.com

Feit Electric, *186*
4901 Gregg Road
Pico Rivera, CA 90660
562-463-2852
www.feit.com

Fellowes Inc., *97, 107*
1789 Norwood Avenue
Itasca, IL 60143
800-945-4545
www.fellowes.com

 FHP, *166*
505 Railroad Avenue
Northlake, IL 60164
800-838-0151
www.ocedar.com

 First Alert, *204*
3901 Liberty Street Road
Aurora, IL 60504
800-323-9005
www.firstalert.com

 Fiskars Craft, *138*
2537 Daniels Street
Madison, WI 53718
866-348-5661
www.fiskarscraft.com

FUJIFILM **FujiFilm USA Inc,** *111*
200 Summit Lake Drive
Valhalla, NY 10595
800-755-3854
www.fujifilmusa.com

 Galderma Laboratories, *64*
14501 North Freeway
Fort Worth, TX 76177
817-961-5000
www.cetaphil.com

 **Georgia Pacific Consumer Products LP,** *105, 168*
133 Peachtree Street
Atlanta, GA 30303
800-2TELLGP
www.gp.com

 **GlaxoSmithKline Consumer Healthcare,** *46, 62*
P.O. Box 1467
Pittsburgh, PA 15230
888-825-5249
www.gsk.com

 Graber Custom Window Coverings, *178*
800-538-9419
www.memberblinds.com

 **Hollander Home Fashions,** *84*
6560 West Rogers Circle, Suite 19
Boca Raton, FL 33487
561-997-6900
www.hollander.com

 HoMedics Inc. USA, *82*
3000 Pontiac Trail
Commerce Township, MI 48390
800-466-3342
www.homedics.com

 Hunter Fan Company, *188*
2500 Frisco Avenue
Memphis, TN 38114
888-830-1326
www.hunterfan.com

 Intel Corporation, *6, 23*
2200 Mission College Boulevard
Santa Clara, CA 95052
408-765-8080
www.intel.com

 ITW Space Bag, *80*
7520 Airway Road
San Diego, CA 92154
800-460-0011
www.spacebag.com

 Jasco Products Company, *175*
10 East Memorial Road
Oklahoma City, OK 73114
800-654-8483
www.jascoproducts.com

JointJuice **Joint Juice Inc.,** *67*
444 Spear Street, #105
San Francisco, CA 94105
888-642-9941
www.jointjuice.com

 JVC Company of America, *132, 136*
1700 Valley Road
Wayne, NJ 07470
www.jvc.com

 Kimberly-Clark Corporation, *82*
2100 Winchester Road
Neenah, WI 54956
920-721-2000
www.kcc.com

 Kittrich Corporation, *183*
14555 Alondra Boulevard
La Mirada, CA 90638
714-736-1000
www.kittrich.com

 KJS Industries Inc., *128*
4245 International Boulevard
Norcross, GA 30093
770-638-3434
service@kjsindustries.com

Vendor Listing

 KLH Audio Systems, *21*
11131 Dora Street
Sun Valley, CA 91352
818-767-2843
www.klhaudio.com

 KRACO Enterprises Inc., *203*
505 E. Euclid Avenue
Compton, CA 90224
800-678-1910
www.kraco.com

 Lexmark International, *106*
740 New Circle Road NW
Lexington, KY 40550
800-332-4120
www.lexmark.com

 The Libman Company, *166*
220 N. Sheldon
Arcola, IL 61910
800-646-6262
www.libman.com

 **Lifetime Products Inc.,** *185*
P.O. Box 160010
Clearfield, UT 84016
800-225-3865
www.lifetime.com

 **LitterPurrfect Company,** *166*
info@litterpurrfect.com

 Logitech, *21*
6505 Kaiser Drive
Fremont, CA 94555
800-231-7717
www.logitech.com

 Magellan GPS, *203*
960 Overland Court
San Dimas, CA 91773
909-394-5000
www.magellangps.com

 McNeil Consumer Healthcare,
Johnson & Johnson–Merck
Consumer Pharmaceuticals Co., *64*
7050 Camp Hill Road
Fort Washington, PA 19034
877-TYLENOL
www.tylenol.com

 **Meco Corporation,** *186*
1500 Industrial Road
Greeneville, TN 37745
800-251-7558
www.meco.net

 **Michelin North America Inc.,** *197*
One Parkway South
Greenville, SC 29615
866-866-6605
www.michelinman.com

 **Mitsubishi Electric,** *19*
9351 Jeronimo Road
Irvine, CA 92618-1904
800-332-2119
www.mitsubishi-tv.com

 Nestlé Waters North America, *165*
777 W. Putnam Avenue
Greenwich, CT 06830
203-531-4100
www.nestlewatersnorthamerica.com

 Neutrogena Corporation, *56*
Los Angeles, CA 90045
800-582-4048
www.neutrogena.com

 Nikon Inc., *117, 139*
1300 Walt Whitman Road
Melville, NY 11747
800-645-6687
www.nikonusa.com

 **Olympus America Inc.,** *137*
3500 Corporate Parkway
Center Valley, PA 18034-0610
888-553-4448
www.olympusamerica.com

 **Optoma Technology, Inc.,** *109*
715 Sycamore Drive
Milpitas, CA 95035
408-383-3700
www.optomausa.com

 **Pacific Coast Feather Company,** *81*
1964 Fourth Avenue South
Seattle, WA 98134
888-297-1778
www.pacificcoast.com

 **Pactiv Corporation,** *166*
1900 West Field Court
Lake Forest, IL 60045
847-482-2000
www.pactiv.com

 Panasonic, *26, 164*
One Panasonic Way
Secaucus, NJ 07094
www.panasonic.com

Panasonic Battery Corporation
of North America, *108*
3 Panasonic Way, 7A-3
Secaucus, NJ 07094
www.panasonic.com

peerless

Peerless Industries, Inc., *18*
3215 W. North Avenue
Melrose Park, IL 60160
800-729-0307
www.peerlessmounts.com

PENTAX

Pentax Imaging Company, *138*
600 12th Street, Suite 300
Golden, CO 80401
800-877-0155
www.pentaximaging.com

Spirit of Wonder
Pentel

Pentel, *105*
2715 Columbia Street
Torrance, CA 90503
800-421-1419
www.pentel.com

Nature Made.

Pharmavite LLC, *70*
P.O. Box 9606
Mission Hills, CA 91346-9606
800-276-2878
www.naturemade.com

PHILIPS

Philips Accessories, *108*
1881 Route 46 West
Ledgewood, NJ 07852
888-PHILIPS
www.philips.com

PHILIPS

Philips Consumer Electronics, *27*
64 Perimeter Center East
Atlanta, GA 30046
888-PHILIPS
www.philips.com

PHILIPS

Philips Sonicare, *85*
1010 Washington Boulevard
Stamford, CT 06902
800-682-7664
www.sonicare.com

**Pilot Pen Corporation
of America,** *105*
60 Commerce Drive
Trumbull, CT 06611
203-377-8800
www.pilotpen.us

P&G

Procter & Gamble Company, *85,*
86, 152, 198
2 P&G Plaza
Cincinnati, OH 45202
513-983-1100
www.pg.com

**RECKITT
BENCKISER**

Reckitt Benckiser, *167*
Morris Corporate Center IV
399 Interpace Parkway
Parsippany, NJ 07054
800-333-3899

Ricardo Beverly Hills, *138*
15905 Canary Avenue
La Mirada, CA 90638
800-724-7496
www.ricardobeverlyhills.com

**RoC Division, Johnson &
Johnson Consumer France
s.a.s.,** *68*
92787 Issy CEDEX 9 (Paris) France
www.rocskincare.com

Samsonite

Samsonite, *138*
575 West Street, Suite 110
Mansfield, MA 02048
800-262-8282
www.samsonite.com

SAMSUNG

Samsung, *25*
105 Challenger Road
Ridgefield Park, NJ 07660
800-SAMSUNG
www.samsung.com

SanDisk

SanDisk, *12, 140*
601 McCarthy Boulevard
Milpitas, CA 95035
866-726-3475
www.sandisk.com

SANYO

SANYO Fisher Company, *164*
21605 Plummer Street
Chatsworth, CA 91311
818-998-7322
www.sanyo.com

International Greetings PLC

Scandinavian Design Ltd., *130*
Penallta Industrial Estate
Ystrad Mynach, Mid Glamorgan
CF82 7QZ United Kingdom
0044 (0) 1443 814917
www.internationalgreetings.co.uk

Non-Drowsy
Claritin
Allergy Products

Schering-Plough, *47*
3030 Jackson Avenue
Memphis, TN 38151
www.claritin.com

Schiff.
NUTRITION
INTERNATIONAL

**Schiff Nutrition
International,** *69*
2002 South 5070 West
Salt Lake City, UT 84104
800-526-6251
www.schiffnutrition.com

iHome
www.ihomeaudio.com

SDI Technologies Inc, *23*
1299 Main Street
Rahway, NJ 07065
800-288-2792
www.ihomeaudio.com

Vendor Listing

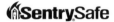

SentrySafe, *108*
900 Linden Avenue
Rochester, NY 14625
www.sentrysafe.com

Seville Classics Inc., *187*
19401 South Harborgate
Torrance, CA 90501
310-533-3800
www.sevilleclassics.com

Sharp Electronics, *28, 164*
One Sharp Plaza
Mahwah, NJ 07430
800-BE-SHARP
www.sharp-usa.com

SONY.

Sony Electronics, *8, 24*
16530 Via Esprillo
San Diego, CA 92127
800-222-SONY
www.sony.com

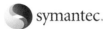

Symantec Corporation, *94*
20330 Stevens Creek Boulevard
Cupertino, CA 95014
408-517-8000
www.symantec.com

Symtec/Wellesse, *67*
1441 West Smith Road
Ferndale, WA 98248
800-232-4005
www.wellesse.com

TDK Electronics Corp., *20*
901 Franklin Avenue
P.O. Box 9302
Garden City, NY 11530-9302
800-835-8273
www.tdk.com

TEAC.

TEAC America Inc., *21*
7733 Telegraph Road
Montebello, CA 90640
323-726-0303
www.teac.com

TOSHIBA
Leading Innovation >>>

Toshiba America Consumer Products LLC, *18*
82 Totowa Road
Wayne, NJ 07470
973-628-8000
www.tacp.toshiba.com

Tripp Lite, *5*
1111 West 35th Street
Chicago, IL, 60609
773-869-1111
www.tripplite.com

True Seating Concepts, *90, 107*
2052 Alton Parkway
Irvine, CA 92707
800-379-9773

Turtle Wax Inc., *203*
625 Willowbrook Centre Parkway
Willowbrook, IL 60527
800-323-9883
www.turtlewax.com

Uni-ball (Sanford Brands LP), *96, 104*
2707 Butterfield Road
Oak Brook, IL 60523
800-323-0749
www.uniball-na.com

Uniden America Corporation, *110*
4700 Amon Carter Boulevard
Fort Worth, TX 76155
800-297-1023
www.uniden.com

Unilever USA, *59, 64*
700 Sylvan Avenue
Englewood Cliffs, NJ 07632
800-782-8301
www.unileverusa.com

UNIVERSAL
FURNITURE

Universal Furniture International Inc., *79*
4190 Eagle Hill Drive
High Point, NC 27265
800-357-0701
info@samsoninternational.com

U.S. Divers, *140*
www.usdivers.com

Verizon, *109*
P.O. Box 26140
El Paso, TX 79915
800-830-9444

ViewSonic Corporation, *10*
381 Brea Canyon Road
Walnut, CA 91789
800-888-8583
www.viewsonic.com

Vizio Inc., *17*
39 Tesla
Irvine, CA 92618
714-668-0588
www.vizio.com

3VTech Communications Inc., *110*
8152 SW Hall Boulevard, #421
Beaverton, OR 97008
800-595-9511
www.vtechphones.com

WestPoint Home, *84*
28 East 28th Street
New York, NY 10016
800-458-3000
www.martex.com

WHALEN STORAGE

Whalen Storage, *187*
1578 Air Wing Road
San Diego, CA 92154
619-423-9948
www.whalenstorage.com

Whirlpool

Whirlpool Corporation, *86*
2000 M-63 North
Benton Harbor, MI 49022
800-259-1301
www.whirlpoolcorp.com

WireLogic
LOGICAL SOLUTIONS

WireLogic, *1, 27*
2967 Michelson Drive, #460
Irvine, CA 92612
877-444-2488
www.wirelogic.us

Wyeth

Wyeth Consumer Healthcare, *64*

Costco Household Almanac
Electronic Edition

Now you can fully interact with the Electronic Edition of the *Costco Household Almanac* on your computer. Hosted by the *Online Edition* of *The Costco Connection*, the *Almanac* is accessible via the costco.com home page by clicking on "In the Warehouse."

Browse the contents page by page or quickly jump to the chapter or article you seek via the table of contents. Cross-indexing lets you browse the index to easily link to topics throughout the book.

"Share" on the navigation bar lets you e-mail a link to friends that will take them precisely to what you want them to see in the book. You can even add comments to the e-mail.

"Print" allows you to send *Almanac* pages to your desktop printer.

"Download" gives you a PDF of the entire book on your desktop, easily navigated via a PDF-reader application on your computer.

The Electronic Edition also gives you the flexibility of having the *Almanac* with you wherever you have Internet access. Take a look and make it a favorite destination. You'll be revisiting it frequently.

Author biographies

Marjolijn Bijlefeld, *lives in Fredericksburg, Virginia, and is editor of* Women in Optometry, *a quarterly publication of Gerber Communications that goes to 35,000 eye doctors.* Your Body, Your Health/"What's new with contact lenses," *38.*

Brenda Borenstein *is owner of Toronto-based The Organized Zone (www.organizedzone.com).* Home Office/"Straighten up and file right," *87.*

Kathryn M. D'Imperia *is a free-lance writer and photographer.* Your Body, Your Health/"Super fruits to the rescue," *50.*

Joyce Tellier Johnson, N.D., *trains health-care practitioners across North America in current health issues and the integration of pharmacological and natural therapies.* Your Body, Your Health/"Protecting your eyes the natural way," *36.*

Donna Lindley *is owner of Organize Your World Inc. (*www.OrganizeYourWorld.net*), based in Rochester Hills, Michigan.* Home Office/"Straighten up and file right," *88.*

Angela Pirisi *is a Toronto-based freelance writer who frequently covers health topics for a variety of publications.* Your Body, Your Health/"Psyched about scent," *42.*

Tami Reilly *is president of Get Organized for Success (*www.goget organized.com*), based in North Vancouver, British Columbia.* Home Office/"Straighten up and file right," *88.*

Lynne Meredith Schreiber *is a freelance writer based in Southfield, Michigan.* Home Office/"Picking the right office chair," *90.*

Kathy Vincent *is owner of Organizing Solutions (*http:// OrganizingSolutions.tripod.com*) in Windsor, Ontario.* Home Office/"Straighten up and file right," *89.*

Front of book

Bruce Morser, cover illustration
Photodisc, ii
Graber, ii
Photodisc, ii
Blend Images, ii
Brand X Pictures, iv, v
Courtesy MaryJane Butters, vii
Ken Broman, viii
Photodisc/Artville, xi

Sight & Sound

Digital Vision, 1
Photodisc, 3
Digital Vision, 4
TrippLite, 5
Photodisc, 6
Photodisc, 7
Corbis, 8
Sony, 9
Viewsonic, 10
Viewsonic, 11
Photodisc, 12
SanDisk, 12 (insets)
SanDisk, 13
Brand X Pictures, 14 (top)
Photodisc, 14 (bottom)
Photodisc, 15 (bottom)
Rubberball, 16

Your Body, Your Health

Chris Crisman, 29
You On a Diet, 30
2004 The Old Farmer's Almanac, 31
Photodisc, 32
Photodisc, 33
Stockbyte, 34
©Mike Watson Images, 35 (top)
Johnson & Johnson, 35 (bottom)
Photodisc, 36
Photodisc, 37
CIBAVision, 38
CIBAVision, 39
Thinkstock, 40
Photodisc, 42
Photodisc, 43
Brand X Pictures, 44 (top)
Photodisc, 44 (bottom)
Brand X Pictures, 45 (top)
Photodisc, 45 (bottom)
Photodisc, 46 (top)
Digital Vision, 46 (bottom)
Sensodyne, 46 (bottom)
Taxi, 47
Brand X Pictures, 48
Photodisc, 49

Stockbyte, 50
Food Collection, 51
Photodisc, 52
Winfried Bruenken (Amrum), 53
PhotoAlto, 54
Riser, 55
Neutrogena, 56
Neutrogena, 57
Neutrogena, 58
Unilever, 59
Iridio Photography, 60
Iridio Photography, 61
PhotoAlto, 62 (top)
Corbis, 62 (bottom)

Bed, Bath & Laundry

Photodisc, 71
Photodisc, 72
Blend Images, 73
Zeta, 74
Ingram Publishing, 75
©2006 Deco Lav, Inc.:
    all rights reserved, 77
Photodisc, 78

Home Office

Veer, 87
Veer, 88
Veer, 89
True Seating, 90
Ken Broman, 91
The Print Shop, 92
The Print Shop, 93
Photodisc, 94
Sony, 95
Photodisc, 96
Fellowes, 97
Fellowes, 98
Brand X Pictures, 99
Stockbyte, 102

Hobbies & Leisure

FujiFilm, 111
FujiFilm, 112
FujiFilm, 113
Ken Broman, 114
Ken Broman, 115
Banana Stock, 116
Nikon, 117
Nikon, 118
Nikon, 119
IT Stock, 120 (insets)
Blend Images, 121
Getty Images, 122
CRI, 123
Bushnell, 124
Image Source, 126

Corbis, 128
KJS Industries, 129
Scandinavian Design, 130
Scandinavian Design, 131
Digital Vision, 132
Photodisc, 134

In the Kitchen

Photodisc, 141
Photodisc, 142
Photodisc, 143
France Freeman, 144
Photodisc, 146
Photodisc, 147
Photodisc, 148
Household Discoveries and Mrs. Curtiss'
    Cook Book, An Encyclopedia of
    Practical Recipes and Processes, 149
Photodisc, 150
Food Collection, 151
PŪR, 152
PŪR, 153
PŪR, 154
Iridio Photography, 155
Blend, 156
Photodisc, 157
Photodisc, 158
Image Source, 160
Glow Images, 161
Photodisc, 162

Design It, Build It, Fix It

Photodisc, 169
Photodisc, 170
Photodisc, 171 (top, middle)
Artville, 171 (bottom)
Brand X Pictures, 172
Brand X Pictures, 173
Jasco, 175
Photodisc, 176
Graber, 178
Graber, 179
Custom Decorators, 180
Custom Decorators, 181
Custom Decorators, 182
France Freeman, 183
Corbis, 184

The Garage

Photodisc, 189
Photodisc, 190
Stockdisc, 191
Stockdisc, 192
Digital Vision, 193 (top, middle)
Eye Wire, 193 (bottom)
Rubberball Productions, 194
Photodisc, 196

Index

Index